CHILDREN OF WAR

The Second World War Through the Eyes of a Generation

Susan Goodman

JOHN MURRAY

© Susan Goodman 2005

First published in 2005 by John Murray (Publishers)
A division of Hodder Headline

Paperback edition 2006

The right of Susan Goodman to be identified as the Author of the Work has been
asserted by her in accordance with the Copyright, Designs and Patents Act 1988.

1

A CIP catalogue record for this title is available from the British Library

ISBN 0 7195 6123 X

Typeset in Minion by Servis Filmsetting Ltd, Manchester

Printed and bound by Clays Ltd, St Ives plc

Hodder Headline policy is to use papers that are natural, renewable and recyclable
products and made from wood grown in sustainable forests. The logging and
manufacturing processes are expected to conform to the environmental
regulations of the country of origin.

John Murray (Publishers)
338 Euston Road
London NW1 3BH

For all of us who were there.
And in memory of my mother.

Contents

Illustrations

The author and publishers would like to thank the following for permission to reproduce illustrations: Plates 1 (HU 36139), 2 (HU 36138), 5 (HU 36214), 6 (LN 4559C), 8 (LDP 325), 9 (HU 36245), 11 (D 8956), 12 (HU 36235), 13 (HU 63736), 14 (P 948) and 15 (D 20152), Imperial War Museum, London; 3, Hulton Archive/Getty Images; 4 and 7, © Bettman/CORBIS; 10, © Hulton-Deutsch Collection/CORBIS; 16, Colin Bickerton. *Integrated illustrations*: p. 1, Hulton Archive/Getty Images; pp. 43 (HU 36163), 83 (HU 36217), 129 (HU 36152), 179 (V110), 253 (HU 36166) and 281 (TR 1643), Imperial War Museum, London; p. 219, © Hulton-Deutsch Collection/CORBIS.

Acknowledgements

First and foremost, to all the former children of war I was able to reach, who helped, encouraged and willingly gave their time to write or talk to me, my heartfelt thanks. Your voices, your thoughts and your memories were with me as I wrote, and they echo through every page. I have set the scene, but this is *your* book.

I am most grateful to the Merseyside Maritime Museum, Liverpool, for allowing access to transcripts recorded for *Spirit of the Blitz: Liverpool in the Second World War*. And to James Roffey and members of the Evacuees Reunion Association, for their kind and generous help.

My thanks also to Marguerite Patten OBE, for her sensible and witty advice, and for her suggested menu for a family supper in wartime using her recipes; to Charles Spencer and Charlotte Lessing, whose memoirs I have used; to Sarah Molloy, Selina Walker and Lisanne Radice, for their friendship and their support; to my editor, Gordon Wise, for helping when I needed it most; and to my husband, Charles, who was with me every step of the way.

All of the following, in their different ways, helped me through, and I thank them: the staff of the Imperial War Museum and the London Library, Anthea Arnold, Colin Bickerton, Robert Blake, Pamela Carr, Bob Davenport, Faith Eaton, Peter Gorb, Hugh Henry, Joyce Imms, Brian Jordan, Caroline Knox, Glennis Leatherdale, Julia Lymington, Yvette McKinnel, Petronella Macnaghten, Britt Mayer, Madeda Mina di Sospiro, Anniken Whitmore de O'Connell, Auriel Reid, Jane Riall, Mary Sheepshanks, Stephen Sklayne, Sylvia Sklayne MBE, Jeremy Strauss, Lawrence Strauss, Roy Tassell, Caroline Westmore, and Tom Whipham CBE.

Prologue

The idea for *Children of War* has been hovering in my head for years.

When I was writing a biography of Sir Ludwig Guttmann, a pioneering neurosurgeon and founder of the Stoke Mandeville Spinal Injuries Centre, I spoke at length with his daughter. As we talked, we found that, although we were much the same age, our wartime experiences had been dramatically different. She, her parents and her older brother had arrived in Dover on a bitter March day in 1939, a highly respected Jewish family forced to flee their home in Breslau, where life under the Nazi regime had become intolerable. They then had to re-establish their lives in the United Kingdom, which they did most successfully despite the stringent wartime conditions.

In contrast, my wartime experiences were typical of a young child's life in the UK at that time: a father who disappeared into the army for six years, several house moves, the usual air-raid sirens, rationing and shortages. Yet the shifting backgrounds and changes in the people around me, as well as the sense I had of deep and frightening uncertainty, affected me both during the war and I believe, for much of my life thereafter. I thought as I spoke to Eva Guttmann, as I do now, that whatever our wartime circumstances, dramatic or not, we children of war all have our stories to tell. And if *we* don't tell them – soon – who will?

I decided to do something about it, and late in the summer of 2002 a small boxed notice began appearing in a handful of provincial UK newspapers:

> Were you a child, toddler or teenager during the war?
> If so, please share your memories and anecdotes: the
> blackout, bombing, evacuation, shortages, absent
> fathers etc. – and the fun. Researching major book.
> Need YOUR help. It's important, for those of us still
> around – and for the future. Confidentiality
> respected. Please reply to Box No. . . .

I waited. What, if anything, would it yield?

Soon, the answer came: well, rather a lot . . . Starting with a trickle, a stream of envelopes was soon flowing through the letterbox, for in quiet corners of Devon and Cornwall, in East Anglia, parts of the Midlands and Wales, those few stilted words hidden away among the classifieds seemed to have touched a dormant nerve. For whatever personal reasons, a hundred or so men and women, all well into retirement age, briefly put aside their garden chores and their interests and, in their hundred or so different ways, contacted the unknown person behind the 'box'.

To a man and woman, they were encouraging. An elderly judge wrote drily, 'I believe it is quite right that this material should be documented. I am willing to help. You may contact me if you wish.' And at the end of several overflowing pages describing her happy childhood evacuation to a Welsh village a woman scrawled, 'P.S. I think it is a lovely thing that you are doing.' (In despairing moments, I have thought of this and blessed her for it.)

Reassured that a lot of people felt as I did, I moved on to nationwide journals and more, mainly provincial, newspapers. Then London, the great northern cities, Scotland, Yorkshire, Tyneside and other parts of the north, the Home Counties . . . And in twos and threes, and sometimes a stack, the replies came in. There was not an avalanche, but there were many hundreds, and each one was read, replied to, and filed.

The response was gratifying, but it was also becoming a problem. I have but one pair of hands, and I needed to impose limits. I wish I could have corresponded with, or spoken to, thousands more children of war out there. But there was an important deadline, the sixtieth anniversaries of VE Day and VJ Day in 2005, and I had to move ahead. About a year ago I stopped most of the research and started sorting the letters by content. And in January I began to write.

I have worked with the large cache of the material that I was able to collect, the contacts that arose from it, my own sources, and relevant reference books and documents. The majority of the wartime children who speak in the book came from backgrounds which might best be described as unexceptional: suburban homes, provincial towns, quite a lot from inner cities and various country areas. A few came from privileged homes, but some had experienced real hardship. I made every effort to use voices from as wide a social and regional background as possible, although understandably Greater London produced a big response. I have also tried to show the impact the war had on different age groups (eighteen and under) – although, no matter what circumstances we lived in, we children who spent those six gruelling years of war in the UK all faced the same shortages and privations. Certainly there were parts of the country which were safer and pleasanter than others, but there was no escaping the realities of war on the home front, or the ever present drone of the bombers.

I have attempted to paint a broad canvas giving some idea of what it was like to be a child in this country from the late 1930s until the end of the war. *Children of War* is part panorama and part ragbag of information on the drab civilian world during the dramatic events of the Second World War. As you would expect, the book is centred on the family in wartime, and I have dedicated it partly to my mother because she was the rock who got us through, as so many mums got their families through. I mean it to be for those mums, and in their memory, too.

Much of it – funny, poignant, humdrum or harrowing – is written by the wartime children themselves. In most cases, names have been changed; the words have been edited very lightly, and only where necessary. If some voices recur, as they do, it is because they have something interesting to say on a number of topics.

In the Epilogue, I have reflected on what we all took from our wartime childhoods. It was a long war, and, like any other environmental factor, it must have affected us all.

Inevitably, *Children of War* is personal and idiosyncratic. It has been a long journey back to my childhood days; it was sometimes rather painful, but I learned a lot that I had not known before: about my family and myself, and about the circumstances and events of the war, particularly on the home front. I find that I look back at that time now quite differently, and I have enormous sympathy for the adults who went through it with us.

The other day a woman who has contributed generously to this book said to me, 'You have made "us" think.' If that is so, for at least some children of war, then I will have accomplished what I set out to do.

Susan Goodman
London
October 2004

I have near perfect clarity of memory of those years. Of scooping up horse manure from the milkman's cart to put on the roses. Of an annual tin of 'Yellow Cling Peaches', for which I used a fork not a spoon to consume the juice, as it prolonged the enjoyment. Of the house backing my grandmother's being hit in the second doodlebug raid to hit London – and the bed I should have been sleeping in that night being obliterated. Of travelling by bus from Edmonton to Tottenham through the devastation caused by a V2 rocket – 'It must have been a landmine,' one of the bus passengers commented. Of the giant map of Europe and Near Asia on our living-room wall, with its row of marching flag pins indicating the ebb and flow of the various fronts . . .

Of being able to recognize every known aircraft then flying – and I still can. Of watching dogfights by day and searchlights and gunfire by night (we were about half a mile from the nearest ack-ack battery, which I passed on my way to school). Of not being able to cross the North Circular Road to school one day, due to continuous streams of army vehicles carrying the white star – and of aircraft suddenly sprouting the black and white bands of the attack on Europe. Of blackouts and rationing; of walking and cycling everywhere; of blast walls along the school corridors; of ration books and Boots Public Libraries (where I worked my way through all the CHs – Cheyney, Charteris and Christie); of Saturday-morning children's cinema; of rare occasions eating out, and the food restrictions – smoked haddock being a great delicacy . . . And so on, and so on . . .

Andrew, aged five when war was declared. His parents were both schoolteachers; the family lived in north London

1

A CHILD'S WORLD
IN THE 1930s

A young boy collects milk bottles in his toy cart in a suburban street, Cardiff, July 1936. With little traffic and not much crime, in the 1930s street play was considered safe for children

Looking back to my schooldays, all the summers were sunny.
That of 1939 seems no exception.
A man reminiscing on a happy boyhood in an affluent London suburb

We were all left to live in this flat – seven of us kids, Mum and
Dad. It was cold and smelt of damp. There were two small
bedrooms. It was lit by gas, and you had to keep buying small
mantles – if you touched them, the outer part of the mantle just
fell to pieces.
A woman who grew up on Tyneside during the 1930s slump

Late in the autumn of 1938 the more than 1 million readers of the dazzling new magazine *Picture Post* pored over the photograph of a twelve-year-old girl alighting from the upholstered back seat of a Daimler motor car – fresh-faced, shiny curling hair, hand outstretched. On the abdication of King Edward VIII two years before and the accession of her father, King George VI, Princess Elizabeth had become heir to the throne, as had been expected in knowledgeable circles for some time. Behind her, as usual, out came her lively younger sister, Princess Margaret Rose.

The children were arriving at the New Dominion Theatre in Shaftesbury Avenue, in London's West End, to see a new production of *Rainbow's End*. Princess Elizabeth's composed and confident manner, even at her young age, already hinted at the unswerving dutifulness she would show in the future. In a very short time, the profound shock of the abdication had been pushed to one side. As if by sleight of hand, the somewhat louche and pleasure-seeking court of Edward VIII's brief reign had been transformed into one of happy and stable domesticity. Pleasingly informal photographs of the new

King and Queen at Royal Lodge in Windsor with their daughters – and their several dogs – struck just the right note of modern family life with the British public. And the two young princesses had quickly become the nation's darlings, icons of childhood.

Looking closely at the *Picture Post* image, beyond the flashlight haloing the two princesses the grainy photograph tells us something about everyday 1930s London life. As the princesses walked up the carpet to the entrance of the theatre, several women and children, checked by the outstretched arms of a policeman, pressed forward to get a better view. The women are wearing long cloth coats and felt hats pulled down to one side; the children also wear quite formal coats, and caps or bonnets – during the thirties, respectability of dress was aspired to by all classes and all ages.

In a world before television, ceremonial events, royal occasions and outings, and even lavish society weddings provided the less well off with a taste of glamour which was remembered, in detail, for a long while after. This was so for a little girl called Iris who was growing up during the thirties in Islington, north London, in a working-class district near the Angel. In 1927, five months before she was born, her father had died of appendicitis – aged twenty-two – leaving his young wife and baby to fend for themselves. In those days, benefits were scant; there was no safety net of state-funded family allowances and health care. In many families where the mother was in reasonably steady employment – a real boon in those jobless times – it was accepted that the other members helped out with childcare. As her mother had managed to obtain full-time work in a bottle-washing plant, when she wasn't in school young Iris was looked after mainly by her grandmother, who lived down the street. 'They took us at three years old at school,' she said, looking back over nearly seven decades. 'We went home at dinner time – me to my gran's. My mum gave me a halfpenny for sweets after dinner, and then she went back to work. Going back at two o'clock, the infants class was laid out with beds and we went straight into them until playtime. I went to that school until I was nearly ten. I had the same teacher all the time – she just moved up with us every year.'

Fatherless from birth, shunted between mother, grandmother,

school and street play, Iris was exposed to the grim realities of working-class urban life during the worst years of the Depression.

It was hard for everyone in the thirties. The poverty was thought of as normal. We only ever saw riches in the cinema, and we accepted that life was for us and them. No expectations of ever becoming *them* . . . A lot of men were out of work then . . . There were always long lines outside the labour exchange.

Cousins across the street lived in real poverty. The husband couldn't get work, and the children were thin and ill. Mum helped out when she could . . . and gave them knickers and socks . . . One of the girls, the same age as me, had heart trouble, and died when she was eighteen . . . Luckily, all those bad years my mother kept the same job.

Times were tough and money was short, and illness requiring a doctor was a disaster. As Iris knew well, tragedy stalked every family in those teeming streets. 'The saddest thing was that so many children died . . . It seemed every month or so one of them went – always one of us, from our school. I think my gran was a sort of professional mourner – they had them then – because she would drag me along to the bereaved house and when the little coffin was brought out she would start wailing and crying very loudly . . .'

Iris's childhood memories are a gritty mixture of harsh deprivation, strong family ties, and a spunky determination to get the most out of life. And among the raw rough-and-tumble of city streets in the late 1930s there was plenty to divert and entertain. She was not one of the children jostling for a better view of the two princesses on that November day, but she well might have been. Royal occasions and ceremonies which were both spectacular and free became, for Iris, memorable family outings.

My gran would always have her fingers in what was going on . . . At the Jubilee of King George V and Queen Mary my mother and I walked to the West End to see the parade, and suddenly a man picked me up and pushed me on to a pillar box just as the parade went by and I saw Queen Mary look at me and smile and touch the King's arm and he turned and smiled as they passed . . .

We walked for miles and miles – and queued for ages – to see anything that was happening. At the lying-in-state of George V we caught a glimpse of Edward and Mrs Simpson. We were always somewhere in the crowd on Remembrance Day at the Cenotaph.

Another little girl of about the same age was also growing up in London at that time – but in very different circumstances. Sandrine, the only child of socially prominent parents, frequently took part in a different kind of spectacle: as a bridesmaid in the grand society weddings of family friends, when the routes to and from the church were also lined with curious onlookers, packed several deep. A luminous photograph records Sandrine perfectly dressed for one such outing: a pretty dark-haired child, straight-backed and poised, wearing a ruched silver-lamé dress with tiny puff sleeves, a little diamond brooch in the shape of a plane – a gift from the bride-groom – glittering on the bodice. She remembered that at the reception 'My great friend Archie and I – he was a page-boy in white satin – crawled about under the tables and drank champagne . . . All our friends then depended on the nannies. If two nannies got on, then the children played together in each other's houses, and that was how we got our friends.'

Sandrine's mother was one of the great debutante beauties of the 1920s, when the most glamorous social butterflies were treated with the adulation of pop stars today. 'It was not easy being the daughter of a famous beauty, I can tell you,' Sandrine said crisply. Years later, at her own marriage (aged nineteen), her mother imperiously can-celled the reception – for no apparent reason – at the last minute. 'Just like that . . . So I was married in my going-away outfit – hardly anyone was there – and I never wore my beautiful Hartnell wedding dress. Extrordinary. I have always assumed that she simply could not bear the thought of anyone except herself being the centre of attention, being queen for a day.'

Sandrine lived with her nurse, then later with her governess, on the floor below the servants in a large house in a smart London square. She rarely saw her parents: 'We never went anywhere as a family – no outings.' Her most vivid memory of her father dates from when she was about six, when she looked in through his open study door and saw him lying fast asleep stretched out on a large white polar-bear rug, immaculate in full evening dress. One evening she was taken down for a brief appearance at a cocktail party her parents were giving in the elegant drawing room, decorated in the pale tones that were then fashionable. High above her head she heard a woman say of her rather dismissively, as she sipped her Martini, 'Of course, she's not a patch on her mother. She'll never have the success she had.'

'Children were never told anything in those days,' Sandrine said. 'I was sent to Frinton on holiday with my governess and told there would be a big surprise when we got back. We found the nursery bathroom had been painted yellow. "Some surprise!" I thought. I learned years after that my mother had been expecting a baby – a boy, who had died at birth – and that was to have been the surprise.'

It is perfectly understandable that children like Sandrine who were with Nanny 'twenty-four hours a day – we slept in the same room' came to depend on the nanny's emotional support and companionship. This frequently led to friction between mother and nurse. 'One night I heard Nanny crying in bed,' Sandrine said. 'I had no idea why . . . but the next day when I got back from school I found Nanny had gone and I had a Swiss governess. Just like that.' Her capricious mother had grown jealous of Nanny's authority – and sacked her. A few years later, when her mother called her into the drawing room to tell her that she and her father were getting divorced, Sandrine remembered that she 'couldn't have cared less. It meant nothing to me. I just skipped back out into the garden and went on playing.'

Picture Post's photograph of the princesses, frozen for ever in their velvet frocks and tweedy coats, gives a glimpse of the pre-war life both of the nationally doted on princesses themselves and of those anonymous London children – like Iris – up for a bit of excitement, craning for a glimpse of 'the toffs'. The princesses also hint at a story which would soon be crucial to the country: the genuine, and rather unexpected, success of their parents in their new roles of king and queen – which they were now playing on a world stage. Not only had royalty become respectable again, but confidence in the institution of monarchy, so severely undermined by the abdication, had also been restored at a critical time for the country. For in the late 1930s, as the country gradually struggled out of the depths of economic depression, the political situation in Europe, which had been rumbling ominously throughout that decade, became darker and increasingly unstable.

When Hitler became Chancellor of Germany in 1933, after years of financial and political chaos, it was soon clear that his aims were dangerously militaristic. Under the guise of securing full employment, the German war machine was rearming furiously, as the rest of Europe watched in horror. In 1936 Germany successfully occupied the Rhineland. By this time Hitler's mad racial hatreds were also causing alarm far beyond the German borders. The Nuremberg Laws of 1935 effectively banned Jews from taking any part in mainstream German life: in business and the professions, in schools and universities, and in virtually all social activities. Anti-Semitic propaganda permeated the country's media, and the cynically orchestrated stirring of racial hatred exploded in November 1938 on *Kristallnacht*, the Night of Broken Glass, when Jewish homes, businesses and synagogues were systematically smashed and torched.

The outside world, appalled, could no longer ignore Hitler's overweening ambitions and systematic cruelty. However, the British Prime Minister, Neville Chamberlain, determined to avoid war at all costs, continued to pursue a policy of calm and negotiation. By now the word 'appeasement' had entered ordinary conversations in pubs and clubs and homes all over the country, but talk of possible war was heard everywhere.

'We knew what was coming – of course we did,' said Alex, who was a sixth-former at school in London in 1938. 'We were brought up on the derring-do adventures in comics like *Beano* and *Boy's Own*, and we wondered . . . It was frightening – we had no idea what lay ahead of us – but I have to say it was also exciting.' Jill, the daughter of a surgeon, who would herself become a wartime medical student, had clear memories of the period: 'We carried on just as usual. I well remember driving through Lancashire – and seeing the terrible poverty – on our way north to visit relatives . . . In 1938 we went abroad, to France, . . . but we all knew war was inevitable by then: my parents didn't have the slightest doubt.'

In the spring of 1938 Hitler annexed Austria, and in cinemas the newsreels showed long lines of jackbooted German troops marching victoriously as the Austrians waved and cheered. But Hitler's ambitions were not satisfied. He next set his sights on Czechoslovakia, and by September of that year a full-blown international crisis had erupted. Chamberlain, backed by powerful Cabinet figures such as Lord Halifax, the Foreign Secretary, retained a naive optimism that some diplomatic compromise with Hitler could be found. Yet, although the sobering preparations for war on the home front were going ahead (the Air Raid Wardens Service was created in 1937 to protect civilians during enemy air attacks, and plans for a possible evacuation of children from the cities were going forward), the majority of people in the United Kingdom stubbornly clung to the hope of peace.

During September 1938 Chamberlain met Hitler three times; the third time he returned, ecstatic, from Munich waving a piece of paper at the crowds as he emerged from the plane and announced 'Peace in our time' – to general, if somewhat sceptical, relief. As Pat, a thirteen-year-old schoolgirl in south London, put it, 'We accepted it at face value, but merely thought, "Thank you for buying us time" . . . We all felt the war was going to happen sooner or later.' Her father, expecting the worst, had already joined the Territorial Army.

Despite so much political uncertainty, Fred, then a humorous young Cockney lad, remembered the Munich crisis rather more light-heartedly: seeing a Jewish woman from Stepney, who barely spoke English, weaving her way through the city crowds, excitedly waving a newspaper and shouting, 'Piss in our time . . . Piss in our time . . .' – which at least raised a laugh.

Although there was fervent gratitude for Chamberlain's apparent last-minute reprieve, the public knew instinctively that all was not well: that Hitler had been briefly 'appeased' – but not satisfied – at the expense of national honour. Popular opinion for and against a tough line over Hitler, whatever the consequences, had been veering back and forth, with women tending to favour the Prime Minister's conciliatory stand. But after Munich, very reluctantly, the country began to swing against this meretricious treaty with Germany, which left Czechoslovakia to fend for itself in return for Hitler's renouncing aggression towards the UK and was judged to be diplomatically disastrous and morally wrong.

During this time of extreme political tension, one of Chamberlain's implacable opponents was Winston Churchill. Though thought by many to be well past it this sixty-four-year-old veteran who had already made his share of tragic misjudgements in the First World War fumed and thundered and openly feared for the future of this country – and all right-minded people – if Hitler and the Nazis were not stopped, and his outspoken stance was beginning to attract wide notice. Sam, then a sixteen-year-old with a keen interest in public affairs, remembered that already he and his school friends 'lusted after' Churchill's powerful oratory. 'Although he did not hold office then, his voice, and his views, were already gaining him a wide following.'

Every day, signs of Germany's increasingly repressive regime and insane racial laws – evils which had now spread to Austria – filtered into the British newspapers. Pathetic advertisements appeared in the personal columns: 'Au pair in cultivated household. Austrian girl 16 (refugee); well educated; will turn her hand to anything' only hinted at the desperation that lay behind the words. German and Austrian Jews, many of whom had fought loyally for their countries in the First World War, were now social outcasts, the men frequently disappearing into detention camps. The only glimmer of hope for the children lay in the *Kindertransport* – trains on which Jewish children with approved papers were permitted to leave for countries willing to admit them.

In Vienna, a fifteen-year-old Jewish boy called Carl, his mother distracted by nursing his sick father, decided to get out of the country at all costs. Under the brutal Nazi regime he was no longer permitted to attend school, and he was sickened by the hatred and bullying and degradation of Jews that he saw around him. He quickly got a job as a messenger with a Jewish organization. Determined to put his name down on a list for the *Kindertransport*, one day after work he locked himself in the lavatory. When everyone had left, he rifled through office files until he found the official papers he was looking for. He then added his name to the waiting lists for trains to the UK, France and Palestine, scrambled out of a window, and ran home, hoping against hope that he would be successful.

In the late 1930s Britain was a class-conscious and rigidly layered society: although attitudes were slowly moving in the direction of the post-1945 welfare state, there were still great social inequities, and prejudices of all kinds seethed beneath the surface. In street gangs, as well as in some of the most prestigious public schools, many Jewish children routinely faced anti-Semitic bullying; petty rituals in social behaviour and rivalries and taboos were rife, and deeply divisive, in all classes. And there was growing bitterness in depressed industrial areas, where men without hope sought a political outlet for their anger.

David, growing up in Edinburgh, was profoundly affected by this deep-seated social unrest. His family lived in a very modest two-bedroom house with 'one cold-water tap, gaslight and a single cooker, a small coal fire, and – total luxury – an indoor toilet'. Most of the neighbours had an outdoor toilet, in some cases shared between up to six families. His father was 'more or less unemployed for two years, and lack of money was a constant worry . . . They could not afford the 2/6d. (12½p) to allow me to go with the rest of my class to the World Exhibition in Glasgow. There were about six of us left in the school that day!'

As he saw for himself, poverty and desperation bred political extremism.

Great mobs swirled around the foot of the Mound where it joined Princes Street – Edinburgh's Speakers' Corner – and there seemed to be an endless supply of demagogues haranguing the crowds of men, mostly unemployed. They were kept in order by the 'Polis', who seemed enormous compared to the ranks of thin, poorly dressed men seeking some meaning and excitement in their lives . . .

The blackshirts [the British Union of Fascists, led by Sir Oswald Mosley] had their headquarters in Thistle Street, and it was common to see men exercising and parading in the lane behind. I also remember a man giving the Nazi salute in a cinema. He was very forcibly removed.

Hearing of trouble brewing one day, he ran off to watch the action.

Mosley's blackshirts clashed bloodily with red-scarved Communists . . . Both groups were baton-charged by mounted police and driven to a cul-de-sac where the Black Marias were waiting. A man pulled me out of the crowd and dumped me firmly down behind a pillar outside the Royal Academy and told me to 'Bide there until the stamash is over'.

There were similar scenes in London. Iris was taken to hear Oswald Mosley 'and his blackshirt marchers' by an older boy cousin. He carried her high on his shoulders above the noisy and baying mob, whipped to a frenzy by Mosley's oratory. Terrified by the violent scene, she started to cry – until he gave her a lollipop to keep her quiet. Her mother was fiercely opposed to the Fascist movement, and when she heard of the cousin's escapade she was so outraged that she 'marched straight across the street and walloped him'.

Yet for all the contrasts of great wealth and soul-destroying poverty, the insularity and silly snobberies, essential fair-mindedness remained British society's hallmark. Even in the most deprived and discontented areas of the major industrial cities during the slump, Fascism – unlike the Nazi party in Germany – never really took hold, although it attracted many ardent admirers. One humane illustration of the country's moral ballast in that period of dangerous social divisions is the contrast in the everyday life and attitudes encountered by young Carl in Vienna and by a Jewish girl called Charlotte, exactly his age, and of similar middle-class background, living in north London in the immediate pre-war years. Charlotte, who was born in the UK, put it like this:

My father came from Vilna, in Lithuania . . . During the First World War he had not yet got his British naturalization and could not be accepted by the British forces, so he joined the Red Cross as an interpreter . . . He got into the furniture trade and at one time he had a factory that started off well, but soon he was nearly bankrupt.

I was fifteen in 1939, and at a private fee-paying school, a day girl. My mother had to tell the headmistress that I would have to leave, as my father's new business – he started importing small pieces of furniture from Hungary and Czechoslovakia – collapsed.

Fortunately the headmistress said that I was too 'promising' and arranged a scholarship . . . I never had any difficulty with religion or anti-Semitism at school. There were a number of other Jewish girls there, and we just missed out the school morning prayers. We also stayed home on important Jewish holidays . . .

Money was always short. My happiest memory, just before the war, was when I could save my 6d. pocket money and go to the Sadler's Wells Ballet for the cost of the fare – and 6d. for a seat in the gods.

Both Carl and Charlotte had been born into civilized countries in western Europe in the middle years of the twentieth century; yet Carl and his family faced persecution and ultimate tragedy, while Charlotte grew up like all her friends, with a normal background centred on school and family life.

Fortunately, both their life stories turned out well. Carl's guts and initiative paid off: his name went forward, and he was accepted for *Kindertransport* to the UK. And on 10 December 1938, smartly dressed and having been given 'lots of advice' by family and friends, he was taken by his parents to a suburban station outside Vienna (Jews not being permitted to use main railway stations) where he would start his journey, alone. The train was already waiting when they arrived. 'Then came the command from the SS: "Eine minute für Abscheid nehmen" ("One minute to say goodbye"). I don't think I cried . . .' Carl wrote as he put down his life story, many years later. 'But I know Mutti did, and I cry now, for it has only struck me forcibly during the last few years what it must mean to a mother to . . . send a fourteen-year-old child to an unknown destiny and destination.'

Carl and the other children being sent away from their homes and families on that December day boarded the train, which had closed windows and drawn blinds. At night, when the children had settled down to sleep, SS men came through the carriages. 'There was a commotion . . . They took all the valuables off the children, including gold fillings in teeth . . . And then we were over the Dutch border . . . At the first stop, one of my clearest memories – people standing on the platform in the middle of the night with hot cocoa, banana sandwiches and chocolate.'

The children travelled right across Europe, and eventually arrived at Harwich. Carl never saw either of his parents again.

He quickly found his feet, rejected further schooling, and chanced his way quite lucratively through a series of jobs. Having acquired what seemed to him a considerable tax bill, he joined the forces as soon as he was eligible and began training with the Royal Armoured Corps.

Both Carl (who had become Charles) and Charlotte set out on their working lives during wartime. A rebellious girl, impatient to get started in work, Charlotte horrified her mother with her favourite, rather daring, 'wine-red corduroy trousers'. Keen to break into journalism, she chucked a secretarial course after three months and at seventeen got a position 'looking after the small ads' on a famous political journal. Bright and creative, and determined to get into print, she managed to sneak a review she had written of *Alice in Wonderland on Ice* at the Stoll Theatre on to the formidable literary editor's desk. 'To my amazement it was published. I think I was never happier than to get my literary debut in the *New Statesman*.'

A little more than five years after his arrival in the UK – knowing nobody, without money, and without speaking much English – Charles drove the second tank on to the coast of France at Arromanches on D-Day, 6 June 1944. After a rough crossing, soon after daybreak, Charles and his mates faced the wide French beaches – and the Germans. 'A sailor swung the lead to ascertain the depth of the water ... the front of the Liberty ship went down like a ramp ... and off we went.' They made it off the beach, and he and his crew survived Day 1. Badly wounded in the leg on Day 2, Charles survived, came through the war, married his wartime sweetheart, and prospered. After making a success of his business early in middle age, he concentrated on his great love of music, a passion he had inherited from his father. He even discovered through distant relatives, decades after leaving Austria, that his and his father's developed musical tastes were identical.

Charlotte more than justified her headmistress's confidence: she persevered, used her talent and her buoyant personality, and became a journalist and, later, a successful magazine writer and editor.

It is painful to realize that at the time of *Kristallnacht* and the Munich crisis, as Europe rushed headlong into another conflict, virtually the entire adult population of this country had memories of what had been so hopefully described as 'the war to end all wars'. A child born around the start of the twentieth century was a teenager during the First World War and by 1938 or '39 was verging on early middle life. After a mere twenty years, so many mental and physical wounds and lingering sorrows still remained from those killing fields that the mere possibility of another war must have been devastating. In 1933, young students at the Oxford Union had voted overwhelmingly for the resolution that they would 'under no circumstances fight for King and country'. Hardly anyone in the land had not lost a relative or a colleague or a friend; a generation of young men, with all their energy and talent and qualities of leadership, both to use themselves and to hand on to others, had been annihilated.

Their absence pervaded every aspect of society. In a country pub in Oxfordshire in 1930, as old men sat on benches and reminisced and told their stories, there were no younger ones to be seen downing a beer. 'There's only the old chaps like us . . . That war didn't do any of us any good. Nothing's been the same since. Forty-two were killed from this village.'

In subtle ways, as they got older, children in the 1930s became aware of the ghosts of the men who were not there. The place names of the conflict bring a haunting chill: the Ypres salient, Passchendaele, the Somme, Flanders, Vimy Ridge . . . Overall Allied casualties were estimated at just under a million; German and French losses were considerably greater. In the first Battle of Ypres alone, in October–November 1914, 50,000 British troops died. A large part of the country's present, and its future, also died in this and other battles. On a simple war memorial in a hidden village in Warwickshire there are twenty-four names; four are from one family, three from each of two others, and two from a fourth. An old-timer remembered hearing from his grandparents that most of the villagers who died were boys, under twenty and as young as sixteen. Such memorials continue to tell their tragic tale in town squares and villages throughout the country – as well as over much of the Continent.

The public schools, breeding grounds for officers, suffered as much as – perhaps more than – any group in proportion to their numbers. During the First World War 1,157 Etonians were killed – a figure above the national average for the public schools, but by no means the highest – and many more were badly wounded. Tim Card, a former Eton vice-provost, observed sombrely in his book *Eton Renewed* that 'there was . . . a feeling that the best had died'. And he also pointed out the simple consequence of these young, unnatural deaths: at Eton, as at all schools throughout the country during the 1920s and early '30s, 'an unusually large number of boys had no father'. Although it might be suggested, tentatively, that the lack of a father is harder for a growing son than for a daughter, all the fatherless children of both sexes must have suffered to some degree; it is impossible to quantify the emotional damage that the carnage wreaked on the formative years of that post-war generation.

'We all had spinster aunts and great aunts, didn't we, when we were growing up?' a writer said, her voiced edged with sadness, thinking of the thousands and thousands of young women whose futures had been blighted. 'They were a part of nearly every family. And so were stories about uncles who had been killed, and the sons of one's parents' friends – some no more than boys.' Amputees were a common sight between the wars. As a boy of eight, in 1938 Charles was walking down Corporation Street in Birmingham with his father; all his life he would he remember seeing a man on crutches, without a leg, begging on a street corner. Millie, who grew up playing with her friends in the back streets of another great city, said that they 'kept seeing a little group of men, all ex-soldiers, one or two without limbs, pitifully singing – one with a mouth organ, or one whistling, and there was usually a penny or two thrown from a window'.

Boys attending Clifton College in the 1930s were taught by the talented head of the music department, Dr Douglas Fox, whose right arm was amputated on the Western Front; he continued to play the organ and the piano, and was one of the first performers of Ravel's Piano Concerto in D Major for the Left Hand.

Even children born several years after the Armistice were still deeply affected by the war's lasting trauma. James, born in 1929, and later educated at wartime Stowe School, said that his and his older brother's childhood games

were all based on the fearful battles of Flanders . . . We occupied ourselves with trenches, redoubts, dugouts. Our equipment was improvised except for a Sam Browne belt, a tin hat, a gas mask, and a Luger pistol in its original holder . . . all probably acquired by our father, who was in the Royal Army Medical Corps throughout the war, at some casualty station immediately behind the lines . . .

He only talked briefly about the terrors of shelling, the fear of gas, the ghastly wounds, and to hint at the absolute horror of it all. He came from a strict late-Victorian Welsh family – his father was a Methodist preacher. But I believe after that he lost any conventional religious faith.

Michael, who in the 1930s was living in Dorset, where his father was in charge of a county institution, never forgot his mother's despair at the worsening international situation; as a nurse in the First World War, she had cared for many terribly wounded soldiers, and kept in touch with some of them. 'My brother and I used to be shown old photographs and mementoes she had kept – the kind of things you see on the *Antiques Roadshow* now . . . I know one particular boyfriend of hers had been killed.' The thought of another war had rekindled her grief, as it must have done for so many women still mourning the loss of husbands, sons and lovers. As sensitive children watched, the results of that bitter conflict now confronted yet another generation.

Many children in their teens just before the war would empathize with Dorothy, living in her family's large Edwardian house in Dulwich. At fifteen – on the verge of womanhood – trying to make some sense of the political situation, she wondered anxiously about her schooling if there was a war, and quietly determined not to be separated from her family, no matter what. And suddenly she too saw her parents from a quite different perspective. 'My father had fought on the Western Front from 1914 before being discharged, having had a hand shattered by shrapnel. So many of those he had fought with had died. Of course, for me at my age then I had no idea of the pain that that generation, with memories so fresh, would be going through . . . Now he and my mother had two teenage children – my brother and myself – and it was all happening again.'

Although many politicians and educators believed that it should be raised by one year, the school-leaving age remained at fourteen. All children attended elementary school, while more able, or luckier, pupils went on to secondary schools. The move to stream all children at the age of eleven into either secondary or vocational schools was gradually being implemented. Children in secondary schools had a better chance of continuing their education beyond the school-leaving age than those who remained in elementary schools.

State education was patchy and varied from district to district, but by the mid-1930s opportunities for able children were somewhat improved. According to Charles Mowat in *Britain Between the Wars*, 'The number of public secondary schools of the grammar-school type increased . . . as well the number of junior technical schools.' The latter provided vocational training. Just under half of all children entering the better-funded secondary schools – including grammar and vocational schools – had free places awarded by the local authorities; fees were required for the rest and this could prove a financial burden on a family with no money to spare. There were also strict uniform regulations.

Pat, who had passed her exam to go to a secondary school in Beckenham in 1934, was told that she did not have good enough grades to go to grammar school. 'If I had managed this I would have received a sum of money to cover clothing, but I only managed sufficient marks to go to a central school (comprehensive), which meant that we would have to find the money for a complete outfit of clothes for both winter and summer. This was a considerable sum – about £30 – and I knew it would be impossible for us.' But the family took this educational opportunity seriously. With her older sister helping out, and clothes made for her by her mother, aunts and friends, the family scraped together the necessary equipment. And this good educational grounding stood Pat in good stead; blessed with a fine voice, her talent was spotted at school, and later – during the war – she trained as a professional singer.

It was noticeable that children from more prosperous areas were consistently awarded more scholarships than those from poorer districts, where the schools were more crowded. In the countryside, many children's education suffered from what were often long distances to the schools, and from young children helping out with domestic chores. Brothers aged eight and nine in Oxfordshire routinely milked four cows each on their father's farm before walking 3 miles each way to and from the nearest village school.

So, although in theory there was a route towards higher education open to everyone, it was still narrow and following it was largely dependent on chance. An enormous amount of the nation's youthful talent was therefore going to waste.

David, in Edinburgh, beat the odds of a poor background to go on to a successful career as a naval officer. He remembered:

In school, we all bought our textbooks, and I was exhorted to keep mine in good order so that they could be sold on at the end of the school year. My mother would bind them in wallpaper or American cloth to extend their lives. In the early primary days we used slates and always kept a sponge to clean them with. After that we moved on to steel pens and used a special pen cleaner consisting of three squares of cloth held by a decorative button – if a girl 'fancied' you she would make one and slip it on your desk. The post of ink monitor, who filled the inkwells daily, was a very important one.

Like many a poor youngster, David hustled in the city streets from a young age to try to make a few pence. 'In Edinburgh,' he wrote, 'a common task for boys was to go shopping for people – known as "doing messages". It was usual for old ladies to lean out of their windows, throw down a scribbled note wrapped round a coin, and say, "Gie's a message, Laddie." They were never refused, and usually paid with a sweetie or a bun.' Aged eight, he got his first real job, 'as message boy for a pair of maiden ladies who kept a small card and trinket shop. I worked after school for two hours each weekday and from nine till one on Saturdays. Morningside ladies wouldn't be seen dead carrying a package in those days. So I would run through the streets to deliver their shopping – and sometimes I would jump on and off a passing tramcar.'

In those days of strict social tiers, whatever a child's background it is fair to say that he or she was expected to obey and to respect authority without much questioning – be it in the form of parents, bus drivers, schoolteachers, shop assistants or any other adult. All who were children then agree on this: 'We weren't told anything . . . You almost never asked, "Why?"' 'My parents told me to . . .' 'It was expected of me . . .' 'We simply didn't ask questions then'.

Ordinary schools and Sunday schools, as well as the smaller, much more involved communities in which people lived, in villages or city neighbourhoods, all reinforced quite rigid standards of behaviour. Although most children were already out working in their mid-teens, and despite the prevalence of teenage marriages, parental authority – and childhood itself – was considered to last longer than today. A parent's, or teacher's, word was law.

Some kind of physical punishment for disobedience was normal, whatever a child's circumstances. A man then living in the outer London suburbs and attending infant school vividly remembered the head teacher, 'who ruled if not with a rod of iron, then at least with a ruler of wood. Any transgression by the five- and six-year-old children would be punished by making the child make a fist. The head would then rap the knuckles very hard with a ruler. And, yes, it was painful!' In most homes the odd cuff or slap – and sometimes a lot worse – was accepted. Explaining the relative lack of delinquency around the area of the East End in which he grew up in the 1930s, Sid wrote, 'There was no vandalism as such, simply because when a boy got in trouble the father would give him a tanning with his belt. Children were seen and not heard.' This was echoed by Steve, who, with his brothers, remembered, ruefully how his own 'strict father – and his big leather belt' acted as a deterrent against bad behaviour. Carla, also living in the East End, said, 'You'd be picked up for "bloody swearing" and told off for saying "ain't".'

The public schools all used caning to toughen the spirit (or so it was supposed) and to exert discipline; older boys – prefects – were also permitted to use the cane keep the younger ones in order. Offences were usually minor. 'The only time I was caned was by a prefect – it was for keeping the lights on too late in my study, I think,' a former public school boy recalled. There is anecdotal evidence that during the 1930s Eton, at least, became more lenient in its attitude to beatings as punishment; a senior boy writing in the College Annals favoured 'the word of mouth' in dealing with offences – a more modern attitude that would become accepted in all the public schools.

Many reasonably affluent parents of the 1930s sent their sons to boarding schools at the age of about eight – despite probably having servants at home for domestic work – before the boys went on to public schools at about thirteen. In E. M. Delafield's enchanting domestic satire *Diary of a Provincial Lady* – which was written in the thirties and poked fun at the rituals of the middle classes – the central character must speak for many a mother's heartache when she deposits her adored son, Robin, in his prep school. She admits to putting on a face of 'hideous brightness' while they beard the priggish headmaster, and then to crying her eyes out 'all the way back to the station'.

Apart from snobbery, there were many perfectly valid reasons for removing very young male children from hearth and home at that time. A lot of parents were busy propping up the flagging Empire in far-flung corners that were quite unsuited to family life and children's education – although a daughter's place was considered to be at home at any cost. Also, the large cities were noxious and foggy – bad for anyone's health, let alone that of a delicate child. Jack, whose health was poor when he was a boy, said, 'I had a weak chest, I was always getting bronchitis, and my parents wanted to get me out of Birmingham's industrial smog. I was sent to a school on the Kent coast. I wasn't very happy there – it seems to me now that the discipline was rather harsh for such young children.'

Even in this private prep school – as in many others – the politics of the recent past, and the present, intruded.

I know our art master, who was fairly tough, had fought in the trenches. So many male teachers in all kinds of schools at that time must have come through the Great War. No doubt they were all scarred by it somehow. The master who taught us maths was foreign and had a heavy accent. He was a Jewish refugee from Germany, of course. This was about 1937 . . . but at eight or nine we had no idea of the significance of his being there.

While brothers and male cousins were incarcerated in their various public schools, girls from the upper middle classes tended to be poorly, or unevenly, educated. Excellent boarding schools for girls – Cheltenham Ladies' College, Wycombe Abbey, Roedean and several others – had existed and prospered since the nineteenth century, turning out well-educated girls, the brightest of whom went on to university. But even in these select establishments the overall emphasis was more on character-building and social accomplishments than on academic achievement. Unless a girl showed blue-stocking tendencies early, the chief concern of most parents was to prepare her adequately for her life's duties: coming out in society, to be quickly followed by marriage and motherhood.

So the girls were sent to largely undemanding day schools, or were educated, possibly with a few friends, by a series of governesses. The higher up the social scale, the more eccentric such uneven learning was likely to be. The lack of conventional educational methods in many upper-class households was balanced by having plenty of books available, by listening to articulate conversation, by music lessons and, possibly, by foreign travel. For an intelligent girl, quick to learn, who took an interest in what went on around her, this could work as well as any other method. A quirky, but successful, example of this type of upbringing is that of the five Mitford sisters, daughters of Lord Redesdale; erratically taught by their mother and governesses in the 1920s and '30s, all were highly literate, and two eventually wrote professionally and extremely well.

Private education largely depended on the quality of the governess: a clever one, with a knack for teaching, could do well by her pupils in most subjects; a governess with limited education herself could teach next to nothing, leading to what Sarah, one dissatisfied former pupil, described as 'the merest gossip of education'. Rose, who grew up to become a poet and a novelist, was privately educated with about seven other children. They were taught by several first-rate specialized teachers and, with access to the library of a famous public school, some of their education was excellent, she said. Compared to their contemporaries, they were 'way ahead in English and history'. But in other subjects, such as maths and the sciences, they were 'totally neglected'. Many well-to-do educated families sought out refined European girls to teach languages, and Rose's family employed an Austrian Fräulein every summer. The moment war broke out, she remembered irreverently, 'poor Fräulein was interned – but we children were thrilled, of course: no more boring German lessons.'

Discipline and manners – or obedience – were taken for granted.

In all classes, this veneer of social formality also extended to clothing. A photograph of unemployed ship-workers on Tyneside in 1936 shows them sombrely but respectably dressed in suits and coats and ties. Hats, whether flat cloth caps, trilbys, bowlers or high silk toppers, were worn everywhere. Men of the middle and upper classes routinely wore black or white tie for dinners and the theatre.

Although that designer of genius Coco Chanel had pioneered a chic, comfortable feminine style including trousers which was much admired and copied – perhaps the beginning of unisex dressing – womens' trousers were kept strictly for sporty or casual occasions. Middle-class women rarely went out of the house without wearing hats and gloves. Children were dressed with similar formality. Boys, when they were not out playing, wore grey flannel shorts or trousers, ties, jackets and caps. For special occasions, little girls from well-off homes were dressed up in exquisite hand-smocked frocks, or frilly pastel net dresses for parties – perhaps with a string of seed pearls or little coral beads.

In contrast, for large families in areas of high unemployment decent clothing was a real struggle. Richard Titmuss, the official historian of the Second World War at home, wrote that the disadvantaged made 'widespread use of pawnbrokers, secondhand dealers and jumble sales . . . and a vast instalment purchase organization, the clothing clubs of the poor'. Boots and shoes – expensive items that children constantly outgrew – were a particular problem. James, who lived briefly in the Lake District, remembered that 'many of the villagers, including the children, wore clogs – wooden soles with iron rims and strong leather uppers protected at the toe with a shiny cap. Others had heavy and unyielding boots, laced to the toe and with well-studded soles.' A little later, during the mass evacuation of children from the cities in wartime, a high percentage of those evacuated had inadequate footwear, many owning only handed-down plimsolls.

Despite the intrusion of the motor car, in large areas of the country life during the thirties was still quiet and tranquil. Market towns, the mainstay of provincial Britain, had changed little for many generations. The typical 1930s market town described by the historian Charles Mowat is still (just) recognizable today:

The wide main street where half-timbered houses jostled the newer ones of brick . . . bowed shop windows of the eighteenth century still displayed the chemist's ointment jars and the carboys of varicoloured waters . . . the town hall, the two or three coaching inns, with panelled smoking rooms and stables in the yard, the grammar school and the alms houses, the old stone bridge over the river, the side street of Georgian houses of brick or stone, drowsy in the sunlight . . .

Victoria was brought up in such a background, and she evokes the peaceful pre-war atmosphere of a small country town and its unhurried way of life: 'The coal cart, pulled by horses, came round on a regular basis; the sacks were carried through the house to the coal bin near the back door. Milk was delivered by cart in glass bottles with cardboard tops. All shops had one "Early Closing Day" – Wednesdays I think. And of course none were open on Sunday.'

Shopping was a much more leisurely, time-consuming business then. Children were expected to provide a helping hand, lugging that household essential, a wicker shopping basket, back home – as Victoria did.

Without refrigeration, shopping was a daily event . . . and we were often sent back to the shops for items that could not be fitted into the basket. I enjoyed going with my mother on Saturdays, visiting in turn the greengrocer, the butcher, the fishmonger and the grocer. One went to each counter in turn for butter and cheese, tea and coffee, tinned food. ('Pork and Beans' – the precursor of baked beans – had the beans with a piece or two of fat pork in them.) . . . It was fascinating to see the butter weighed out. The assistant would carve off a small piece, then with two wooden 'patters' shape it and bash it into the right size and shape before wrapping it in greaseproof paper.

In provincial towns, in the cities and in the countryside, younger children, largely unaware of the political situation, were oblivious to their parents' worries as the situation in Europe deteriorated and the Munich crisis came and went. Their lives were measured by family and school and going out to play – joining gangs of friends and making up games with whatever implements were at hand, as children always had done. Most of this play was imaginative; even very privileged children who might have been given an exquisite doll's house or a Hornby electric train set for a birthday or Christmas present had far fewer *things* – toys and puzzles and books and clothes and games of all kinds – than is usual now.

There were no televisions, and few children's programmes on the radio – if a family was fortunate enough to own one. Apart from the occasional cinema treat, local theatricals and travelling fairs – and, for the lucky child, the odd visit to a theatre or pantomime – there was no entertainment for children outside the home. Yet, remarkably, nobody of that generation, looking back, mentions the dreaded word 'boredom'. On the contrary, Sandrine, who was eight when the war broke out, remembered playing happily for hours, often on her own, in the large and beautiful garden of her grandparents' house in Surrey; the nostalgia for a far less pressured childhood which her comments reflect is shared by many who have similar memories:

The wonderful freedom children had then . . . amusing oneself. I made a trapeze out of an old broom handle and spent many happy hours hanging upside down, pretending to be a bat . . . We had tremendous independence and resourcefulness. I fell off my bicycle one day trying to demonstrate that one could ride with no hands and no feet and made the most appalling mess of my face. I crept into the back of the house and patched up things as best I could before presenting myself to a grown-up in order not to cause trouble. You can still just see the scar on the side of my face now.

Making their own fun, boys living in the country or on the edge of big cities made use of the local rivers and ponds: swimming, diving, skimming stones. Like so many of his generation, Brian recalled the pleasures of his boyhood fishing expeditions in the late 1930s, so redolent of those quieter, slower days:

We had two favourite places to go fishing for sticklebacks, minnows and similar small fish, rarely more than about 2 inches long. The nearer one was about a mile away and had a dew pond – we always used a stick, cotton and a bent pin, baited with a little bread . . . The other involved a round trip of perhaps 4 miles. We would go to the local sweet shop, which sold fishing nets – fine mesh nets on a wire loop at the end of a cane. This was about 3d., or three weeks' pocket money, unless a kindly relative had pressed a threepenny bit into a grubby hand on leaving.

There was a special spot on the edge of the water near the bridge where we could be sure to catch a few unfortunate tiddlers. We went with a jam jar, with a string round the neck as a handle to carry it home – filled with water – hopefully in triumph . . . The net would be kept for catching butterflies.

Helping out on allotments was another pastime. A lad who often gave his father a hand on the family patch said that when they cycled home he 'sat on the crossbar – there was a piece of string in front which made me a pair of stirrups. Once, we had a sack of potatoes on the mud-guard over the back wheel. As we cycled along the main road, the sack came undone and the spuds fell all over the road . . . Along came a bus – and sliced up all the spuds . . . We thought there ought to be a plaque put up on the allotment saying we were the first people to grow chips!'

And of course there was cricket. Terry, living in one of the newly built suburbs around Birmingham, had fond boyhood memories: 'In the summer, every fine evening and most of the weekends were taken up with cricket. Behind our houses there was a field that the builders had not yet started on. Between us we had managed to scrape together the bat, ball and stumps, courtesy of older brothers who had moved on to other ways of passing the time (such as taking girls to the pictures), and our game nearly always went on until it got dark.'

Ken, another sports-mad boy was a loyal supporter of Arsenal's football team at the young age of seven. He always met his father at the ground before games, and was given 8d. by his mother, the fare being 4d. each way; his father then paid the 4d. admission to get into the ground. 'One Saturday when I got off the tram there was no Dad: he had met up with a pal. So I paid my 4d. to get into the ground. I didn't have the fare back, so I walked home – 6 miles. My feet ached something rotten, but it was worth it – my team won!'

Each child had his or her own small domestic pleasures, which were infinitely more meaningful at a time when sheltered daughters of the well-to-do had few sources of amusement or stimulation outside the home, except for school. In an elegant stucco house in a leafy neighbourhood of London, Faith's biggest treat was to be invited to the kitchen by Cook – 'only when Mother was out, of course – and then being given my favourite Bird's custard. I adored it, but Mother always made me have the proper kind, made with eggs sent up on the train from Devon every week in a covered basket and collected at Paddington station. Cream and butter were sent up that way too. It was a regular service.'

Poorer city children, who had only small backyards at best, made up their own games and managed to have a thriving street life mucking about with whatever bits and pieces they could lay their hands on. In Newcastle, children in a large family who lived cheek by jowl in a two-bedroom tenement above a shop spent hours playing outside 'in the back lane'. In areas with small, overcrowded houses, the street was the natural meeting place, where relatives and neighbours and their children got together to gossip and play. These are among some of the happier memories of a girl called Vi, who lived through the Depression years in grim conditions: 'Those days everyone would be out there in the street – mothers, fathers, sisters and brothers. It used to be very friendly, playing Skippy, having concerts . . . Some people would make toffee cakes or toffee apples and sell them for a penny or so . . . I used to love to be rolled down the lane inside an old car tyre . . . We used to make dolls' beds out of matchboxes and used patches of old dresses for blankets.'

In the noisy bustle of Islington, north London – a largely working-class area, mostly impoverished, but full of vitality – there was always something going on for children to watch or take a hand in. Iris, who had lived there since her birth in 1927, reminisced:

We were lucky that we could roam the streets in those days, and after the market closed we poked about and brought lots of useful odds and ends home . . . One stall had cut fruit, so mothers would get a couple of halves of orange – or pears or apples – when the stallholder picked out the fruit going bad . . . We chalked on the pavement to play hopscotch, and sometimes we got hold of a piece of hearthstone that was used for whitening the front steps – that lasted for ages. We played marbles along the kerbstone, and we called them 'glarnies' . . .

On Sundays the muffin man came along with his handbell and a tray of muffins on his head. Another excitement was the barrel-organ man. He stopped outside the pub, and it was magic when he turned the handle – the children danced wildly to the music, throwing up their skirts, and a jolly crowd gathered tapping their feet, and sometimes a couple of young women would give a turn . . .

'I suppose', she finished wistfully, 'we only remember the happy times.'

Many people recall with real pleasure that close community life in which families – all poor – had known each other, and helped each other out, for generations. It was a way of life that social change, slum clearance and high-rise blocks of flats were to destroy for ever. Largely because the streets were always crowded, and people automatically looked out for each other, they were assumed to be safe for children. 'There was a murder once a few streets away, I know that. But otherwise I don't remember anything bad happening,' Elsie, who lived in the East End, said. 'Mum used to tell us, "Come home when it gets dark." That was all.'

With little or no organized entertainment, the underprivileged made do with spontaneous outbursts of high spirits, as this former city child remembered all her life:

Summer Sundays, late afternoon, without any sort of arrangement we would be sitting in the street on kerbs or against the area railings and all the young wives came out. Someone brought out a sturdy rope and it would be turned by two adults stretching across the street, and the young women would skip – running and skipping through the turning rope, with much laughing – and all along the street on doorsteps would be the older women and men looking on smiling and clapping . . . We children thought it was just wonderful, in awe of it all.

Middle-class children experienced a few more genteel amusements: the pantomime, a trip to the zoo, bucket-and-spade holidays by the sea. For a very sheltered child, living close to London's West End, Faith said that rare visits to the theatre with her parents were truly memorable occasions. 'Our lives were really rather mundane then, so treats were very special. I was an only child, so I paid a lot of attention to what was going on around me. I noticed things.' Apart from the excitement of the production, Faith said that all the beautifully dressed women who glided in and out of the theatre were 'literally, a fashion parade'. She developed an eye for colour and telling detail, and in later life became a world expert on dolls and doll's houses.

Dressing up, and dressing appropriately, was an important part of 1930s etiquette. For one evening theatre outing just before the war, when she was about thirteen, Faith wore a dress of 'pale apricot taffeta, covered in apricot net, with a long, wide sash – and bronze dancing slippers'. Her elegant and fashionable mother might have worn her favourite violet-coloured velvet evening coat with leg-of-mutton sleeves and white fox-fur collar; her most spectacular accessories of the period, which Faith has kept and treasured all her life, were a clutch bag covered with sequins and matching gold and silver kid shoes.

Before the war, boating was a popular family amusement among the better off. Harry, well into his teens in the late thirties, is positive to this day that winters were colder and whiter when he was young. He recalls 'snowy winters in our Thames-side village . . . and many leisurely hours in the summer on the river before motor boats and noisy cruisers destroyed its tranquillity . . . When I was at prep school in Surrey close by the then new Gatwick Airport . . . we used to wonder curiously why our headmaster should want to dress up in white tie on some summer afternoons to go to a mysterious place called Glyndebourne.'

For all children then, the cinema was the biggest treat of the lot. Walt Disney's *Snow White and the Seven Dwarfs* and Judy Garland in *The Wizard of Oz* were hits that endured into the early war years: children would chant and sing to the catchy tunes, and often change the words – 'Roll along, Mussolini, roll along; Abyssinia won't be yours for very long' – for most of their wartime childhoods. All through the 1930s, up and down the land, they queued for twopenny seats in their local children's cinema club on Saturday mornings – and this was the highlight of most children's weeks.

'In 1937, I think, our local Odeon started the Mickey Mouse Club.' Peter remembered – in every detail – the shows at his boyhood club, although it was nearly seventy years later:

It was sixpence to join, and for that we received a membership card (with a pink deckle edge) and every Saturday morning we paid our twopence to see two hours of films – cartoons with Mickey and Minnie, Donald Duck, Goofy, Horace and Horsecollar, and there was always a cowboy film with Roy Rodgers or Tom Mix. The show always ended with the heroine being left tied to the railroad track or the hero hanging off a cliff until next week.

All these children of the thirties were growing up against a difficult, discordant background: socially, politically and economically. The historian Angus Calder, echoing Dickens, said of the decade, 'It was the best of times, it was the worst of times.' Entrenched wealth and power were enjoyed by the few, but privation was endured by many. During the meandering travels that formed the basis for his 1934 book *English Journey*, in the depths of the Depression, the literary all-rounder J. B. Priestley visited Tyneside. 'There is', he wrote, 'no escape anywhere in Jarrow from its prevailing misery, for it is entirely a working-class town. One little street may be rather more wretched than another . . . one out of every two shops appeared to be permanently closed . . . There were men hanging about, not scores of them but hundreds of thousands of them.'

Violet was born at the beginning of the 1930s into just such an area in the north, close to the town Priestley was describing. 'I was the eleventh child. My mother was then forty-five years old,' she wrote, nearly a lifetime later.

I was born in a small bedroom. There was one more bedroom, a living room and a small scullery. Three of the children were already married, so that left Mum, Dad, myself and seven others . . . We were all left to live in this flat above a butcher's shop. The flat was lit by gas . . . From the scullery there was a flight of stone stairs into the backyard. In the yard there was a toilet.

We had a double bed in the big room for my dad and my three brothers; the small room had a single bed in which three of my sisters slept. Usually one of them got kicked in the body by someone's feet. In the living room there was another bed in which my mother, sister and I slept . . . Through the night you kept scratching. The next morning you had these red spots which were very itchy . . . They got a shovel of hot coal and held the shovel under the wire springs on the bed and you could hear the bugs cracking and they would fall out dead. It had to be done quite often.

This was part of Violet's early childhood experience in the north of England in the mid-1930s. Conditions were bad; there was no security; only the sticky emotional glue of family life kept the social structure going. Hardship among the working classes was widespread – on farms as well as in big cities – with little or no safety net. Studies in York and Bristol in 1936 concluded that some 18 per cent of the population had 'insufficient income for the basic needs of food and housing and healthcare', and it was the children, and their futures, that suffered most. Unemployment and poor health were the worst evils. In economically bad times, Violet's father had found work in a paint factory, which did his already weak chest no good. 'Sometimes he would have to stand against the wall in the back lane when he came home from work to get his breath.'

In depressed industrial areas such as South Wales and Tyneside, where the old industries of coal mining, shipbuilding, steel, cotton and the like had virtually shrivelled and died, even part-time shift work was at a premium. Colleen was a teenager in 1938. Her family lived in a run-down part of Liverpool, and her father picked up bits of work along the docks when he could. 'It was hard in the 1930s', she recalled. 'Dad used to go out at five o'clock in the morning and stand with a group of others waiting to be called on to get a day's work. If your face didn't fit, you didn't get it. And that's how it went. But he brought us all up – all five of us. And Mum used to take in washing and do cleaning. So we could get by.' During the war Collen joined the Wrens – the Women's Royal Naval Service – and later became a nurse.

A family in Inverness experienced a bitter twist of fate as their father, the breadwinner, regained employment – through another war. Evelyn said of her father:

He was a casualty from the First World War. He had his right leg amputated and many other wounds. He was on an 80 per cent pension. He had trained as a cabinetmaker and was employed by Lord Roberts Workshops in Inverness. In the thirties the workshop closed because of the slump. It opened again just before the Second World War, so ironically war provided us with the economic security which we could only dream of during peacetime.

The south of the country, although generally the most prosperous, also had areas of severe unemployment. 'I was born in Dagenham in 1930,' a woman wrote, looking back to those hard times that seriously affected her health. 'My family had moved there after the General Strike in 1926 in hopes of finding work. To say that we were poor would be putting it mildly. I developed bronchial pneumonia at the age of six months, which in turn affected my eyesight because my parents were too poor to pay for doctors' fees.'

Money was so tight at home that for some years she was placed in the care of a religious order. It was a deeply scarring experience. 'While . . . in this home I was mentally and physically abused . . . I can remember from the age of four having to scrub a floor – which I could not see properly because I had a patch over my good eye and was trying to see through the one that was nearly blind – and being beaten across the back with a broom handle because I had missed some water that I had not wiped up.' She was finally sent home in 1937. 'This was in time for the Jubilee celebrations . . . I recall having a flag put in my hand to wave about and a good old "knees up" as the Londoners call it.' She also got to know her two older brothers and sister for the first time.

At the opposite end of the social scale, light years removed both from the privations of the thirties' poor and, at least for the present, from the harsh and levelling realities of wartime, lay the sheltered nursery worlds of the children of the privileged. And over these secure and comfortable oases, in quite ordinary middle-class homes as well as in the houses of aristocrats, it was Nanny who presided.

In the early 1930s there were more than one and a quarter million women in service. Even an ordinary middle-class home would routinely employ two domestic servants – perhaps a nanny and a daily maid or gardener – while numbers increased dramatically further up the social and financial scale. Most nannies were country girls, straight out of school at fourteen, needing employment at a time when it was scarce, and probably recommended by a close friend or relative who had been similarly 'in service'.

In the grandest families, long-serving nannies were much treasured, occupied positions of entrenched respect, and were handed on down through at least two generations. Ursula, who was brought up in a magnificent country house, had a childhood that was, she wrote,

very sheltered and secure. We lived in two rooms, a day nursery and a night nursery, just going downstairs – having changed into organdie or velvet – from 5 to 6 p.m. We also went down the back stairs in the mornings to play in the garden and the park . . . looking after bantams, making bows and arrows, birds-nesting etc.

In the afternoon, Nanny and the nursery maid changed into grey costumes (the rest of the time Nanny always wore white and the nursery maids print dresses) and we went for a formal walk. (I remember the awful pinching leather gaiters!) Nan taught me to read when I was four, and then we had a governess when we were about nine . . . as well as a French mam'selle and a German Fräulein in the holidays.

Few children, even then, can have experienced quite this degree of wealth and formality. But even in more ordinary circumstances the availability of a nanny, and therefore of reliable, round-the-clock childcare, was taken for granted by the fairly prosperous middle and upper middle classes in the 1930s – although the majority of these mothers did not have their own careers. Even in homes with a conscientious mother about, Nanny still exerted a strong influence on her charges at a young and malleable age. One woman remembered that when there was talk just before the war of her and her brother being evacuated to Scotland, her brother, aged five, had immediately enquired not about his mother, but 'Will Nanny come too?'

Tens of thousands of pre-war families in country market towns, in farmhouses, in Edwardian villas and in the new suburban houses that had sprung up round big towns employed these young, usually untrained, girls who were known as 'Nanny'. These stable little 'nannied' kingdoms were based on a fairly rigid routine: meals, walks, bedtimes, bathtimes, and times spent with Mummy and/or Daddy, depending on an individual family's outlook and way of life.

Faith, who was the third generation of her family to live in its large stucco Victorian town house in a quiet area of London, said, 'I was the most overprotected child you could imagine. Mother was terrified of my being kidnapped . . . When I went out for a walk, or on my tricycle, with my governess I always had to walk or ride beside or directly in front of her.' A brother and sister, whose father was then a busy politician, saw their parents only at regular times in the late afternoon. 'But Mummy and Daddy would – occasionally – come in and read to us when we were in the bath.'

An author who grew up in a quiet country town said, 'I remember once on Nanny's afternoon out it began to drizzle and Mummy let my brother and me off our walk to stay in and finish a jigsaw puzzle. "But don't tell Nan", she begged us.'

A child's nursery regime was safe and secure, and, apart from occasional family outings, a little dull. Clothes were 'aired' on guards in front of nursery fires; tiresome, restricting leggings, and matching coats and hats with velvet trimmings – the smartest bought at Rowe's in Bond Street – were all part of the uniform of the well-brought-up 1930s child. The thought of combinations (all-in-one underwear contraptions with a buttoned trap door) – always Chilprufe (i.e. pure wool) – made one woman laugh out loud at the memory. 'Horrible, scratchy, itchy things they were too . . . And they can't have been very hygienic.'

Over the decades, the nanny culture evolved its own vocabulary. 'Nannyisms' – simple but stern, no-nonsense sayings, which were repeated day after day – tended to have a lifelong effect on the impressionable young. Elderly and distinguished men and women have been known to wobble at the knees on hearing 'Somebody's eyes are bigger than his tummy'; 'There's no such word as can't'; 'Finish it up – just think of the poor starving children'; 'Cleanliness is next to godliness'; 'Somebody has big ears'; 'Waste not, want not' – all Nanny-type reproofs which took former charges of all ages, and no matter what their station in life, right back to that safe, strict little nursery world where backs were kept straight and Nanny's word was law.

The ultimate Christmas and birthday presents for middle-class boys and girls of those pre-war years were Hornby electric trains for the boys and elaborate doll's houses (probably coming from Hamley's in Regent Street, with a little metal plate to prove it) for the girls. Approved nursery reading might have included Richmal Crompton's

'Just William' stories, A.A. Milne's *Winnie the Pooh* and Kathleen Hale's *Orlando the Marmalade Cat* for the young; Peter Cheyney and Leslie Charteris were devoured by older children.

A cosseted young girl remembered that she was never allowed to read newspapers, which were considered quite unsuitable for her age; only Arthur Mee's *Children's Paper* was permitted, and perusing this as seriously as her parents read their newspapers made her feel 'very grown up and superior' among her friends. The most popular nursery games were snap, ludo, rummy, happy families, snakes and ladders, and Monopoly. And on many a nursery bathroom wall hung a hugely popular Mabel Lucy Atwell plaque depicting the artist's trademark coy, chubby little 1930s child:

> *Please remember,*
> *Don't forget,*
> *Never leave the bathroom wet.*

Furthering the ideal of middle-class family life, in 1936 a series of occasional articles began appearing on the court page of *The Times*. They were nicely crafted pieces purportedly written by a well-off married woman who lived a charmed life in Chelsea with her architect husband and three children – and who did not work outside the home. The editor had thought up the idea to give the page more female interest, and the narrator was considered to have a lifestyle which most women readers of *The Times* could identify with – or aspire to. These articles, which were soon being devoured by both male and female *Times* readers, were written by a woman also living in Chelsea, in somewhat similar circumstances – Jan Struther, an author and journalist.

The writer's biographer, Ysenda Maxtone-Graham, would later describe the imaginary 'perfect' family that Struther created:

She had three children, Vin (Etonian, liked fishing), Judy (took her doll out in new red dress, chain-sucked barley sugar on journeys), and Toby (small, unfathomable, made guitar out of photograph frame and eight elastic bands). Clem was a perfect piano-playing husband and father. They lived in a stucco-fronted London square, where they gave dinner parties.

At weekends, when they were not invited to a country house party, they went to their cottage in Kent called Starlings.

What no casual readers could have foreseen was that a romanticized version of these entertaining pieces would soon form the basis of one of the major films of the coming war, *Mrs Miniver*. Though its plot was highly improbable, the film was a huge commercial success both in Britain and in the United States. Many British children – or the girls at least – will have carried for a lifetime the memory of the glamorous Mrs Miniver (Greer Garson) lying in bed and dreamily contemplating her delicious and wildly extravagant confection of a new hat, wartime or no.

A little earlier in the decade, pottering about the country for his *English Journey*, J. B. Priestley – who would soon be broadcasting bracing homilies to a people at war – found a nation that in broad terms seems oddly familiar today: the countryside, its picturesque villages, cottages and castles; the depressed heavily industrial areas; and the new manufacturing towns and suburbs, where modern, lighter industries were burgeoning and starting to create new prosperity. He travelled through 'the England of arterial and by-pass roads, of filling stations and factories that look like exhibition buildings, of giant cinemas and dance-halls and cafés, bungalows with tiny garages, cocktail bars, Woolworths, motor coaches . . . factory girls looking like actresses'. It was a brighter, brasher Britain, and its presentation, he suspected, was heavily influenced by the United States. Bicycles, typewriters, radios and the like were now desirable objects, which many more people – people living in the neat rows of houses in the spanking new suburbs – could afford. With the old industries in terminal decline, the new type of light manufacturing was the way forward. (But Coventry, in particular, would soon pay a heavy price for its sudden industrial prosperity.)

Despite Priestley's gloomy dislike of the increased traffic cluttering the roads and byways, the craze for the motor car had started in earnest. Importing goods from the Empire helped keep basic prices down, and those in work were starting to earn well and to prosper, so during the 1930s the motor car – from humble Ford to stately Rolls-Royce – became the status symbol for any family lucky enough to be able to acquire one. 'Motoring' and taking the family 'out for a spin' on the much improved main roads were leisure activities of choice. And by 1939 there were some 2 million cars careering up and down the modernized highways of Britain.

Family pride in car ownership was so great that in many mechanically minded boys it inspired a lifelong passion for anything to do with motor vehicles. Eddie was fifteen when, in 1932, his family acquired a second-hand Wolseley – which he still remembered fondly many years later. 'As family legend has it, it cost £40, although that seems extremely cheap for a two-year-old car even in those days. It was bi-coloured – dark blue below with a black roof – and had a six-cylinder twelve-horsepower engine. There was no boot, just a luggage rack, but there was a running board and a little vase for flowers . . . My father once got it up to a hair-raising speed of 55 m.p.h., but only briefly.'

Travelling by car in the thirties was an adventure. It could also be extremely dangerous. In 1934, with 1½ million registered vehicles, 7,000 people were killed in road accidents. No driving tests were required until 1935, when they became compulsory and cost 10 shillings (50p), and dipped headlights were not introduced until 1937. Unreliable cars and highly individual driving skills made for unexpected excitements – and mishaps – as Eddie also recalled.

My father must have read that under-inflating your tyres caused excessive wear. He extrapolated from this that the harder the tyres the longer life they would give. So he laboriously blew them up using the hand pump which came with the car . . . Somewhere near what is now Heathrow Airport, then just fields, there was suddenly an almighty bang as one of the rear tyres burst. That meant unloading the large suitcase strapped on to the luggage rack, putting on the spare wheel, and deflating the others before we could continue . . .

I remember a trip to see family in Dorset one Easter, and as we approached Shaftesbury along a winding lane we passed children picking primroses at the roadside. They turned and waved to us – cars were not so commonplace then.

Along with the fascination for the motor car came an even newer enthusiasm – aeroplanes. Hendon had a major aerodrome in the

1930s, and this was a big excitement for children living in the vicinity. Robin, who lived less than 5 miles away, remembered that from his garden he got a good view of the action: 'I would often see small planes passing low overhead, and from time to time one would make a forced landing in the fields . . . Once a very small plane didn't even make the fields and got caught in a large tree.'

One of the major events of the year was the Hendon Air Pageant, which Robin and his brother followed avidly. 'It was a small-scale Farnborough Air Show, with the RAF showing off its latest aircraft . . . I can still visualize the little biplanes swooping low over the airfield to drop bags of flour to give fairly realistic bomb bursts round the target.' These harmless dustings of flour would in time be followed by the real destruction, some of which Robin and his family experienced.

One of the many dichotomies of the festering and discordant decade of the 1930s is that, despite the poverty of so many, and the deteriorating international situation, the highest reaches of London society still glittered brilliantly. The numbers involved in the almost tribal merry-go-round were very small – a mere fraction of the population as a whole – but it was in this formidable web of high-ranking intermarriages and alliances, some reaching back for hundreds of years but constantly revived by new blood, that much of the wealth, the land and the political power of the country was then concentrated.

The members of this entrenched establishment – the aristocracy, the landed gentry and the aspiring newly wealthy – continued the tradition of 'bringing out' their seventeen- and eighteen-year-old daughters into the same social milieu. Both sons and daughters were expected to marry within its ranks, thus perpetuating its class and rituals and highly privileged way of life.

In the summer of 1939 somewhere between 900 and 1,000 of these well-connected girls were presented at court to the new King and Queen; with feathered headdress and exquisite, trailing ballgown, each girl in turn was announced and curtseyed low – probably coached by Madame Vacani, dancing teacher to royalty and to London's elite. A small percentage of these debutantes would have 'done' the season (which ran from late April through July) in the full sense: being given a dance of her own, receiving invitations to perhaps three others a night, plus a non-stop round of tea and cocktail parties, punctuated by the usual fashionable events like Ascot, Goodwood and Henley.

Having a debutante daughter doing the season in some style was an extremely costly business. A run-of-the-mill dance, held in a hotel or a smaller London house, and often shared with another girl, might cost each set of parents upwards of £1,000 – equivalent to two very reasonable middle-class yearly incomes. But for what could be called the 'hard core' of the debutantes – those with both the means and the desire to sparkle and charm and dance the nights away – the season of 1939 was, one said, like

being suddenly catapulted into this fairy-tale world where everything was champagne and flowers, strawberries and cream. It was deliriously marvellous. Having been brought up to believe that one was plain and stupid and uninteresting . . . and suddenly to have admirers . . . I remember going on the bus down Park Lane on a wonderful May morning and looking out, and all London was absolutely golden, with the sun shining, and I remember thinking, 'It's marvellous. Life is wonderful.'

In her book *1939: The Last Season*, Anne de Courcy gives a vivid picture of the time, trouble and artistry devoted to some of the season's grandest balls. She describes a dance that Lady Astor gave in her house in St James's Square for her debutante niece, Miss Dinah Brand, with a dinner for forty people beforehand:

[The] oval dining table, with its unusual centrepiece of an eighteenth-century Chinese pagoda [was] hung with tinkling silver-gilt bells . . . Even in this era of lavish floral decoration, the flowers were exceptional – brilliant gold tassels of laburnum swaying overhead, great masses of mauve, pink and purple flowers in the ballroom itself, white gardenias and pots of arum lilies in the small sitting-room, whose exotic, languorous scent drifted out.

At all the dances, the food was delicious and looked spectacular: lobster, salmon, strawberries, ices, a 3 a.m. breakfast of eggs and bacon – with champagne available throughout. Eligible, or at least suitable, young men – always scarce, and always in demand – could take their pick of invitations. The impecunious ones ate their fill, for nothing, for months; if bored by the company at one dance, they could usually manage to sneak off to another. Chaperones for the girls were insisted upon, and only the most daring deb managed to slip off to a nightclub with a young man.

People who took any part in that 1939 season, and who still remember, speak of it as having had a special quality of brilliance – perhaps because the threat of another war lent an added urgency. It is also generally agreed that the indisputable climax to all this glittering sociability was the ball held at Blenheim Palace on 7 July.

The dance was to celebrate the coming-out of Lady Sarah Spencer-Churchill, the seventeen-year-old daughter of the Duke and Duchess of Marlborough. But this was no ordinary debutante dance, for the cosmopolitan guest list, which included diplomats, political leaders and top establishment figures as well as the gilded young, transformed it into the final private extravaganza of that last pre-war summer.

The words used over and over to describe Blenheim Palace that night were 'magical' and 'magnificent'. The ball was also believed to be the last grand occasion in England when footmen, wearing eighteenth-century Marlborough livery, powdered their wigs (usually with flour from the kitchen). It might also be said that the setting, commemorating a glorious military success of Britain's past, was ominously appropriate.

Anne de Courcy wrote, 'All was splendour, magnificence, glamour, with the great golden façade of the Palace, lit by powerful floodlights, gleaming in the distance as guests drove towards it down dark country roads.' A young debutante guest remembered the 'floodlighting and music and the lights in the garden among trees and shrubs . . . great masses of pink malmaisons all over the house . . . I remember dancing . . . masses of waltzes . . . all the marble statues all down the long passage . . . And at a certain moment the whole of Blenheim was floodlit. Oh, fantastic!'

Among the guests – fittingly, as Blenheim was both his birthplace and his ancestral home – was Winston Churchill. A young girl spotted him, strolling up and down one of the terraces, smoking and talking to another politician, the handsome and debonair Anthony Eden. The same girl, one of the popular debutantes of the season, recalled that her partner, seeing Churchill, said of him quite dismissively, 'Look at that poor old has-been. My father says he's still a potential troublemaker, but he won't get any public life now.'

As dawn broke and the floodlights faded to darkness, the guests melted away and the curtain came down on the Blenheim ball and on an era. Sixty-eight days later war with Germany was declared. Within six months the 1930s, which the poet W. H. Auden called 'a low dishonest decade', were over.

Ten months after he had paced the Blenheim terraces on that summer night, at a party given for a tall young girl with red-gold hair, Winston Churchill became Prime Minister. And nearly everybody's life had in some way been altered.

Schools, charged with the care of the nation's youth, were in the forefront of this change, and emergency shelters and evacuation procedures had already been arranged. In the autumn of 1938 the headmaster of Malvern College had been informed that, should war break out, the college buildings would be requisitioned. Finding alternative accommodation for so many boys, as well as their classroom and sports requirements, was extremely difficult; but, after the country had been searched for premises, the national treasure of Blenheim Palace was suggested.

The Duke of Marlborough had patriotically offered the palace to the country for as long as it was needed, and, although he had expected orderly government offices to move in, he sportingly agreed to allow Malvern College to take up residence instead. There is a story, possibly apocryphal, which has it that the deal was clinched by the experience of the catering at that final ball; after they had wined and dined the hundreds of guests that night, the headmaster was confident that the palace kitchens would be well able to cater for 450 Malvern boys and staff.

For a Malvern schoolboy of fifteen called Nigel, who was longing for a bit of wartime action, this was a thrilling turn of events. Shortly after Lady Sarah and her friends, hardly out of the schoolroom themselves, had danced and partied through them, the great rooms were being put to a very different use. Nigel remembered it very clearly: 'The grand state rooms were our dormitories, and initially also classrooms – until wooden huts were built in the front courtyard.'

Whatever the dangers facing the country at the time, these Malvern College boys were, understandably, both intrigued and a little awed by their stately new surroundings. But not too intimidated to have some fun: 'To our delight the winter of 1939–40 was very cold, freezing the great lake for many days of skating and much tobogganing in the snow down to the bridge.' And while the world waited for the cacophony of war to begin, the boys – many of whom would soon join the services – began training enthusiastically. Nigel, who later became a naval officer and saw active wartime service wrote:

The school Training Corps became a unit of the Local Defence Volunteers (later named the Home Guard) and we patrolled the Blenheim estate at nights, always hoping to challenge a German parachutist . . . I also spent several nights on the many acres of the palace roofs . . . As Churchill had been born at Blenheim Palace, we were assured it was the target for enemy bombers, so we really felt to be in the front line.

For Nigel and his classmates, for the fetching Sandrine, living at the top of her family's house in a smart Kensington square, for the chipper Iris, battling her way through a hard inner-city childhood, and for millions of others in all kinds of backgrounds up and down the country, life was about to change dramatically.

To the last boy and girl, they were about to become the children of war.

2

'THIS STRANGEST OF WARS': AUGUST TO DECEMBER 1939

Sunday 3 September 1939, 11.27 a.m. People run for safety in Whitehall, a woman clutching her little girl, when the first air-raid siren sounds minutes after the declaration of war. This was a false alarm, but at the time it seemed that the nation's worst fears of immediate air attack were being realized

In August, my friend, also five, tells me, 'My daddy knows a man who knows Hitler and there is going to be a war.' That was my first knowledge that something 'big' was going to happen.
A child in Newcastle, who later became a lawyer

Rather than be afraid, we were all just trying to carry on as calmly and normally as possible.
A London schoolgirl, fifteen struggling with exams, getting seven honours in her matriculation – but failing maths 'miserably'

By the end of August 1939 the summer-holiday season was drawing to an uncertain close. As many remarked, if this was a run-up to war it was the longest preamble to armed conflict in history. Since the Munich crisis the previous autumn, the whole country had been on tenterhooks, hoping for the best but secretly fearing the worst.

A stream of government leaflets, starting in the winter with a hefty publication *The Protection of your Home against Air-Raids*, delivered to every household, had put a damper on family holiday plans; many chose to stay close to home that year, worried about immediate petrol rationing and chaos on the railways if war broke out. July and August brought yet more unwelcome practical advice: *Your Gas Mask* and *Masking Your Windows* were among the depressing official leaflets dropping through letterboxes. Understandably, none of this was conducive to a jolly holiday mood.

All the same, an unusually long spell of good weather late in the summer raised spirits, as always with the British, and, as August ended and the days imperceptibly drew in, many seaside towns were still crowded with last-minute holidaymakers. On holiday with her parents and older sister in a rented house on the Norfolk coast, Carola, a four-year-old who lived in Cambridge, was playing in the garden. 'There was a swing, and I remember swinging on it one lunchtime and hearing from the wireless inside the house the high, ranting voice of Hitler.'

The hypnotic and slightly crazed tone, the screeching, and the timing – it was the day before war was declared – made those moments stick in her memory. And she was not unusual. In fact Hitler's complex, demonic personality continues to exert a terrible fascination on generation after generation. An experienced lecturer on wartime evacuations, who often gives talks in schools, has found that more than sixty years later even quite young children recognize a photograph of Hitler far more readily than they might a contemporary politician.

The mood of the country was sombre rather than jittery. With the Scottish jute industry struggling to keep up with the demand for sacking, the price of sandbags had doubled to 5d. since Munich. Dorothy, the fifteen-year-old from Dulwich whose father had served in the last war, and whose older brother was intending to join the RAF shortly, made the most of the warm sunshine and spoke nostalgically of 'staying with friends in their house in Cornwall . . . a last idyllic peacetime holiday'. Many families, deciding at the last minute that the war could wait, had done the same. A sign saying 'Half a mo', Hitler, let's have our holidays first' appeared on the back of many family motor cars. A week for a family of four in a good small hotel in a choice holiday spot in the Lake District or Devon, or on the Welsh coast, would have set the head of the house back some £20 – a decent sum in 1939.

Economically, times were a good deal better for most people than they had been five years before: although there were still more than a million unemployed, a healthy sign of expanding middle-class prosperity was the increase in car and home ownership, shorter working weeks, and a steadily rising standard of living. And, despite all the talk of war, there was much to enjoy for those holidaymakers who could afford it.

Ice cream was slower to attract the mass market in Britain than across the Atlantic, but during the 1930s sales soared and it became a national passion. Wall's, the sausage-makers, had shrewdly spotted the trend, and by 1939 it had thousands of ice-cream salesmen trundling along Britain's roads on tricycles fitted with refrigerators bearing the slogan 'Stop Me and Buy One.' Children playing along the front in Brighton, or anywhere else, paid 2d. for their choc ices and tubs. The giant American chain store F. W. Woolworth had become a feature of most British high streets; keen pricing (it was known as the '3d. and 6d. store') made it a target for children's pocket money, and it sold nearly everything – including sweets and toys and records and the newly available Penguin paperback books for 6d. each.

The traditional attractions such as Blackpool's tower and pleasure gardens, a big draw for holidaying families for generations, were now getting competition from Butlin's holiday camps, which had started in 1935 in Skegness, and had become increasingly popular with parents and children.

For the more adventurous holidaymakers, determined to get a last peacetime look at the Continent, the cheapest fare from Victoria to Paris was £3. But the war clouds were gathering fast. Molly, a girl of seventeen from Nottingham, who would soon find herself working as a wartime land girl, was happily cycling through the Burgundy vineyards; she was astonished to be told by a French boy, quite seriously, that a group of young Germans staying at the youth hostel were suspected of being spies. Another girl, the daughter of a surgeon, who would enter medical school during the war, was holidaying in Brittany with her family that month: 'We were certain this was to be our last holiday, and I think that made it very special. We all remembered every single thing we did during those two weeks.'

Also 'certain' were many of the young men and women who would be called upon to serve their country if war came. So many couples, in all strata of society, were rushing into matrimony that registrars struggled to cope with the demand for their services. Keeping to his principle of resolute calm – or out of touch with the gravity of the situation, as many now thought – the Prime Minister went north to take his annual fishing holiday in Scotland. The King and Queen and their daughters were at Balmoral as usual. One of the 'cleverest minds in England', the playwright George Bernard Shaw, was so convinced there would be peace even at that late stage that he wrote to *The Times* complaining 'everyone except myself is frightened out of his or her wits.' But the public knew better.

During those last days of peacetime summer, Terry, a lively six-year-old from Palmer's Green, north London, was parked with friends on a farm in Devon when he came down with chickenpox. 'The people I was staying with must have loved that,' he said wryly. 'Anyhow, my parents were away in Annecy in CPP 197, our trusty black Ford, and as the political situation worsened they had to rush headlong back across Europe – not that a Ford 8 did much rushing anywhere – to be one of the last cars to be accepted on the ferry. After that it was foot passengers only and you left your car on the quayside.'

At the seaside in Northumberland, Sue, aged four, her brother (five years older), and her parents and grandparents were finishing their 'last family holiday. Brother Derek had just passed the eleven-plus exam. I still have the last ciné films of this holiday – the last ciné film until I was twelve or thirteen years old, because no film was available during the war.'

Debby had just left school and was about to enter the Civil Service. She was staying at the remote family holiday bungalow, also in Northumberland. 'On 27 August there were violent thunderstorms throughout the land,' she wrote. She remembered this particularly because she was so terrified of lightning that she 'spent several hours hiding under a travelling rug'. She was cured by living in the tropics later in life, but at that time of threatening catastrophe the severity of the storms struck her as ominous.

All over the country, older children – reading the papers, watching newsreels in cinemas, and listening to their parents – were becoming acutely aware of the gravity of the international news. A family holidaying in Cornwall decided to return home early 'for reasons we all understood', Dorothy, fifteen, remembered. 'The terrible realization that war was actually going to happen became obvious. Travelling home, as the train got closer and closer to London, more and more men in uniform got on at each stop. I felt at the time a sort of doom closing in on us which was frightening.'

Returning home, holidaymakers found that shoddy, brick-built public air-raid shelters had erupted in towns all over the country, and the miles of uninviting trenches dug for air-raid emergencies in the green acres of city parks were falling in and very damp. Householders had been given serious warnings and, taking no chances, were digging in to protect their families. 'Mounds indicating newly dug-in shelters had appeared in gardens all around where we lived,' Carola said of her return to Cambridge after the family holiday. 'Soon ours was at the bottom of the garden too, some 20 yards from the house.'

Parliament was recalled on 22 August, and the Emergency Powers Defence Act, which set in train the wartime regulations, such as the blackout, that would govern everyone's life for the next six long years, was passed soon after. Schoolteachers were called to report to their jobs on 24 August. On the 31st the fleet was mobilized and all reservists, including the Territorials, were recalled to duty.

Despite all this serious military activity, for most people life went on as usual – outwardly at least. But the political situation was never far from anyone's mind. The mounting uncertainty and the impossibility of deciding on any future plans were making people understandably glum. The threat of 'national emergency' – euphemism for the dreaded word 'war' – loomed over everything.

In parks and streets and gardens, children were skipping and chanting to the catchy, rhythmic ditty of

> *Under the spreading chestnut tree,*
> *Neville Chamberlain said to me:*
> *'If you want to get your gas mask free,*
> *Join the blinking ARP.'**

In fact, despite what the song alleged, all gas-masks – including Mickey Mouse imitations for small children, and weird air-pumping contraptions for babies – were free, and some 38 million had been handed out since the Munich crisis of the previous September.

Even when they were out playing, children were encouraged to carry their masks slung across their chests, and to practise getting them on and off. For putting them on, the magic words, instilled

---

* ARP – standing for 'air-raid precautions' – was also used to refer to the Air Raid Wardens Service.

relentlessly, were 'Chin first'. The historian Angus Calder describes the horrid, slimy objects as 'grotesque combinations of pig-snout and death's-head'. But the need to carry them at all times was driven home starkly by the Ministry of Information. A sinister poster of a black, saturnine Hitler, which was widely distributed, threatened, 'Hitler will give no warning.' As was intended, it put the fear of God into the public – particularly parents of the young, who knew of the horrors of gas from what had been experienced in the trenches in France twenty years before. But most small children found gas masks alien and deeply frightening, and mention of them, even today, brings a shudder. No one has forgotten the rubbery feel – or, particularly, the smell. 'I hated the smell. I can smell it now' – nearly seventy years later, this woman, then a young child, spoke for eveyone who lived through the war. Others are convinced that their childhood experience of gas masks set off a lifelong struggle with claustrophobia.

All the same, despite the tiresome precautions, the national sense of urgency also brought a whiff of irresistible excitement to the young – of all ages. Richmal's Crompton's *William and A.R.P.*, published in May 1939, captured the attitude of many youngsters. It begins with William and his friends the Outlaws contemplating forming their own ARP unit:

'Well, I don' see why we shun't have one, too,' said William morosely. 'Grown-ups get all the fun.'

'They say it's not fun,' said Ginger.

'Yes, they say that jus' to put us off,' said William. 'I bet it *is* fun all right. I bet it'd be fun if *we* had one, anyway.'

'Why don't we have one?'

'I asked 'em that. I said, "Why can't we have one?" an' they said, "Course you can't. Don't be so silly." Silly! S'not *us* what's silly, an' I told 'em so. I bet we could do it as well as what they do. Better, come to that. Yes, I bet that's what they're frightened of – us doin' it better than what they do.'

'What do they do, anyway?' demanded Douglas.

'They have a jolly good time,' said William vaguely. 'Smellin' gases an' bandagin' each other an' tryin' on their masks. I bet they bounce out at each other in their masks, givin' each other frights. I've thought of lots of games you could play with gas masks, but no one'll let me try. They keep mine locked up. Lot of good it'll be in a war locked up where I can't get at it. Huh!'

There was a pause, during which the Outlaws silently contemplated the absurdity of this situation.

Five-year-old Andrew took a cheerful, if competitive, attitude to his strange new accessory:

I felt that a gas mask in a material bag, like my friend Keith's dad had as an ARP warden, was much more sophisticated, and therefore more desirable, than the standard-issue box-on-a-string that I had to carry round with me. Unlike some of my contemporaries (mainly wimpish girls!) I didn't feel claustrophobic in my gas mask. But I definitely didn't like the smell – similar to masks they used for anaesthetic gas.

It was during this edgy, beginning-of-war period that the Anderson shelter first entered many people's lives. Around 1½ million were handed out free to householders with gardens; the better-off paid £7. Named after Sir John Anderson, the Home Secretary, who had done much to galvanize the rather piecemeal preparations for war on the home front, these half-buried shelters were by no means easy to erect. They were simple corrugated-steel structures with a curved roof, 7½ feet long and 6 feet wide, and were inserted in a hole 4 feet deep and covered with soil; the entry was sandbagged. Sitting or lying in one was described by a boy of seventeen, who later spent a lot of time in his, as 'rather like being entombed in a small, dark bicycle shed, smelling of earth and damp'.

In the grim days and nights that were to come, these clumsy contraptions, which frequently flooded, proved highly effective and undoubtedly saved many lives; but in the late summer of 1939 they were chiefly a source of entertainment to children. Sammy, who lived in Coventry and was no more than three or four in 1939, vividly re-created the mind of a child at that time with simple, snapshot memories of things going on around him which made no sense: 'This weekend my father and some neighbours have been digging a large hole. This is fun and I want to help. Is it for sandcastles? When it is finished they all go home and it starts to fill with water. It is to be our air-raid shelter.'

Brothers of about five and six were forbidden to enter their brand-new Anderson shelter near Glasgow – which of course made it all the more enticing. After playing all round it all one afternoon, jumping on and off, they finally ventured inside. 'There was so much water in it that it came right over our Wellingtons. I remember us running in crying to Mum.'

For little girls, this strange new 'room' which appeared at the bottom of the garden was an ideal spot to play house. 'Dad installed two little bunk beds for us children,' Sally, who lived in Ipswich, remembered. 'There was a table, and an oil lamp too. It was a tight squeeze, but it was quite cosy. We played "house" in there before it started . . . but once it got nasty we wouldn't go near the place unless we had to – and that was often enough.'

Over the first weekend in September the weather turned sultry. The political temperature also started to rise rapidly. Early on 1 September German troops moved into Poland; Warsaw was heavily bombed soon after. In the UK, Operation Pied Piper – the official evacuation plan to remove children, some mothers, the elderly and the disabled out of the cities – swung into action, and people of all ages, but mostly children, streamed by bus and train into the remoter parts of the countryside.

At sunset that Friday, 1 September, the blackout went into operation. There had been many half-hearted practice runs – mostly bungled – but this was official. The whole country was instantly united in gloom and irritation; no one, of whatever age or station in life, was exempt. Mothers, sisters, daughters and working women everywhere were forced to down tools and sew special-purpose government fabric (heavy black sateen, about 2 shillings a yard – it soon ran out), or whatever they could lay their hands on, into chink-less lightproof window coverings. Carola remembered them clearly: 'Ours were made of a thick, dull-black material and hung on all windows behind the normal curtains.' Others struggled to concoct a dye which a government leaflet recommended to make any fabric, or shutter, lightproof. It was, one handy young boy said, a 'repellent-looking mixture', which he helped his father 'cook'. But it was used, in desperation, by many, and it apparently worked well enough. The blackout was rigidly enforced, and would profoundly affect everyone's life, in town and countryside alike, for the duration.

Scarcely remarked upon at the time, the world's first television station, the BBC – which reached about 20,000 people, mostly in the London area – was shut down indefinitely on 1 September, slap in the middle of transmitting a children's Mickey Mouse cartoon.

While all this profound social disruption was bearing down on every man, woman and child in the country, at the beginning of that momentous weekend the Prime Minister still clung stubbornly to slim hopes for a continuing peace. Eventually his own Cabinet staged a revolt. They had had enough of prevarication, which was being interpreted as weakness by Germany and which led nowhere; the time had come for Britain to face up to this evil and aggressive enemy. According to Angus Calder, the drama of Neville Chamberlain's confrontation with his Cabinet on the night of 2 September was heightened when a ferocious storm, with thunder and lightning, broke immediately above the Houses of Parliament – 'A regular Old Testament hundred-percenter flogged London with a faint premonition of floggings to come.' In Berlin, a final ultimatum, that Germany immediately withdraw its troops from Poland, had been delivered by the British ambassador.

Sunday dawned. From all accounts, once the storms had passed over, the morning of 3 September 1939 was exceptionally fine – brilliantly sunny, with a hint of autumn tang. In the past days, people had devoured every word of the staid BBC news bulletins, hoping against hope for a last-minute reprieve; but there was by then also a resignation, a real feeling of 'let's get it over with.' At 10 a.m. came a brief official announcement: the Prime Minister would address the nation at 11.15.

By mid-morning the country was hushed and stilled, with little traffic on the roads. Despite feeling a bit foolish, Mary, who was sixteen and worked on a farm in Sussex, took care to have her gas mask with her when she went about her milking chores that day. Wherever possible, friends and families instinctively came together and huddled round their radios, as if seeking a spark of human comfort. As Kevin, whose home was in a village near Cardiff, recalled many years later, the focal points that morning were the family and the wireless. 'I remember my brother and I and our parents gathering round our small Bakelite wireless, bought specially because of the crisis – the first one we had.'

Dan, a teenage boy from Newcastle, camping with his friend in Northumberland, joined a gang of children playing along the riverbank and went to listen in the village shop, specially opened for locals for the occasion. From that spot, as he remembered all his life, you got a fine view of the hills and the surrounding fields and countryside – a timeless landscape which was steadying at that period of uncertainty and danger.

All over the country, in the face of national crisis, worried neighbours were speaking across garden hedges, and innate British standoffishness was slowly crumbling. Fortunate householders owning a wireless – and in 1939 many did not – invited round those who were without. James, a future social historian, who was then living in a Manchester suburb, said, 'This was the first time the family next door had ever been inside our house, though we had lived side by side for nine years.' Small children were gathered on to laps, dogs were controlled, and windows were opened wide on to sunny gardens so that those working outside could also hear, and the country fell silent.

I am speaking to you from the Cabinet Room at 10 Downing Street. This morning, the British Ambassador in Berlin handed the German Government a final note, stating that unless the British Government heard from them by 11 o'clock that they were prepared at once to withdraw their troops from Poland, a state of war would exist between us. I have to tell you now that no such undertaking has been received, and that consequently this country is now at war with Germany.

When the Prime Minister had finished speaking, the national anthem was played and many people rose to their feet. The writer Norman Longmate, who would later so brilliantly chronicle that time, was then aged thirteen. He wrote, 'That was how the war began for my family and for millions of other families throughout Great Britain.'

Chamberlain's desperate attempts to secure peace in Europe had failed, and for the second time in the first half of that bloodied century the country was preparing to fight Germany – now usurped by Hitler and his Nazi party. The Prime Minister was then a man of seventy, and his voice came over as old, tired, sad and a little querulous. (Scratchy recordings still attest to this.) The intense strain had also taken a terrible personal toll: he was probably already a sick man, and he died of cancer little more than a year later.

Many people who were children then still remember listening to that short, simple address: the atmosphere in which it was received and the awesome realization of what was happening have never quite left them. Even those who were very young then remember, hazily, their bewilderment at watching the reactions of the grown-ups around them. After the Prime Minister had spoken, the whole tenor of the country had changed, and with it the lives of every one of its citizens. Even those as young as three – with no understanding of the meaning – seem to have absorbed, and retained, the extreme gravity of the moment.

These are just a few of their memories of that luminous Sunday morning: simple, honest, poignant.

Jane, then six, for whom that declaration would presage personal tragedy, said, 'I remember sitting in Grandmother's small front room with all the family and hearing Chamberlain speaking. The feeling of anxiety is still with me . . . Being hugged by crying aunts . . . all their men, and my father, being career servicemen.' She and her family were in Portsmouth. Her sense of 'anxiety' was prescient: two years later her father, a naval officer, was lost on HMS *Barham*. He was thirty-two.

A seven-year-old boy called Robin was living in a village in Kent, not far from the coast. He remembered, amused, the cosy domestic scene in the living room of their cottage that morning. 'Our next-door neighbour came running around and said to my mother, "Oh dear, Olive, what are we going to do?" My mother replied, "Don't worry, dear, they say it will only last a couple of weeks. Now let's have a nice cup of tea."' A year later, much had changed. His father had been called up into the services, and the once quiet blue skies above the village were the setting for many of the deadly dogfights of the Battle of Britain. Robin, who watched avidly from the garden, became a first-rate plane-spotter; it was his passion for making model aircraft that eventually led to a lifelong career as a professional woodcarver.

Across the Channel from this Kent village, in Brittany, a little girl called Yvette, with her twin brother, an older brother and sister, and her mother, had been spending the summer in their seaside holiday home. Many years later she wrote:

My father, who was French, had come to London . . . to work in a French bank in the City and met my mother, who was from Yorkshire. They married and lived mainly in England. As was the custom for many French families, we used to spend our summer holidays in the country. For us it was Brittany. In 1939 Father bought a small bungalow, standing alone facing the bay, at Quimiac, 30 km from Saint-Nazaire. That summer, into September, we were at Quimiac. There was talk of war. My father, intensely patriotic, thought it would be safer for us to stay in Brittany than return to London, our home, in case of bombing. So when he returned to work in London, we stayed on.

Never dreaming that France would capitulate, the family remained in the Saint-Nazaire district. After the fall of France in June 1940 they were trapped, and endured many perils during the following five difficult and dangerous years.

In East Anglia on that fine September morning, Shirley and her parents set off for an ordinary, carefree family outing. 'My mum and dad and myself had gone for a day by the sea. We were walking along the pier at Great Yarmouth when a newspaper-seller came along shouting "War is Declared", and although it was still only just past eleven in the morning my dad said, "We'd better get back home straight away!"' Shirley said she often wondered, later, 'what on earth good he thought that would do'. But most people's instinct, like her father's, was to get the family into familiar home surroundings as soon as possible.

In a village outside Sheffield, an eleven-year-old boy called Jim was cleaning his bike as he listened to the Prime Minister's announcement through the open kitchen window – the family having recently got hold of a second-hand radio. 'My mother had just returned from a holiday on the Isle of Wight, and she brought me back a stick of rock and a pair of Woolworth's binoculars. With these, I immediately began to scan the skies for enemy aircraft.' He said that, for him, Chamberlain's words were a relief because they 'ended the uncertainty'. He and his friends eagerly devoured the heroic actions of 'Flash Gordon . . . the *Beano* . . . and the *Knockout* comics. And as a child, with little thought to the consequences, I have to say that it was a very exciting time.'

Very young children, alert to adult emotions, quickly picked up on the apprehension all around them. In Coventry, Billy, who was four, was 'playing on the floor with Dinky toys that Sunday and my aunt had joined us. I remember the wireless being on and all the adults listening intently. I had no idea what was going on. I asked what was the matter, and my father said that a war had started between us and Germany. I said we would win, and my aunt replied, "Yes – but how long will it take?"'

David, who lived in Birmingham, has retained crystal-clear images of that morning all his life:

A Sunday. I am 3½. We are visiting my uncle and auntie. They are listening to the wireless. In a little while my auntie takes me by the hand and leads me to the door. She points. 'Look at that balloon, David.' I can see it, silver against the blue sky. Nobody tells me what it is for. My mother, unusually firm for her, says that if ever she tells me to lie down in the street I must do it right away. 'Even if I am wearing my new coat?' I ask. 'Yes.'

A young mother in the Midlands was desperate to get her small son away from the depressing atmosphere of the adults talking in the sitting room after the Prime Minister's speech. She remembered taking his hand and walking with him in the sunshine right to the bottom of the garden and watching a train go by. Waving at it with her little boy, she wondered fearfully what would become of them all.

Edith was twelve, living in a working-class area of London, and well aware that war was imminent. In her street, she was the only child who had not been evacuated from the city with her school. Her father had died before she was born, and her mother had recently remarried and had another daughter. That warm Sunday morning, with her playmates gone off to their temporary homes in the country, she was playing with her baby sister in the backyard. 'My mother and stepfather had the wireless on in the kitchen. Suddenly I noticed the stillness – it was as if everyone in the world was holding their breath . . . I heard the words that the Prime Minister was saying and I heard my mother shriek, and they were both crying when I went in.'

Because her mother felt she needed her help and support at home, Edith was never put down for the government's evacuation scheme. She believed this was a real hardship for her, and she resented it all her life. A year later, in the thick of the Blitz, she spent fifty consecutive nights in a cramped, dank brick air-raid shelter in that same backyard.

In the kitchen of their farmhouse in Devon a family had gathered, as they did every Sunday morning. 'I was sitting with my mum, dad and three brothers,' Sylvia remembered clearly. 'One of my father's friends was there too – he usually visited my father on Sunday mornings for a chat and a glass or two of his home-produced cider. They often talked of the last war (1914–18), which they had both served in.' But that morning they listened in silence round the wireless. After the Prime Minister had spoken, she had, she said,

a fear in the pit of my stomach: what would happen to me, a girl of ten years? . . . But the Sunday passed as usual – Mum's scrumptious roast beef for lunch, Sunday school in the afternoon, fancy cream cakes for tea . . . As dusk fell I had to shut the hens in for the night – this was my chore on the farm. The field in which the henhouse was placed was about half a mile from the house, and the only thing that had ever bothered me was shooing the bull away . . . But that night I gazed anxiously at the sky, afraid that German soldiers might be parachuting down.

Instant communication was not to be taken for granted then as it is today. Debby, who had just left school, was on holiday with her family in an isolated part of Northumberland. They had no wireless or newspapers, and did not know that war had been declared, she said, until 'people began arriving in taxis (few people had cars in those days), escaping what they thought was going to be an immediate bombardment. I had to return home in one of those taxis that afternoon, and I was petrified when we got near Newcastle and saw barrage balloons aloft for the first time.' Although she could not know it at the time, the war changed all her plans. She soon went into the Wrens – 'And that', as she wrote looking back down the years, 'is when my real life began.'

Peggy, from Inverness, whose family had known real hardship through her father's unemployment during the worst years of the slump, never forgot an odd incident that happened to her that Sunday morning. 'One hour before war was declared, I was sitting on my front doorstep humming a popular tune when a neighbour caught me by the collar and, peering into my face, asked me if I knew that singing on the Sabbath was sinful and if I didn't stop I would be sent to the "burning fire". I was eleven years old.' Brought up in poor, and very narrow, social conditions, Peggy came to believe that the war had widened her horizons, creating opportunities she would never have had otherwise. Leaving school at fourteen, she took a job as a junior clerk in a lawyer's office (for 10 shillings a week); she enrolled in wartime night-school classes to complete a secretarial course and also to sit the Royal Society of Arts English examination. There were no books in her home as a child, but she soon became, and has remained, a passionate reader. And there was another door this coming war would open for her: with certain entry standards relaxed, she was eventually able to join the Civil Service and have a fulfilling career.

Picture five-year-old red-headed twin boys, with their two elder brothers, all squashed in the back of their parents' car, driving from Birmingham on that hot Sunday morning to stay with friends in Leamington Spa. If war broke out, their father was convinced that Birmingham would immediately be targeted by enemy bombers. As they drew into a petrol station, one of the twins remembered his father asking the attendant, 'Any news?' and being told that war had been declared only minutes before. The family stayed on in the Midlands, and the following year the twins witnessed the devastation of Coventry that turned the night skies into an inferno.

Pamela, a future WREN, was nearly fourteen:

I saw a long crocodile of young children – all labelled and each carrying a gas mask and some kind of case – en route from the railway station to the Sunday school hall, where they would be chosen by the strangers they'd be billeted with. We lived in a reception area, halfway between Leeds,

Bradford and Manchester. The first evacuees came from a very poor part of Bradford, and some of my old dresses were given to the two who ended up living next door, for them to use as nightdresses.

Peter, also nearly fourteen, had a lucky escape that weekend:

Our Boy Scout troop used to go over to Jersey for the annual summer camp. The cost was £2 for a fortnight, including the fare. We went to St Helier on the last Saturday to check up on the sailing times. We were told that our boat, the SS *St Julian*, had been commandeered by the Admiralty – 'because there's going to be a war tomorrow'. We finally got home after sailing through the night. When I walked into our dining room, Mum and the neighbours were listening to the wireless and Mr Chamberlain was speaking. Why didn't we stay in safety in Jersey? I thought.

Henry, twelve, in Portland, Dorset, went to church as usual with his younger brother. During the service, the vicar placed 'a wireless on the pulpit rail so the congregation could hear the Prime Minister's broadcast'.

Such memories were echoed by a girl of seven, Mary, who was living in Scotland, near the Clyde, with her mother and sister. Her father, a naval officer, was posted abroad in Alexandria, Egypt. 'I can clearly remember the day war broke out,' she said, 'and my mother – always so cheerful – saying she had so hoped she would not have to live through another war.' In the years to come, Mary's chief wartime discomfort was not bombs but the cold; when nobody was looking, she used to run the hot tap and hold her hands under what tepid water there was, and her feet were 'constantly covered with chilblains and had to be rubbed with Zambuck [an all-purpose medicated ointment that children of the 1940s grew up with]'.

Martin, who was five, cheerfully remembers 'sitting on Ma's knee to hear Neville Chamberlain . . . and going the next day to Parkstone, in Dorset, to stay with my aunt (nearer to the enemy!)'. Later in the war his family experienced tragedy through random violence from the skies – which was common during wartime. His uncle was killed. Martin recalled his father making the sad journey to Portsmouth to identify his brother's body. 'He had been killed while walking past a pub that received a direct hit . . . My father brought back my uncle's crumpled cigarette case. He left a widow and seven children.' Another member of his family, Martin's grandfather, was luckier. 'One day during a raid in London he ran for his bus home and missed it. He learned later that it was passing a local outfitting shop when it was hit.'

A mother who had evacuated herself and her two young children to stay with friends in the West Country was taking the children for a Sunday-morning walk on 3 September when she heard the Prime Minister's voice come crackling out of an open cottage window. She stopped in the sunshine to listen.

The Prime Minister had not long finished speaking – the last notes of the national anthem had barely died away – when the first air-raid siren sounded, a mournful wailing lifted right across Greater London at 11.27 a.m. A little later the long, dreaded moan, rising and falling for two interminable minutes, was taken up over East Anglia and the Midlands.

It had been assumed that in any future war devastating air attacks would be made on the cities; it was also thought that these raids would follow swiftly on a declaration of war. (Secretly, appalling casualty figures of hundreds of thousands were believed possible.) So at those first, gut-wrenching siren notes, as if on cue, parts of the country feared the worst: bombs raining down on vulnerable civilians; buildings flattened; gas attacks; mass panic; mayhem; death. In fact a stray French plane had unwittingly breached British defences – but it had tragic consequences. British fighters were scrambled and, mistakenly, a friendly-fire dogfight ensued. Two planes were shot down; one pilot was killed. It was a grotesque false alarm – the first of many – but it gave a terrifying glimpse of what was to come for people who were still struggling with the enormity of yet another war.

For many who heard those first air-raid sirens, the fact that their warnings proved false made no difference; for the rest of their lives they would speak of the sheer terror of that moment. Virginia, a teenage girl from a wealthy and rather rigid background – who would shortly find dangerous ambulance-driving during the Blitz 'liberating' – thought it the greatest ordeal of the war. 'Nothing was ever so bad again.' A fifteen-year-old girl called Margaret fervently agreed. 'My father had reinforced the cellar of our old Edwardian house in the manner of the trenches,' she said – 'great solid pillars of wood supporting the walls and ceiling. We went down there, and I clearly remember my knees shaking, uncontrollably, due to my fear. I don't believe this ever happened again, I'm glad to say.'

But life went on that day, war or no war. For one man the date of 3 September 1939 would always hold a particular, and affectionate, significance. In east London, a Jewish family was preparing for a wedding, and at the exact moment when the siren sounded the eighteen-year-old bride was being helped into her long white wedding dress. Nerves held – including the bridegroom's – the all-clear sounded, and, despite some anxious looks at the sky, the wedding took place, as planned, later that afternoon. 'I was born in Airthrey Castle, Stirlingshire, on 24 June 1941,' the couple's son said, looking back across the years. His parents had evacuated to Scotland soon after war was declared. His father's business – he was a tailor – had been relocated to a Scottish factory, and some of his fellow workers had gone too.

What the good citizens of Alloa made of this bunch of East End Jews . . . with heavy Russian or Polish accents . . . remains a mystery. The castle was built in 1791 by Robert Adam . . . and I can claim without fear of contradiction that I was the first, and only, Jew born there. When my father went to Glasgow to schlep a mohel (for the circumcision) up from the grime and smoke of the city, he got out of the train, breathed deeply, and proclaimed, 'Oy, a machya!' – 'Oh, what a pleasure!'

Newspapers indicate that, when the first sirens wailed, most people queued – 'quietly and politely' – to get into the newly erected public shelters; others stood in the doorways of their houses, peering for approaching aircraft. Silvery barrage balloons, intended to hamper low-flying enemy planes, floated in the deep-blue skies. Although they were never very effective, they did bolster morale; residents in the Chelsea area of London became devoted to theirs, nicknaming them 'Flossie' and 'Blossom'.

For the young, despite the coming dangers, this new wartime era also had its amusing side. That day, Sally, looking out of her terraced house in Battersea with the sirens shrieking, collapsed in giggles at the sight of an eccentric elderly lady running down the street to a shelter wearing only a nightdress, hair-curlers and a gas mask.

Maisie, an older girl of seventeen, who had left school that summer and was about to start her first job, was on a bus on her way to a station when the first sirens went. 'Suddenly the bus stopped,' she recalled. 'We were all ordered off. We all thought, terrified, "This is it – the war has really begun." A policeman grabbed me and pushed me into a nearby Lloyd's Bank, where, with a lot of other people, I was led down into the vaults in the bowels of the earth. It all seemed quite unreal – but it was probably a very safe place to be . . . They let us go when the all-clear sounded.'

There was shock, too, now that the unthinkable was actually happening. In Holland Park in London it was only when policemen on bicycles pedalled by shouting 'Take cover!' that people began 'to run frantically . . . diving for any open door they could see'.

Helena, then ten, the daughter of Greek immigrants, remembers being in the flat above their grocery shop in a Birmingham suburb and hearing the siren wail. 'My knees were knocking together with weakness, and I thought I was going to be sick. I glimpsed that already all my known world was toppling about my ears. Mum put the kettle on. She said we might as well have a cup of tea as sit there fretting.' Jennifer, a year older, from a military family, kept a stiff upper lip. 'It was nerve-racking, of course,' she agreed. 'But I don't believe we were really afraid, neither my brother nor I. We children were much tougher in those days.' Stella, who was in London that day, repeated an old story of her parents': 'A friend of my father's was stuck halfway over Westminster Bridge when the sirens went. He couldn't decide which bank to make for, and ended up sheltering in the House of Commons.'

Jilly, then a cheery eight-year-old who was already stubbornly refusing to be evacuated, remembered a bit of family drama. 'On 3 September 1939 we were living in Kent . . . My father and my big brother were busy in our small back garden implanting the Anderson shelter when the first siren sounded. My auntie promptly had a full-blown case of hysterics on our back doorstep. Mum gave her a bit of a shake and a glass of brandy . . . She said that whatever we had to face couldn't hurt us if we were all together.'

In a beautiful and isolated part of Wales, untouched by the sound of those first morbid sirens, a small girl was playing in the garden with her older brother. They were staying at the much loved home of her grandparents, a long, low white farmhouse that had been inherited. 'Its magic was handed down too,' she said. She had just listened, with the rest of the family, to the declaration of war. Even then she showed the perception of the novelist she became. Though having no real understanding of what was happening, she nevertheless remembers 'being aware of the gravity, the deeply solemn atmosphere' of the moment. Trying to make some sense of all this strangeness, she asked her brother, 'who was into digging trenches in a big way, if Daddy would become a soldier ... "Yes." "Might he be killed?" "Oh, yes" (enthusiastically).' Her father came through the war – and her brother, as his early interests foretold, later had a distinguished military career.

An equally bewildered girl of seven, living in a country district near Worcester, had listened fearfully to the conversation of the grown-ups as they crowded round the wireless to hear the Prime Minister. Feeling ignored, and with nobody bothering to explain what was happening, she crept out into the flower-filled garden fully expecting to see German soldiers approaching across the fields. As an adult, she believed that the timorousness she had so much trouble overcoming in later life might have developed around this time.

An eighteen-year-old girl called Connie was staying at her grandmother's large family home by the sea that September weekend. Only weeks before, she had been a debutante in the 1939 season, flitting from party to party, her mind filled with her first serious boyfriend, clothes, and gossip with friends. 'We were all to meet at the appointed hour of 11.15 around the wireless set,' she reminisced. 'I can see us all vividly, and can remember consciously saying to myself, "This is the most poignant moment of your life to date, and you will never forget it." . . . The drawing room was heavy with the scent of great bowls of roses, cut lavender drying on the wide, sunny window seats, and foreign cigarettes. Here, we foregathered.' She never did forget. She married her boyfriend soon after, and was widowed, with a weeks-old baby, in 1942.

Pamela, who had also danced and laughed the nights away in London ballrooms that summer, came to believe that the war had 'saved' her from a vacuous life of pleasure-seeking. With many of her friends, she entered the services and worked hard and seriously. Later there was no question of returning to her pre-war existence – the way of life, and her own outlook, had changed completely.

Education was not negotiable for stoic, middle-class parents whatever dangers the country faced; many of the smaller private prep schools were able to arrange for suitable temporary premises away from the cities and the south coast. In the centre of London, a ten-year-old called Christopher, kitted out in his new school uniform, was en route to his boarding prep school for the first time from his home in the suburbs. He had been due to start at his school in Sussex three weeks later –

But as war seemed imminent, and travel through London might be difficult or dangerous, the school invited parents to send boys back to start the autumn term three weeks early.

It was on 3 September that I was taken to Horsham by train by my parents, complete with trunk, cricket bat etc. We arrived at Paddington station at about 11.20, just after the declaration, and heard the very first siren of war sounding. My parents acted very calmly, as though it was all quite normal! I think I felt more excited than anything.

Douglas, a nine-year-old who had just returned (early) to another prep school, watched with his friends as the wartime preparations accelerated:

We were intrigued by the rapid erection of enormous lattice towers quite close to the school. Unknown to us at the time, these were the start of the radar chain along the south coast, warning the RAF of approaching planes . . . We also had strict air-raid drills in the school shelters built on the tennis court. Initially exciting, the drills soon palled and my abiding memory is of a wet, cloying smell accompanied by unpleasant claustrophobia.

A little girl in Greater London, taking the government's sinister warnings of gas attacks to heart, immediately donned her gas mask – and could only be persuaded out of it, through hunger, late that night. And after the first siren went a young mother in Birmingham, to her horror, saw a warden running down the street excitedly – and mistakenly – twirling a wooden rattle that was supposed to be used only in the event of gas attacks. 'I clutched my two-year-old, sent aloft a prayer, and waited for the worst,' she remembered. 'Of all things, gas masks went completely out of my mind.'

On that same day Tom, idling on a friend's launch in the Thames before the end of the summer holidays, saw a policeman pushing his bike along the towpath, shouting over the water, 'It's happened, it's happened.' In Chester, a girl of seventeen was horrified to see her father, whom she had always feared as 'a hard man', weeping openly as he recalled his own bitter experiences in the trenches twenty years before. A schoolboy in Cheltenham was ecstatic: he and his pals had somehow got hold of the idea that, if war was declared, all schools would be closed indefinitely. They weren't. Instead, he found his had been doubled up with a school evacuated from the Midlands. But some 7,000 Borstal boys and other young offenders were luckier: they won the jackpot when they heard that they were to be released immediately and were told to go home.

Older children, some on the verge of adulthood, reacted more soberly to the news of war. Louise, from Birmingham, was about to enter teacher-training college, and had been fully absorbed in her busy school and social life, hoping that there would be no complicating wartime to interfere with her plans. Now she wondered anxiously if these plans would have to be altered. (They weren't: teachers were largely exempt from call-up duties, and she qualified as a teacher later in the war.) Cyril, a sixth-former who had set his heart on reading history at university, remembered his father's horror stories of the First World War; he thought glumly about his academic plans and the timing of his call-up, and despaired of his future. (His degree course started in 1940, was interrupted by war service in the army, and was finally completed in 1948.)

Many people who were children on that fine late-summer evening remember larking about in what seemed like a holiday atmosphere, out of sight of worried parents. In Oldham, the daughter of a strict headmaster played out in the lanes behind the houses with friends until long after dark, something never allowed before, the adults being far too preoccupied to call them in.

The diffident King George VI broadcast at 6 p.m. A poor speaker, cursed with an appalling stammer, he nevertheless played a significant part in steadying his shocked country that evening, calmly expecting the people to 'stand firm and united in this time of trial'. The country responded warmly and affectionately to this dutiful and decent man, whose innate good instincts made him an admired figurehead during the darkest times of war. He steadfastly refused opportunities to be spirited away to Canada; nor would he allow his family to be separated or sent far away from London. When the bombing came, and especially after Buckingham Palace was hit, he appeared to 'take it' like the rest of Londoners. His family life was exemplary. His Queen – shrewd, pretty and charming – was adored, as were his two young daughters. Pictures of the princesses' sparkly Christmas pantomimes at Windsor Castle would cheer and amuse thousands of colour-starved children in the hard and dreary years ahead.

In response to urgent national crisis, the country came together in prayer. Attendance was high in most congregations across the country that Sunday night, with many parents also choosing to bring their children. In Birmingham – significantly, as the city would suffer greatly the following year – a girl then seventeen would never forget the row upon row of gas-mask boxes she spotted lining the pews at evensong.

That same evening – while the pubs hummed, and the most patriotic hymns rang out lustily, and overexcited children romped unchecked, and worried parents tried to plan ahead – the severe disruption of wartime was already being endured by a good half of the youthful urban population of the country. Children evacuated through the government scheme from London and Liverpool and Manchester – and other obvious target areas – to quiet parts of the countryside were finding themselves in the extraordinary and bewildering position of being cared for in temporary homes, by total strangers. The story of evacuation – an event which has never quite gone away for most of those who experienced it, however briefly – will be told more fully later. For now, suffice it to say that on that particular night thousands of these relocated children were settling down in strange beds, in unfamiliar surroundings, away from their parents – and engulfed in what must have been a dark and frightening country silence, interspersed with alien sounds of birds and animals.

All these city evacuees who were old enough to write were given postcards to send home to their parents, letting them know their whereabouts and that they had arrived safely. We may picture one such child travelling all day by bus or train, being herded into some village hall used for as a reception area, and finally ending up, worn out, in some strangers' home. This dispirited, anonymous little boy, homesick and unhappy – but still hoping that tomorrow might be brighter – scribbled home, 'Dear Mum, I hope you are well. I don't like the man's face. I don't like the lady's face much. Perhaps it will look better in daylight. I like the dog's face best.'

So much had happened, so rapidly. Yet on the surface, at least, as one blazing day followed another, for most people little seemed to change. The massive air raids, expected at any moment, did not materialize and, after the high drama of the declaration, life generally carried on relatively normally. There was even a strange feeling of anticlimax – which did not help already jangled nerves. But during those first tense, difficult weeks and months of war, the comedian Robb Wilton's daft signature joke – quintessentially British, inexplicable to any foreigner – always raised a laugh among old and young alike. It was the flat, deadpan delivery, the mournful tone, that seemed to finger the sheer absurdity of the present situation:

The day war broke out, my missus said to me, 'It's up to you – you've got to stop it.'

I said, 'Stop what?'

She said, 'The war.'

It made everyone smile – and feel a bit happier.

Inevitably, the most profound disruption in the lives of many children during that autumn was when fathers began disappearing into the services. For younger children, especially, this was both frightening and inexplicable. As a man who was about four at the time said, 'What *was* a war, I wondered? What *were* the Germans? What *was* fighting? I didn't know; it meant nothing to me. But all the changes – people leaving, talk of our moving – were very upsetting.'

Sarah, whose father, a lawyer, was also a Territorial officer, was four. She has odd, vivid memories of the family's summer home, on the Dorset coast, where they were living that August. 'It was close to the beach and a ferry that ploughed back and forth across the harbour all day. Going across on it with Nanny was the biggest excitement . . . I can still hear the chains grinding on the jetty and smell the seaweed. Then our father, who I don't remember very clearly at that time, simply wasn't there any longer.' He had been called up, and Sarah and her brother, who was nine, scarcely saw him again for six years.

All over the country, thousands and thousands of children like them were about to go through the same experience: the mystifying disappearance of a close family member and the start of an extended period of one-parent care – during their crucial formative years. Many would echo Sarah's belief, looking back after more than sixty years, that 'After my father left in 1939, nothing in our family life was ever the same again.'

Robert, in Scotland, age six, never forgot his mother answering the telephone sometime during the first weekend in September. It was his father. 'I can still remember my mother's horrified cry, "O no! David", as she took the call from my father to say that war was imminent and that he had agreed to transfer from the Territorial Army to the regulars . . . I was told then that Daddy had become a soldier and that we were going to move to my paternal grandparents' house.' On the whole, he was pleased:

Their house was a large Edwardian edifice, not far from Glasgow, complete with my grandfather's offices, stables and outbuildings, standing on about an acre and a half of gardens. My parents' home had been quiet . . . There it seethed with activity . . . My grandmother was a small, intensely active person, very interested in politics, and from the moment Mother and I arrived she saw to it that I understood just what was going on.

Getting to know grandparents better was frequently one of the happier aspects of the war for children.

Like many children, after 1939 one six-year-old girl from East Anglia would not see her father again for six years. She wrote this intense, moving little memoir over sixty years later:

World War Two

My Dad was in Regular Army when Mum met him. He joined when he was eighteen.

Then war broke out in 1939.

I was six years old. My sister was born 1941.

Dad was called overseas. Was taken Prisoner of War by Japanese, sent to work on Burma Rail Lines. Just a handful of raw rice a day.

Survived on bananas/coconuts monkeys threw down.

Later on reported missing or dead.

Mum went back to work. Grandparents brought us up. My aunts took in forestry girls, also evacuee boy from Dagenham Essex.

Times not always bad.

But we dreaded the bombs, doodlebugs.*

Air raids overhead. German planes. I had two uncles in Home Guard.

Dad survived. Lived with us twenty years. Bad health. Died at work. Angina. 53 years old.

These memories I treasure now as I'm nearly 70 years. Mum died 86 years old.

Treasured memories now.

Suddenly bereft of their fathers, older children frequently took on parental responsibilities, helping out with domestic chores and taking care of younger siblings more than they had been used to. Lonely mothers also looked to them for companionship. A girl then living in Ipswich said that 'As I was the eldest child and our dad was called-up into the RAF, my mum used to talk to me as an adult.'

A great many children of wartime would come to accept family separation – and frequently tragedy – as normal aspects of their lives. But most who were youngsters in 1939, caught up in the preparations for war they saw going on all around them, remember the excitement more than anything else: helping to fill sandbags; taping windows with sticky tape – '2-inch-wide brown paper gummed on one side' – to prevent injuries from shattering glass; marvelling at the shiny barrage balloons; remembering to carry their gas masks.

* Pilotless planes, with fiery tails, which crashed and exploded when they ran out of fuel.

All this busyness could have been made for young boys. Andrew, then aged six, with an active mind and a feel for mechanics, said that he 'actually enjoyed those early days of war . . . It was a period when things were literally "happening" every day. When staying with my grandmother, I could walk to the nearby park to watch the barrage-balloon installation filling the balloons from lorries with a fixed pyramid of high-pressure bottles of hydrogen – and the searchlight-battery personnel at work on what I regarded as the best torches in the world.' Another boy of Andrew's age, living on the outskirts of a large city, wrote that he was thrilled to bits to see 'the very first preparations for war, the anti-aircraft guns being installed, as well as an experimental system of "smoke pots", which would screen the area during air raids'.

Two brothers living in a village in Surrey threw themselves enthusiastically into the home-front war effort. Their father was a businessman who commuted to work daily; all of a sudden that autumn he 'blossomed forth as the leader of the village first-aid party'. The boys' eager participation lends a true *Dad's Army* feel to its well-meaning, if bumbling, activities. For when the first-aiders had studied the St John's Ambulance handbook 'they then sought victims,' one of the boys remembered. 'My younger brother and I were ideal. They bandaged and splinted us up until we were immobilized, and then carted us about on stretchers. Their party trick was to heave the stretcher over a 6-foot brick wall, or to lower it out of an upper window. You needed lots of confidence in the ability of this motley group to tie knots. At nine and twelve we did not weigh much – and, mercifully, they never dropped us.'

One girl went on holiday in the West Country with her family on her tenth birthday – 3 September – and came back to face real domestic sadness. 'Our lovely cat was put in the cattery as always, and when we returned from holiday all the animals had been put to sleep' – by then the first air-raid warning had sounded, and the staff had understandably panicked. In fact thousands of pet owners had been quietly agonizing for months over what to do with much loved animals when faced by air raids, possible evacuation or the ultimate horror of gas attack. For many, despite the sorrow caused to countless young children, a painless demise seemed a kinder option than fear and suffering. Vets and the NSPCA (the National Society for the Prevention of Cruelty to Animals) were quite unable to cope with the large number of dead domestic animals which had then to be disposed of.

London Zoo, the scene of so many happy family outings in the pre-war years, was also facing grave decisions. Some of the animals were sent to other zoos such as Whipsnade, but the poisonous snakes from the reptile house – which might have got free and slithered danger-ously about London in bombing attacks – were killed with chloro-form. The aquarium was drained to prevent the release of 200 gallons of water in the event of severe damage to its structure.

For the middle classes, perhaps the biggest shock of those early days of war was the immediate disappearance of domestic help of any sort. Nannies, cooks, butlers, cleaners and gardeners simply melted away – most to the services, others disappearing into the weapons and aircraft factories which were gearing up as fast as possible for the war effort. (For many employed in domestic service – and most young nannies starting out were no more than teenagers – reasonably paid factory work must have seemed an attractive option.)

Even in quite modest households, this sudden lack of help meant a big adjustment for the family; for grander establishments, dependent on servants to maintain house and garden and lifestyle, the rapid staff exodus delivered a stunning blow. Mansions were requisitioned for various kinds of war use, or used to house evac-uated schools, or fitted out as convalescent centres. Many big town houses were emptied of valuables, sheeted, and shut up and aban-doned for the duration, the owners evacuating themselves and hoping for the best.

Caroline was living in a large terraced house overlooking Regent's Park in London. 'I don't remember exactly when – or why – but Cook, Nanny and the maids all left fairly soon after war was declared,' she said, looking back in wonder at her young self, then living in a very different world.

I distinctly remember being astonished at seeing Mummy with a duster in her hand, polishing something. I had never seen her do anything of that sort before in my life. I was ten. I also remember her telling me and my sister to follow her into the kitchen. I can see it now: there was a swinging green-baize door – truly! 'Come on girls,' she said. 'We're going to learn to cook.' . . . We did too – or at least she did.

Looking back, I can't believe our lives were like that before the war – Mummy discussing menus with Cook. But she did . . . My father had rejoined his regiment and the house was too big to manage, so we moved to a rented house in the country, near my grandparents. My father was killed in the North African campaign, and my mother remarried quite soon after. The London house was badly bombed at some point in the war . . . We never went back.

But Mummy did learn to cook – and very well too. I really take my hat off to people like her, that generation. They just had to get down to it – and they did.

This admiration is also felt by another woman, then a girl in her teens living in a large house where there were always live-in staff before the war. 'Mother was absolutely marvellous,' she said. 'She saw the way it was, what had to be done, and got on with it. She kept the house going throughout – despite the terrible anxiety. She was always worried for my father, who was in charge of fire services in east London during the worst of the bombing.'

In later life, so many people who were children of the middle classes when war broke out looked back with amazement at how their mothers' lives changed so suddenly, in a matter of a few weeks. Women who had led lives of comparative leisure were now faced with full-time childcare and all the household chores, none of which they had done alone before. More and more husbands went into the services, depriving wives of their partners. Communications were difficult, and few mothers were able to follow their husbands' various postings around the country. Women running large homes found that either these had been requisitioned or they were required to have army personnel, or perhaps evacuees, living with them. They were also coping with great uncertainty: perhaps planning an evacuation themselves, or living parked on in-laws or other relatives. On top of all this change, petrol rationing was introduced two weeks after war was declared. This meant that these same women, many of the better- off having become used to the freedom of a car, were now likely to be stuck at home or at the mercy of increasingly unreliable buses and trains.

Cynthia, who was seven, clearly recalled the fraught domestic circumstances in which many children suddenly found themselves. Her father went straight into the army that September, and she and her mother went to live in her grandparents' house. Young as she was, she sensed the obvious tension; she became aware that 'This was quite a trying time for Mum – and for thousands of others in the same situation too, of course.' Used to going out and about in her own car, her mother was now restricted to her in-laws' home in the country. 'Almost no one was able to drive a car, because suddenly there was no petrol. But my mother was thoroughly put out at having to travel on buses, and unable to understand why buses didn't wait for her to arrive to catch them. She was always just missing the bus into town and arriving back in a fury, slamming the front door and letting forth a very unladylike stream of invective.'

For all the domestic frustration, day after day after day the weather stayed glorious that September – reinforcing the sense of unreality that was widely felt by people of all ages. Commentators remarked on the difference in attitude between 1939 and 1914: in 1939 there was no jingoistic hysteria and intense patriotism, but instead an anxious, slightly grudging, acceptance. It was also noted by an American journalist that on buses and trains and the underground the usually taciturn British travellers had, amazingly, begun speaking to each other.

And a single voice of national leadership had begun to emerge. Winston Churchill, whose powerful speeches had already caught the public's imagination during the prelude to war, had made a swift political return, despite his reputation as a 'has-been' and his vehement criticism of Chamberlain's post-Munich government policy. He had accepted the Prime Minister's magnanimous offer and joined the War Cabinet – ironically, in the same position he had held in the First World War: as First Lord of the Admiralty. But in spite of all his failures (mixed with successes) in commanding naval operations, his personal popularity had held, and on the day of his appointment the jaunty message immediately transmitted to all ships was 'Winston is Back.'

Autumn 1939. Although there was frustratingly little news on the war front, the brilliant weather held. The novelist Elizabeth Bowen observed 'in parks, the outsize dahlias, velvet and wine, and the trees on which each vein in each yellow leaf stretched out against the sun'. Imagine London's Hyde Park as it verges on to Marble Arch: trenches zigzagging across the precious grassland; office workers snatching a sunny lunchtime break – but no deckchairs to sit on: they were forbidden, as they might hamper people running for cover in the trenches and public shelters when the anticipated air raids materialized.

And there would have been very few, if any, children scampering round; the majority had been evacuated by one method or another, and parents were unlikely to bring children into central London in wartime. More and more men, and some women, were seen about in uniform, and a novel all-in-one tailored woollen garment, zipped right up the front and known as a 'siren suit', was on display in a shop window in Oxford Street. This outfit would soon become the favoured wartime attire of young children, some women – and the Prime Minister.

In the absence of hard war news, rumour and gossip circulated madly. A then sixth-former, who later became a college lecturer, recalled that young children were warned sternly by their parents not to pick up strange objects on the road, as they might be booby traps dropped by the Germans to try to destabilize the civilian population. No such devices were ever found; that such crazy, outlandish fears were held by normally sensible people was all part of the feverish anxiety of the time. Some witty lines of the humorist A. P. Herbert, who was extremely popular with both adults and children, poked gentle fun at the scaremongering tattlers:

> Do not believe the tale the milkman tells;
> No troops have mutinied at Potter's Bar.
> Nor are there submarines at Tunbridge Wells.
> The BBC will warn us when there are.

But fantasy flourished in such an overheated atmosphere, and people were ready to believe anything of the demonized Hitler and his Nazi gang. The febrile imaginations of the young, especially boys, were awash with traitors and secret messages; Michael Frayn's 2002 novel *Spies* perfectly re-created the sinister nuances of that period when nothing was allowed to be quite what it seemed.

A teenager called Jack, who lived near Nottingham, later remembered being preoccupied at that time with a supposed local spy – a curious episode that he had never forgotten. During the autumn of 1939, he and his best friend became deeply suspicious of a neighbour who spent hours every night in his garden shed, his torch flicking on and off, seemingly in a quite deliberate pattern, in the blacked-out darkness. The boys, keen readers of all the adventure comics, were convinced that he was sending coded messages to the Germans. 'Everything about the man seemed mysterious to us. We used to follow him down the street and try to track him. We had heard – and read – so much about spies and traitors.' Jack begged his mother to inform the police – which of course she did not. But the boy's imaginings did have an eerie sequel:

This happened about two years later, when we were experiencing frequent heavy air raids. On the other side of the road from our house was a long wall with trees overhanging the pavement. One night, under these trees, a car was parked, and in it sat a man apparently trying to use a Morse-code transmitter. We could hear, but we couldn't see him properly because it was dark. But we told my mother, and even she was scared. We had no phone, so she went round the back and got a neighbour to telephone the police . . .

And this is the strange bit. Much later I was told that there had indeed been a spy in the area, using radio to direct enemy airplanes to raid a very large and vitally important ball-bearing factory nearby. I have wondered so often if our schoolboy theories were right after all.

This uncertain time of waiting – the beginning of the period which was later named 'the phoney war' by the Americans, or 'this strangest of wars' as Neville Chamberlain referred to it at the time – played on everyone's nerves. The better-off, who naturally had more choices, appeared to have felt especially fragile. At least 2 million middle-class families evacuated themselves privately from the cities to rented houses in areas considered safe, or to stay with family members. Every day there were reams of classified advertisements in the papers for what were jocularly named 'funkholes' – accommodation available in 'safe' areas of the country and aimed at the well-to-do. Personal columns in *The Times* offered country houses and cottages for rent 'In the event of war . . .'

The favoured destinations were Wales, Devon and Scotland. A six-year-old called Jean remembered the personal drama of leaving her family's big flat in London, which had been shut up for the duration, and setting off for a rented home in Yorkshire. 'I was squashed up right next to all the luggage, sitting on my mother's knee clutching the birdcage and our budgerigar in it. He was furious at being bounced up and down, and screeched and screeched.' Jean grew to like Yorkshire, and still goes back and visits the friends she made. But she remembers too the wrench of leaving behind everything familiar, like her toys and friends and nursery school. And understanding so little about 'war' – and having nothing explained by the grown-ups – was mysterious and frightening.

Some of these sudden family evacuations involved considerable culture shock. One nine-year-old and her mother went to live in a three-room cottage in Wiltshire. There they found 'no running water or facilities for washing, no electric light, and no sanitation – just a little shed in the garden with a toilet that somehow was mysteriously emptied, I suspect by the man next door. Our water came from a well outside our window . . . We had never lived like this, but took it all in our stride.' Their cheerful attitude got them through the ordeal quite happily and, besides the greater safety, they soon found much to enjoy in their rather basic new surroundings. 'I was quickly accepted by local children: we learned together and got along fine. We had nature walks with the teacher, who was wonderful – walked us for miles and made it fun, pointing out wild flowers and trees and plants.'

Another middle-class option for sending children to safe areas without the disruption of moving house was to bundle them off to boarding schools deep in the country. This course left mothers free to follow servicemen husbands on their various postings all over the country without a child in tow. Sally was sent away to school – aged five – right at the beginning of the war. She and her mother were living with her grandparents, and her father was about to be sent abroad for an extended period. Her mother – lonely and wretched, and wanting to spend as much time with her husband as she could – decided that, although Sally was so young, boarding school was the best choice. 'It sounds worse than it was,' Sally said, trying to understand her mother's very difficult situation. 'This was the school my mother had gone to, and the same very lovely and benevolent headmistress was still there. I was the only boarder when I arrived – in floods of tears of course. So this dear, sweet but very fat lady let me share her bed. I have such a perfect memory of her huge, white-nightie-clad bottom next to me – and, I must say, of the sounds and smells which emerged from it!'

Judy was ten, a pony-mad only child living in the Home Counties. When her father went to work full-time at the War Office, she was bundled off to boarding school. Her mother, she said, 'had never really lifted a finger' before the war, and when her daughter's governess left she felt very restricted. 'I didn't mind at all', Judy remembered – 'I was rather thrilled to be going away to school.' But no sooner had she arrived than the school was evacuated to Taplow Court in Buckinghamshire – to Lord Desborough's mansion. 'It was wonderful: all those jungle beasts staring at us from the walls, mixed up with his ancestors! But the house had far too few loos for all us girls.' She remembered a happy and cheery time there, and was quite unfazed by the lack of academic work. 'I suppose we must have had lessons and learned something, but what sticks in my mind is playing polo on our bikes on the lawn, and the wind-up gramophone we brought outside, and Judy Garland singing "Somewhere, over the rainbow . . ." – we played it over and over.'

Inexorably, the realities of war were impinging in all sorts of unexpected ways, some of them close to farce. Serena, a sixteen-year-old who had just left school and expected to spend a year at finishing school in Switzerland before doing the London season, had her plans abruptly changed, and immediately got down to a secretarial course.

At about this time, just after war was declared, she was told by a crusty elderly uncle of his shock when, on dining at his club, Boodles, he found all but two of the waiters had been called up; also, for the first time in its history, dining members were not required to wear evening dress. 'It's hard to believe those manners and mores existed in my lifetime, when I was already in my teens,' Serena said recently.

By late autumn, and with no sign of the dreaded enemy bombing attacks, the mood relaxed a little; children who had been evacuated during the weekend that war was declared began drifting back to the cities in growing numbers. Bored young mothers with their babies led the way, soon to be followed by older children who were unhappy and lonely or who were brought back by their fretting parents, who naturally missed having their children at home. The authorities, who had worked so hard to evacuate these children from coming danger, were appalled – and quite unprepared for their rapid return. Many city schools now had to be equipped with regulation air-raid shelters before they could be reopened. During this hiatus, children roamed the streets without schooling or discipline; for a lot of them, the often very poor and fractured education of wartime, which would seriously hamper many in their future lives, had already begun.

Although bombs were not yet falling on the industrial centres, German mines and U-boats were wreaking havoc on the merchant-navy convoys plying the Atlantic, and terrible losses were inflicted. In addition to lives being lost, the German grip on the UK's supply line was tightening. After much government dithering bacon, butter and sugar were the first foods to be rationed, in January 1940. During the previous autumn, although the polling organization Mass-Observation found that only one person in five thought the war would last as long as three years, wary householders were beginning to hoard. Sales of blankets and knitware soared; non-perishable foods and medicines were snapped up, as were sugar, flour and children's daily doses – rose-hip syrup and various types of cod-liver-oil and malt preparations.

This hoarding instinct had some humorous consequences. 'Mummy overdid bulk buying at the beginning of the war,' recalled Anna, who then lived in a large, very grand house. Her mother's excesses turned out to have amusing, and long-lasting, consequences:

She had been told that there would be shortages of paper and rubber. So she ordered from a smart London store quantities of hot-water bottles and loo paper. My mother was Danish, and as a foreigner was never very clear about the odd designations of quantities in English. A very large number of hot-water bottles arrived, but that was deemed to be A Good Thing – and they occupied an entire room in the house.

Then came a large Harrod's van full of loo paper. Each smart box had a ream of flat 6 by 8-inch sheets of shiny thin paper that crackled as you worked to soften it to make it effective in any sort of way.

Then, lo and behold, two more large van loads rolled up, both full of loo paper . . . After some consultation with our governess, it was decided that the entire delivery should be accepted.

That same paper was still in the loo of Mummy's last abode sixty years later.

An older woman, whose father had fought on the Somme and who well remembered the shortages of the previous war, was asked by her granddaughter what to stock up on. 'Hairpins, Kirby grips and above all *knicker elastic*, dear,' came the crisp reply.

As the first Christmas of war approached, some relaxation of the strict blackout regulations was allowed for lighting in shops, presumably to try to improve wavering spirits. Cinemas and public entertainments, all of which had been closed immediately after the declaration of war, had reopened and were being used normally. The two young princesses were spotted Christmas shopping in Woolworth's in Scotland – which sounds a suitably dreary wartime expedition.

The Harrod's children's toy fair that year was a shadow of its magical pre-war self, with far fewer children than usual attending. Warlike toys were much advertised, and became highly desirable Christmas presents. Hamley's best-selling gift for handy boys was a toy described as 'Build Your Own Maginot Line' – that being the supposedly impregnable French fortification against German encroachment. The eerily realistic assembly kit had tiered dugouts, in which toy soldiers performed a variety of military duties. (The lucky boys who received this had to make use of it while they could, as the famed Maginot Line collapsed effortlessly the following spring when faced by Hitler's blitzkrieg rolling across Europe.)

As winter set in, the optimism, even slight insouciance, of the autumn had vanished. The complacency of what many had decided was 'the bore war' was wearing off; opinion polls found that people generally believed that the situation was 'bad': that Britain was poorly prepared to fight, without good military leadership, and hopelessly vulnerable to invasion and to attack by the Luftwaffe.

With the nights drawing in and the blackout rigorously enforced, one bright spark that made both adults and children shriek with laughter was the BBC's new comedy series, *ITMA* (short for 'It's That Man Again'). The comedian Tommy Handley and his talented team of mimics found that they had a surprise smash hit on their hands. Its zany humour, catchphrases and loony characters – Funf, the ineffectual German spy; Handley himself as the 'Minister of Aggravation' in the 'Office of Twerps'; Vera, his secretary; bibulous Colonel Chinstrap – pressed all the right buttons and made a nonsense of the high seriousness of the moment. For a golden half-hour each week the entire country roared with laughter.

To Jennie, living in Hull, *ITMA* conjured up the spirit of her wartime childhood all her life. She remembered especially the fun and relief it brought in that strange winter of 1939–40. 'We wouldn't have missed it for the world,' she said. 'It was the highlight of our week . . . I can hum the signature tune now.' Donald, then a first-year university student living in Manchester with his family – and soon to be called up into the army – was similarly nostalgic. 'Later in the war, our dog used to hear the siren before we did if we were listening to *ITMA*. And he went on barking until, reluctantly, we retreated to the shelter.' Several people, remembering their own particular favourite whacky character, believed they had never heard any radio programme since that was so genuinely funny yet devoid of malice, and that so firmly united the country. Throughout the war, its crazy brilliance continued to draw families together in laughter; it was to make people feel that life was, after all, worth living despite the present gloom.

As that first wartime year came to an end, people had reluctantly become accustomed to the tiresome chore of the nightly blackout. Ghoulish children in Cambridgeshire were chided by the local magistrates for pretending to be ghosts and spookily jumping out at passers-by from the cemetery. Torches had to be dim and pointed downward, and pillar boxes, kerbs and stationary cars suddenly became dangerous objects after darkness fell. 'It was a funny feeling walking home in the dark,' sixteen-year-old Ted later remembered. 'Tripping over a kerb was like falling into a hole. Many a lamp-post and postbox got an apology in the dark for being bumped into.' A doctor's daughter in Wales said that, driving along country roads with her father, they frequently stopped in isolated areas to give servicemen or pedestrians a lift – 'Nobody gave a thought to the possible danger of picking up a stranger.'

It is notable that although the blackout could be treacherous for bumps and falls, no one seems to have felt physically threatened by others, although in the early months, while there was still a quite normal traffic flow, there was a rise in accident statistics – particularly for children. The blackout quickly became a fertile source of wartime jokes, and one enterprising publisher brought out *The Blackout Book*. Packed with puzzles and harmless jokes, double-entendres and mishaps while canoodling under cover of darkness, this was aimed at adolescents, in a far more sexually innocent era.

For all its annoyances, the blackout also brought about an unexpected joy at this bleak time, and many people who were then children recall clearly the extraordinary beauty of being in a town without lights at night. Playing outside until late, children became very aware of a magical black mantle that descended, creating a vast, velvety and mysterious sky. A girl who spent most of the war in Cambridge, and who was often out playing after dark – quite without fear – said 'Nowadays you would have to go to the depths of the Highlands of Scotland to find the intense darkness we enjoyed in the centre of our town . . . When you were out at night the stars shone like brilliant jewels. It was an enormous pleasure to look up and feel oneself so tiny, almost nothing, in the universe.'

And all his life, Peter, who lived in Wales, would remember those wartime skies in a way that was very personal – and also strangely prophetic. 'January of 1940 was one of the coldest winter months I can remember, and one evening my father called me to come outside quickly.' Standing in the heavy darkness, they watched enthralled as streams of light radiated across the black night sky. 'It was the Aurora Borealis. It was the only time in my life that I ever saw it. It was almost as though it was anticipating the searchlights and the anti-aircraft guns and the bombing that lay ahead. This was my first memory of that fateful year – a year that was to change our lives for ever.'

3

GET THE CHILDREN OUT!
FROM SEPTEMBER 1939

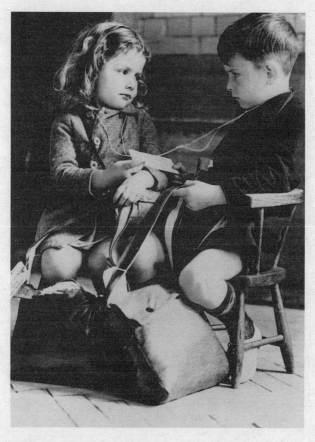

A little girl shows her evacuation label to her older brother,
September 1939. Both children have serious expressions, far
beyond their years

The evacuation scheme set out to save life, and this it did. It also did something else of importance; it served as a safety-valve for several million mothers and children, as an outlet – a voluntary escape path if only for a few weeks at a time – from the cities that were being bombed.

Richard M. Titmuss, *Problems of Social Policy* (1950)

All the children loved the place; it had a tidal river, the Downs, an airport. What more could we want? It was a big adventure for inner-city children.

Nine-year-old girl evacuated from London, with her older brother, to the south coast

We was miserable ... Our plan were to get to the station and hide on train when the guard weren't looking, only we didn't have no money for a platform ticket ... So we go back.

A boy, aged six, evacuated to a village in North Wales with his eight-year-old sister

For those old enough to remember, and for many who are not, the very mention of September 1939 conjures up a chilling sense of dread, as searing pictures of war and death and destruction tumble through the mind. But there is one image, above all, that has come to symbolize those first anxious days of the month: it is Friday 1 September, and photographs of bewildered young children, tagged with plain luggage labels and clutching suitcases, gas masks slung round their necks, standing about on sunny railway plat-forms – children who, whether they stayed in the safety of their rural home-from-homes for three weeks or three years, would be known for ever more as the evacuees.

This is Annette:

It was said I was the youngest evacuee – five years and three months, going away on my own, carrying my gas mask. It was 1 September. All the children wore labels, so I must have too. At the station there were makeshift toilets, and I was mortified to have to sit on one that was wet . . . I was chosen by a lady in a floral overall to go and live with her . . . I remember watching the shelling from the guns – we were right on the south coast – and being put to work in the fields. We were given a piece of bread and cheese and a beer bottle full of cold tea for our lunch, and sent out to work at about 8. When, at my age, I felt hungry, I decided it must be lunchtime ('lunch' meant little to an East Ender) and ate my food. I must have been very hungry by nightfall!

Annette's mother was having another baby, and had already been sent out of London with other expectant mums. When her father found out about the work, he brought Annette back to London, where she spent the war with her mother and baby brother.

Luggage label, suitcase, gas mask – these three articles have come to define these children, whether they came from London or Liverpool or Manchester or Newcastle or Edinburgh or any other city or suburb. Over the years, the word 'evacuees' has taken on an emotive, almost nostalgic, aura. Nobody, the world over, with any knowledge of the damage wrought on the cities during the Second World War would think of asking, 'Evacuees from what?' In grainy old films and photographs, of that crucial summer, it is these evacuated city children with their luggage labels and gas masks who seem to convey most powerfully both the stoicism and the vulnerability of the British home front as it faced up to the hard, dreary slog of a long war.

Newspapers reported that early-morning passers-by stared at the long crocodiles of young children – 'Hundreds and hundreds of us, marching through the streets of London that morning' – in stunned silence. Nina, nine, whose parents had decided to keep her with them in London, watched from a window of her home. 'It was a real bird's-eye view of the faces of the bewildered children, labels on their coats, their gas masks over their shoulders. Several of the pupils were my classmates, and I remember my feelings of joy that I did not have to join them.' The mothers, she said, put on a brave face that day, 'but there were many tears, as they did not know their destination and the parting was very difficult.'

A boy of nine called John, whose house was immediately opposite a school playground where the evacuating children gathered, was also watching that day. He stood at the front-garden gate with his mother, his heart in his mouth. 'There were several double-decker buses. They were all lined up, and the children – with cases and their gas masks – were beginning to climb aboard . . . some crying, others waving and kissing their mothers good-bye. Nobody knew where they were being taken to, only that they would be safer away in the countryside and not left in the towns. I don't think I shall ever forget that scene.' His mother, no doubt torn like all the rest, offered to quickly pack a case for him to leave too. But he told her firmly, 'I don't want to go. I'm staying here.'

The children who had been signed up for evacuation from the cities by their parents during the spring and summer of 1939 knew by the end of August that the time for them to leave was getting close. As war now seemed inevitable, the schools opened a week early, and children who were being evacuated spent the time with their teachers, practising long walks in crocodile or, one teacher said, in singing. 'I can never hear "Ten green bottles hanging on the wall" without thinking of that time – those innocents sitting round waiting.' But a boy who was seven and not at all sure what the evacuation fuss was all about later remembered the preparations in his school as fun. 'My gas mask was in a cardboard box which also had boiled sweets and a handkerchief inside. And we practised for the evacuation . . . We lined up in the playground and the register was called and our name labels were tied on by teachers. Buses came to take us to the station, and the register was called again. Then back we went to school. This was a carefully contrived operation, and somewhat more hectic when it was real.' One mother picked up her two children from school every afternoon that week, clearly worried and dreading the separation which could come at any moment. 'Mum bought us big ice creams every day,' her daughter May, then seven, who was going with her older brother, remembered. 'She said, "Heaven only knows when they'll get another."'

The signal to begin the evacuation was given over the radio on the evening of 31 August, and early the following morning the children, clutching suitcases and sandwiches and perhaps a sibling by the hand, left home for their assigned meeting places in school yards. Their teachers were waiting with lists and banners and labels, and as the sun rose across the country the exodus began. Few parents had the time, or opportunity, to say goodbye before their children were off, marching to the buses that took them either directly out of the towns or to main-line railway stations to catch the special trains painstakingly laid on for the evacuation. They then faced long and tiring journeys to destinations that neither they, their teachers, nor their parents had been told of.

Close to seventy years later, one common factor is apparent from what the 'evacuees' write and how they speak of this corner of their past: whatever their personal experience of evacuation, whether enriching or dull or unhappy or an uneasy mixture of all three, it has stayed with them – powerful, but often hidden deep – throughout the rest of their lives.

Eva, a pretty twelve-year-old with long, curly hair, was one of the children evacuated from east London that day, and the clarity of her memories demonstrated the significance this experience still had for her. She and her sister, who was two years older, were marched with their classmates to buses which took them to Liverpool Street station, where they were put on a train for Norfolk. In the village church hall where the children ended up, they were eventually paired off with an older couple who had no children, and were taken to live in their cottage. It was an odd, unsatisfactory arrangement, and the girls were not happy.

The woman was house-proud and made us take off our shoes every time we came into the house. And the man was awful. I hated him. I avoided him whenever I could. We were given awful food – things like rabbit that we had never eaten before – and I could hardly swallow it. When our parents came to visit, my mother, who worked for a dress manufacturer, brought the foster mother a dress as a present. But they were so rude they wouldn't even let them come in, and made them stand outside the house.

They confiscated food and sweet parcels sent to us by our parents . . . and they were really most unkind to us. I remember sometimes I got so desperate that I walked down to the main road and sat on the kerb and tried to stop anyone in a car to give me a lift home.

The school friends who were evacuated with them were luckier: they were placed with families who were good to them, and they settled in well. The girls particularly envied certain classmates who were billeted in a nearby big house, surrounded by orchards, where a landowner known as 'the Major' lived, and who had servants to help look after them.

Eva found that, because her parents had insisted on keeping her and her sister together, she had trouble fitting in at school. Because of the age gap, schooling was always a problem when siblings were sent away together, and in her case she found herself by far the youngest child in the school, which is always a dubious distinction – although even in school her appealing good looks were an asset, and she was noticed.

After a visit home over the Christmas of 1939, their parents insisted that the girls return to their foster parents, worried for their well-being and believing the countryside was safe from the bombing that would certainly come. But after a few more months both sisters were still so homesick and unhappy that their parents let them come home, and later in 1940 the whole family endured the onslaught of the London Blitz.

Altogether, Eva's evacuation was a miserable, unpleasant experience that she was glad to put behind her. But some sixty years later it had a happier outcome. She wrote:

'I am seventy-six now, and every week my sister and I attend a club where we have tea and entertainment. One week there was a trio to entertain us, and when they announced the name of the violinist I thought it seemed familiar. After the concert I went up to speak to him, and before I could utter a word, he said, 'I remember you – we were evacuated together to Norfolk in 1939.'

I was astounded to think that he could recognize me. My sister, who was with me, was flabbergasted. A few days later he sent me a photograph of the class and I was standing right behind him. He was a very handsome young man at the time, and quite honestly he was the only person I could remember in the whole class. But then I always did have an eye for the boys.

Eva believed that, though she had been able to accept her unhappy evacuation as a part of her childhood, which in no way hindered her full and interesting later life, deep down it had rankled. But all of a sudden, with that unexpected recognition over a cup of tea, the misery of more than sixty years before, of being a homesick child stuck in remote countryside in wartime with strangers, had become a harmless distant episode that at long last made her, and the sister who had been there with her, smile.

In 1995, with the support of the Imperial War Museum, James Roffey founded the Evacuees Reunion Association 'For the 3.5 million British children who were evacuated during the Second World War'. As a former evacuee from Camberwell in south London to Pulborough in Sussex, where he stayed for four years, Roffey himself had lived through the tribulations, as well as the pleasures, of an evacuated childhood. The association has done much to focus national attention on the phenomenon of the evacuees, as well as bringing them together in groups to commemorate events, to share their memories, to find former playmates, and to forge new links.

Roffey finds that for most evacuees the significance of their various experiences, whatever they may have been, has increased, not faded, with time. In older age and retirement, the distant parts of our lives become more interesting and more important to us. There is also more time for contemplation. He believes that the experience of long-term evacuees runs deep, and in many cases has strongly influenced their later lives. And he gave this illustration.

One of the association's members gave a talk, with discussion, at a Women's Institute branch in East Anglia. At the end, a woman came up to the speaker and told him that she had been evacuated to East Anglia from London during the war and had stayed with 'wonderful' people who had treated her as their own. Although she really didn't know why, she had not spoken about this evacuation experience for many years, she said, even though it had been a very good one. And she then broke down in tears.

This emotional reaction – by no means unusual – hints at the damage that is likely to occur, even in the best of circumstances, when parents and young children are separated, for whatever reasons. The historian Richard Titmuss had the great gift of leavening the driest of statistics with eloquence and insight. Considering the overall evacuation, and its long-lasting consequences, he wrote, 'While the institution of the family remains as the basis of human society it cannot, in the long run, be wholesome to break it into fragments and to risk depriving children of their need to give and receive affection.'

The daunting concept of mass evacuation of children (as well as the old and the disabled) from the cities in the event of war had been considered as long ago as the 1920s. The Zeppelin raids on London and other city centres during the First World War had caused both destruction and civilian panic, and the rapid development of air power and its devastating effects in the Spanish Civil War and in Abyssinia (Ethiopia) in the 1930s had fundamentally changed how wars were fought. Thereafter it was accepted that in any future war there would be immediate aerial attacks on large cities and industrial sites.

Faith, who still lives in her parents' and grand parents' town house, remembered her mother telling her when she was a child about a stick of bombs that had fallen round the corner from that house during a German raid in November 1918. The whole neighbourhood shook with the blast, a row of houses was destroyed, and several people lost their lives. This was such an unnerving event that her mother insisted that she never felt quite safe again, even in her own home.

This feeling of terror was widespread; war had moved away from the distant trenches and into the familiar territory of streets and shops and houses. Families were now in the front line too.

Some idea of the most extreme level of parental anxiety felt in 1939 can be obtained from the findings of Mass-Observation, a new and much respected polling organization that gauged popular opinion. Astonishing though it now sounds, trained researchers recorded a 'significant' number of men who were prepared, in the direst of wartime circumstances, to kill their own families. Perhaps remembering the shocking photographs of war-torn Spanish cities, 'I'd sooner see kids dead than bombed like they are in some places,' one mother despaired.

As we look back, we see very clearly what a painful and difficult time this must have been in which to shoulder the responsibilities of parenthood. To us, so much more atuned to the emotions, removing young children from their homes and families seems cruel, almost bizarre, whatever the circumstances. But we have to recognize that, in the conditions of the time, the government felt it had a moral duty to do its utmost to protect its citizens living in likely target areas – particularly the young.

Throughout the politically ominous pre-war years, parents in city and suburban areas began to face up to the threat of bombing raids. A former head teacher in a school in the East End of London spoke of holding a parents' meeting around the time of Munich in 1938 at which the government's new evacuation scheme for children was to be explained. It was a scene he never forgot, and which goes straight to the heart. The men, still in their flat cloth caps, having come straight from work, stood round the sides of the room; the women were seated in the centre. The government's line was firm: if war was declared, getting the children away from cities was the best and safest option. The atmosphere in the hall was grim, and many decades later that head teacher could still visualize the sea of stricken faces before him as the reality of what was being asked of parents sank in.

The gist of the scheme devised by the government, working closely with local authorities, was this. The country would be divided into safety and danger zones. The main industrial centres – London, Liverpool, Birmingham, Leeds, Manchester, Newcastle, Edinburgh, Dundee and so on – were designated as 'Evacuation' areas: those thought to be most at risk from air warfare, and so likely to suffer the worst casualties. The designated 'Reception' areas – almost entirely rural: country districts with low population density and little industry – were believed to be 'safe'. The rest of the country, where nothing much was expected to change, was described as 'neutral'.

After the Munich crisis, the evacuation programme was given a high priority. Evacuation would be organized through the schools, where parents who wished to would sign up their children. The children would be accompanied to 'safe' areas by their teachers; with classes of younger children, a few mothers who were able to leave would go along as helpers.

Local councils in the country areas to which the children would be sent were alerted, and arrangements for accommodation and schooling requirements were hastily put in place. All households in these districts were compulsorily inspected for whatever spare accommodation was available; space for extra children was found in local schools wherever possible, and empty halls and buildings that might be suitable for temporary classroom use were requisitioned.

Receiving householders were given government allowances of 10/6d. (52½p) per week for the first evacuee and 8/6d. (42½p) for each additional child. On a means-tested basis, which was never rigorously enforced, parents of evacuated children contributed to the authorities an average of 2/3d. (11p) for each child. A quarter of parents of evacuated children paid nothing.

Despite the genuine concern, and the government's best efforts – 'Sign Up For Evacuation!' was the stern advice given to vulnerable parents in industrial areas – the take-up was disappointingly low. Understandably, large families tended to send several children, while only children were likely to be kept at home. In the autumn of 1938 more than 80 per cent of London parents said that they would want their children evacuated; by the following summer this had dropped to two-thirds – and when it finally came to the crunch fewer than half the eligible schoolchildren from the county boroughs of England and Wales were evacuated.

For reasons nobody understands, numbers varied considerably throughout the country: Lancashire sent away the highest proportion (two-thirds) of children, the Black Country sent one-quarter, and only 15 per cent made the exodus from Sheffield. In all areas the numbers who left were far lower than the authorities had hoped. But, despite official mutterings and misgivings, evacuation remained voluntary throughout the war.

Even quite young children knew from their friends what was happening and, no matter what their parents wanted, and even though family discipline was then considerably stronger, a lot of those living in unsafe districts resisted leaving their homes. Kate remembered her eight-year-old self in this situation as though it were yesterday – and she spoke for many. 'I flatly refused to join all the other kids with their labels and gas masks waiting for the trains to carry them away to the country,' she said. 'And I really believe my mother was quite relieved.'

Equally, just as many parents would prove reluctant to part with their children, bombs or no bombs, many householders were less than pleased to open their homes to unknown city children. In exceptional circumstances, if extra housing was needed desperately, local authorities were empowered to billet evacuees on whomever they chose. But, throughout the war, this was rarely necessary. However doubtful they may have been, the majority of rural householders in the reception areas seem to have been reasonably good hearted and determined to do their best, at least in the initial evacuation.

The evacuation scheme – code-named Operation Pied Piper – had been in high gear since the late summer of 1938, although it was thought wise to play down the urgency so as not to cause undue alarm. Children in cities were targeted as well as their parents, often successfully, being persuaded by their schools and teachers that evacuation was some sort of 'jolly' – an opportunity to spend time in the countryside with their friends; a more interesting option than the usual school routine.

James Roffey of the Evacuees Reunion Association believes that a good deal of 'brainwashing' took place, with children being assured that they were going 'on holiday – to have a lovely time'. And, with a sizeable percentage of families in the cities living close to the poverty line, even a train journey was a genuine adventure for disadvantaged children who rarely went anywhere.

By the time the school summer holidays were under way in 1939, a three-point evacuation alarm system was already in place: 'Prepare for Evacuation', 'Standby', and 'Evacuate Forthwith'. When the Evacuate Forthwith order was given, on 31 August, it precipitated a series of well-rehearsed and complex travel arrangements that over the following three days moved nearly 1½ million children, teachers and young mothers out of the cities: trains and buses were assembled, normal schedules were put on hold, and some main roads leading out of cities were closed to ordinary traffic. The first – and by far the largest – of the three major evacuations of the war had begun.

According to James Roffey:

The first departures probably began at 4 a.m. on Friday 1 September 1939, when thousands of children were taken to the gates of the Ford Motor

Works at Dagenham, ready to board the fleet of boats, many of them paddle steamers . . . that were anchored on the Thames or alongside the Ford jetties. As the hundreds of children gathered at the gates, many of them having been brought there in the backs of baker's vans or on milk floats, the Ford workers switched off their factory machines and went out to carry the youngest children to the waiting boats.

A little later, at 5.30 a.m., a mother in East London, like thousands and thousands of other mothers across the country, had the 'terrible task' of waking her children, daughters of eight and nine. The younger broke down in floods of tears, but took heart from her sister's composure. Two hours later mother and father watched grimly as the girls marched off from their school in a crocodile, their teachers leading the way, to board the buses that would take them to the main-line station – and into the lives of strangers. Tim, who was seven, said that his memory of that day started with 'when my mother told me that she wasn't coming with us. None of the mothers were. "Look after your little sister," she said. But who was going to look after me?' Like many parents of younger children, his mother tried to cheer up the pair of them with the idea of having a good time: 'She told us that we were going on holiday, and only the children could go.'

We can only guess at the feelings of parents all over the country that day: their hope and their despair, praying that they had made the right decision, that their children would be safe and well cared for – and that they would be reunited soon. Those who had chosen to keep their children at home – some at the very last moment – crossed their fingers and hoped for the best.

A small boy in north London, Dan, then aged five, saw – uncomprehending – his mother's despair then: 'I sat on the stairs of our little terraced house. I can still remember looking back along the hallway to where my mother was making sandwiches for us. She wept as she made them, which puzzled me at the time. I must have thought we were going on holiday with other children from the neighbourhood.'

Further north, a bewildered little girl of five called Sue was also being evacuated, dressed in her 'best Sunday clothes, matching coat and hat – and my gas mask in a cardboard box. I was standing on

Newcastle upon Tyne's central station with my mother, who was a helper, and hundreds of children.'

Most children, having been necessarily enthused by parents and teachers, felt ambivalent towards this great, open-ended upheaval in their lives. 'I wanted to go and I didn't want to go. I didn't want to leave my mother' was how one girl aptly put it. Others thrilled to the adventure. On his way from West Kensington to Paddington station with his brother, a nine-year-old called Robert remembered feeling only 'intense excitement . . . then boarding an enormous hissing and panting train going to an unknown destination . . . Mothers could not come on to the platform, and I couldn't understand why my mother and most other women were crying. We all thought it was simply marvellous . . . I remember pleading with God that we would be taken somewhere close to the sea and go and live with a duke or a lord or anyway people who were rich.' The boys ended up in a labourer's cottage in Dorset, not far from the sea, but with no great riches in sight. Although the living conditions were basic, they settled down reasonably well, made friends, and stayed for three years.

It was over the transport that some of the official plans went badly awry, leading to a good deal of confusion about timing and, later, to chaos in the reception areas. Many of the children who had been signed up for evacuation failed to turn up at the school meeting places. Undoubtedly this was due to nerves and changes of mind by both parents and children – but, however understandable, it played havoc with timetables and numbers. Timetables had to be kept to, so on arrival at the stations children were marched willy-nilly on to whatever train was waiting – not always the one intended. This naturally caused problems when they arrived at their destinations.

Once on the trains, for some the real tedium set in. Many of the trains did not have corridors and lacked basic toilet and washing facilities, adding to the discomfort and fractiousness of young children. 'We seemed to be on the train for hours,' Adam, who was eleven, said. 'I remember asking our teacher where we were going. He said, "Ely." I was puzzled, as I thought he had said "Ealing" and I knew that was part of London . . . Hours and hours later we arrived at a village in the Cambridgeshire countryside.' A girl being evacuated from London to the Sussex coast, a short distance in normal times, remembered that the journey seemed to take all day, with much waiting about and long delays.

Messed-up schedules at the main stations produced some odd results. When a group of hefty schoolboys arrived in a small mining town in South Wales, Mike 'sensed some consternation as we – aged thirteen and fourteen – were a good deal bigger children than our host town expected . . . All the same, everyone greeted us with friendliness.' Boys from another school – their ages between eleven and thirteen – got off a train in Surrey 'to be met by a bemused group of mums bearing teddies and toys, meant for about a hundred five-to-seven-year-olds, who had been sent elsewhere'.

These kinds of mishap were happening all over the country, and added to the fluster. Cambridge, in particular, received far fewer evacuees than it had expected and prepared for. And getting the trains out of the cities on time made for at least one genuine anticlimax during those dramatic few days: eager would-be foster parents waited on a railway platform in Sussex for a train packed with evacuees, only to have it eventually arrive empty.

For all children, trains were then glamorous and exciting objects. Thrilled to be on this outing with their school friends and their packets of sandwiches, many of them happily made the most of it. Dan, a six-year-old on his way to Devon with his classmates, remembered that 'as the train thundered along, the children were holding their handkerchiefs out of the windows so that they fluttered in the wind. Of course, I had to do the same, and the wind was too strong for my surprised young fingers, so the handkerchief blew away.'

Rob, a confident nine-year-old from Essex, was evacuated with his younger brother. The boys came from a decent and caring family, but one in which there was no spare money for outings and holidays. All his life he would remember that bright September morning as an 'exhilarating experience'. His widowed mother, he said:

must have been given a list of the things we had to take with us, and so for the first time in my life I possessed a toothbrush and a tin of tooth cleaner like a slab of soap. There was no suitcase in our household, and so my mother took my brother and me shopping in Marks & Spencer's, where she bought one for 5 shillings. It was quite small, but easily contained what clothing we owned between us . . . I have very little recollection of the journey except the wonder of Paddington station – I thought it was Crystal Palace that I had seen in illustrations – and the sight of Malmesbury Abbey as we approached our destination . . . I remember calling out to my companions, 'Look, there are some ruins for us to explore tomorrow!'

Given the desperation of the authorities to get the children out of the cities as fast as possible, buses also were pressed into service. Kate, then aged four, said, 'I clearly remember my grandfather putting me on a bus in the Kennington Road: I had a luggage label tied on to my coat, and a small toy attaché case with a doll and a square of pink silk that I used to wrap her in. I had no idea what was happening . . . I was sent to Devon, and I clearly remember sitting quite happily in a beautiful garden and being read Bible stories.'

Minnie, aged twelve, was evacuated with her younger brother to the south coast. The children's parting from their widowed mother made an indelible impression. 'I vividly remember my mother's sadness,' Minnie wrote years and years later. 'She had only lost our father two years before, so she had no one to advise her as to whether she was doing the right thing . . . She saw us off that Sunday morning in double-decker buses with our gas masks, labels tied to our coats and our small cases, not knowing where we were going. I looked after my brother – and we made the best of it.'

Arrival at whatever town or village had been selected meant more herding and hanging around until a billet with a local householder could be arranged. So we must picture these same children, some with siblings in tow, by now thoroughly exhausted and bedraggled, fetching up at various halls in the country reception areas, while harried teachers attempted to keep some control. There the children were faced with strangers from all walks of life who, braced to receive these unknown youngsters into their homes, had assembled to inspect and claim – rather gingerly – their new charges.

The situation was fraught and difficult on both sides. In many of these rural venues there was pandemonium as hosts attempted to pick out a child, or children, who seemed on first sight to be tolerable. As Richard Titmuss aptly put it, these were 'scenes reminiscent of a cross between an early Roman slave market and Selfridge's bargain basement'. One after another, the recollections of the evacuees confirm this.

Sisters of twelve and fourteen who had come from London finally arrived in Norfolk quite late that evening. Phyllis, the younger girl, said, 'We were herded into a church hall . . . and the householders came to choose whichever children they fancied. My sister, who was two years older than me (fourteen), was rather skinny and did not look too strong. I was a plump, quite pretty child. They came over to choose me, but they did not want my sister. We told them that we could not be separated. Unfortunately, we were left to the very end.' These girls eventually went to live in quite a large house with a middle-aged couple who were both bad tempered and displeased at having to take in evacuees. The girls' experience of country living, which had started badly, turned out to be a difficult one.

Some left-to-the-last children's experiences, such as this one, make for sober reading. In many cases the vicar had to take home whatever children remained until other arrangements could be made.

Sue, who had travelled from Newcastle, found herself in the yard of a village school in Cumberland. She was, she said, 'sad that my really best friend had gone to another unknown place. Mother was a helper, and we were being chosen like cattle. An unmarried brother and sister in their sixties said they would pick my mother, but she said she had a little girl. They didn't want a child, but she said I was very good and they accepted us both. That was 1 September 1939 – two days before my sixth birthday.'

Her birthday fell on Sunday 3 September, when she and her mother went to church. It was a harvest-festival service, and when the words 'All good gifts around us are sent from heaven above' rang out Sue thought excitedly, 'Now I am definitely going to get a doll for my birthday' – as she had been longing for. But she had already been warned not to expect much in the way of presents, 'because there was a war on – a phrase we were to hear a lot in our childhood . . . However, I was deeply disappointed to receive only a ball and a bar of chocolate, not the desperately wanted doll . . . I still cannot hear this hymn now without the tears welling up.'

Ruth, then aged nine, remembered that

We thought we were going to a camp, so of course I wanted to go . . . We seemed to travel for hours, and eventually arrived at a small country town . . . Coaches then drove us to various villages. We went to a school where we were given cake and lemonade and the village ladies walked amongst us plucking out the children they fancied . . . One child was immediately chosen by a lady who whisked her off in her car. I was taken by an old lady, and we went back to her cottage. It was now very dark, and I was introduced to the lavatory down the bottom of the garden – in a shed: just a bucket. I was put to bed by lamplight. There was an old dead tree with owls outside.

This creepy and unpromising beginning presaged an unhappy evacuation for Ruth. 'We evacuees were blamed for everything in school, even though one of our own teachers was there.' Later she was quarantined, through illness. She was often lonely, with the beauty of the surrounding country her only consolation – 'I used to take Jock the dog walking round the lanes, and wander through the woods picking many wild flowers.' After three difficult and mostly unhappy years she returned home to Barrow-in-Furness. Yet, for all her tribulations, and several different foster homes, in later years she still kept in touch with a few of the people she had met during this bleak time of her young life.

In agricultural areas, strapping lads were quickly snapped up by local farmers looking for an extra pair of hands. Brothers and sisters, and friends wanting to be billeted together, were always a problem. Two girls of twelve, best friends, were each in charge of a younger brother, aged seven. The four children were determined to stay together, as their parents had hoped they would. 'A retired headmistress and headmaster were willing to take two boys and two girls,' Grace, one of the older girls, recalled. 'But they lived some way away, and this meant we were taken from our teachers and other school friends.' The children had managed to stay together, but they missed their friends badly. Their foster parents, although responsible, were cold and strict – and they treated the children quite harshly. The girls were required to do all the housework – a common complaint of many older girl evacuees – which they had never done at home. The small boys, who were then not very strong, also had to turn their hand to domestic chores. 'They were expected to chop the wood and bring the coal in . . . When I look back, I often wonder how they coped,' Grace added sadly.

A glimpse of a rural household receiving two young evacuees is given by Sheila, at that time a girl of ten living in Derbyshire. She clearly remembered the doorbell ringing one evening:

The billeting officer was standing at the door with two little pale-faced children. They looked very frightened – as well they might, having left their parents and having no idea what was to happen to them. Round their necks were labels giving their names and their gas masks in cardboard boxes. They had come from the East End of London, and were aged six and four.

These two children opened my eyes to an aspect of life I knew nothing about. Although we had given them a bedroom with two beds, they slept in one bed with their arms round each other. They were very fussy about their food, refused to eat a lot of it, and wanted 'brown sauce' with everything. So much for my nanny's constantly telling me that I had to eat everything up! They told us they were given a penny each day to buy their lunch, and their greatest treat was pineapple chunks. Billy, the elder, stood up to my brother's teasing with 'I'll tell my dad of you, and my dad's a boxer and he'll knock your block off.'

These children came from a loving family who were anxious for their welfare. 'My mother received a touching letter from their father thanking her for giving the children a home.'

This was a positive evacuation, as the children stayed on for a couple of years, were occasionally visited by their parents, and missed the worst of the air raids. And the story had a good ending. Years later, Sheila's parents again had a knock on the door. A nice-looking young man stood outside. 'I'm Billy,' he said. This was the pale and scrawny little evacuee, now grown up and making his way in the world. 'I really think the evacuation was the making of those children,' Sheila said some sixty years later. 'I think it made a big difference. I know my parents kept in close touch with the family, and were very helpful and encouraging in many ways. Both the children did very well in life.'

A little girl of eight called Sally, arriving with her school at Leeds station, immediately faced a second journey into the country. When the children got to their final destination, she later remembered, 'some ladies and gentlemen came and sat behind tables and they came to choose amongst us.' It was the usual scene that was being witnessed in halls throughout the countryside, with children of certain characteristics being 'booked' in advance. 'A man with fair hair came and asked if I would like to go with him, but someone said I was booked. In the afternoon a lady with black hair done in earphones came to fetch me. Apparently she had booked me by asking her friend, who was helping, to look out for a little girl about eight years old.' This turned into a contented evacuation on both sides – one that lasted for most of the war, and formed enduring relationships.

Although the government had not wanted siblings evacuated together, so many parents had insisted that it was forced to yield. This was undoubtedly a comfort to both parents and children, but it greatly complicated billeting and educational arrangements in overcrowded country schools with a limited number of teachers. Anecdotal evidence suggests that the older siblings took their duties seriously, like upstanding thirteen-year-old John, who remembered 'feeling or sensing that I had the responsibility of taking great care of my four-years-younger sister'. When billets were being assigned, siblings consistently tried to stay together, even if it meant several moves and inadequate schooling, in the wrong class, for at least one of them.

Many first billets were hastily and haphazardly organized, with no attempt to match child and foster parents, and were quite unsuitable and soon had to be changed. A Jewish brother and sister from a moderately strict religious home found themselves sleeping on camp beds in the loft of a pork butcher, above his shop in a small town in Devon, with most of the neighbourhood friends who were evacuated with them. Dan, who was the younger, managed to swallow a little of the unfamiliar food, though he found it disgusting:

Everything seemed to be cooked in bacon fat – I still recall the pervading odour. I ate what I was given, but my sister refused and subsisted on Wrigley's penny chewing gum from a slot machine fixed to the wall outside the butcher's shop. She quickly became very skinny . . . Needless to say, we were unhappy, and the billeting officers soon transferred us to another home . . .

This was with a widow from World War I, whose late husband's clothes were still in the wardrobe in the loft, again where we slept . . . There was no bathroom, so we had a commode near our beds, the pot of which we had to carry down the ladder from the loft to be emptied every morning in the latrine at the bottom of the garden.

The children were also unhappy there, and after yet another move they finally went to live with the family of the local GP. 'This was a quality home, where we were happy. I remember both our parents coming to see us there and having tea, served by the maid, under a huge weeping willow tree in the garden.'

Dan became a doctor, and he wondered, many years later, whether his sister's early eating trauma, combined with the shock of her alien surroundings, could have triggered the serious intestinal disease she suffered from when she was older.

All evacuees had been given cards to send home to their parents to let them know where they were, and that they had arrived safely. As one former evacuee pointed out, 'Phones then were a rarity and only used in the most extreme emergency.' In any case, except in some large homes, few telephones existed in the rural areas in which most evacuees were settled. Although few of these cards and letters can still remain, most children in those early days must have been unhappy and desperately bewildered, and many must have attempted to communicate this to their parents. A thoroughly miserable child wrote pathetically to his mother in Liverpool, 'Dear Mam, I want to come home. Pleas come and tack us home.'

Some, however, were cheerier and happier – or perhaps putting on a braver face. A boy of eleven called Peter, evacuated to the south coast with his school, was clearly not smitten by terrible homesickness, as so many evacuees were. He wrote to his parents, 'Everybody is enjoying themselves. We have a dartboard here. It is very nice food. Will you send my bathing costume down please and a shilling or six. I have one penny. Will you send by post another towel please. Lots of people talk to us and ask us where we come from. Hope you have not been bombed yet. I think we have to go to school next Monday. I am quite well.'

On 4 September, reporting on this mass evacuation, *The Times* got the figures badly wrong, greatly inflating the numbers to 3 million. It commented blandly that for 'all but a few [it was] an enthralling and happy adventure, and homesickness and shyness quickly fled'. It was certainly a far more complex experience than these words indicate – and the consequences, for most, were long-lasting. Nevertheless, despite the heartaches and the confusions, the wrongly filled trains, school parties that got separated, and many disastrous first billets, the authorities and their thousands of helpers had done very creditably in 'getting the children away'. Whatever emotional damage may have been done that day, not one accident or physical mishap to any child was reported.

The above fragments of the initial experiences of evacuees during those early September days illustrate the bewildering disruptions the war was already causing in the lives of children, their parents and their teachers – as well as their foster parents. And they were not alone in facing sudden change. From the end of June through to the September of 1939 nearly one-third of the population was on the move. Men – and now women too – were called, or recalled, to military duties; others left their jobs and simply joined up. Large parts of the Civil Service moved to temporary accommodation outside the capital, as did some of the bigger firms of lawyers and accountants; the Bank of England abandoned the City and buried itself in the safety of Hampshire. Some of the nation's greatest treasures, peerless paintings from the National Gallery in London, suffered the indignity of being transported to an old slate quarry in North Wales.

Over the weekend that war was declared, some 5,000 people left Southampton by boat, many of them children. During the following year, with the growing threat of German invasion, the idea of leaving the country became an increasingly attractive option for those who had the means to do so. With offers of help from the United States, and from countries that were then British Dominions, the government announced a limited scheme to send school-age children, with adult carers, to pre-arranged billets. An enormous number of parents immediately applied on behalf of their children, but it was clear that it would not be possible to arrange passage, or suitable billets, for more than a fraction of them.

In the following months, several thousand children – some in school parties and some privately; some with government help or through the auspices of various organizations – were sent to the United States, Australia, Canada and New Zealand. But by the spring of 1940 German U-boats were making the seas around Britain increasingly dangerous, and after the tragic sinking of the *City of Benares* in September that year, with the loss of seventy-three British children and the six adults who were looking after them, the scheme was abandoned.

All told, some 13,000 British children spent all or part of the war in the safety and relative comfort of foreign countries. Of these, 11,000 placements were privately arranged; the rest were government-assisted. It is ironic to think that roughly similar numbers of children were being sent into the UK: approximately 10,000, during the nine months before the war – mostly Jewish children from Germany, Austria and Czechoslovakia, sent away by their desperate parents to seek freedom from Nazi persecution. And after war was declared many of these newly arrived children also found themselves being uprooted to safer areas – for the second time in their young lives.

So by the end of 1939 the destructive upheaval of war in Europe was already having a profound effect on the social mix of the UK, with lasting post-war consequences of greater equality and tolerance. All in all, there had never been such an extensive and diverse cobbling together of ages and jobs and schools and backgrounds right across the land; but it was still the young evacuees, falling into exhausted sleep in their unfamiliar beds in strange surroundings, who gave the most visible, and perhaps most lasting, picture of that shifting time.

With up to a million urban children in all age groups parked on dwellers in the countryside, loosely organized in school parties, the results were bound to be very mixed indeed. Britain in the 1930s and on into the 40s was a multi-layered society, perhaps best described as tribal. And each layer had its own nuances. A former evacuee remembered that, when he was about eight and living in south London, children a few streets away were allowed to join the Boys' Brigade, whereas his own parents, living round the corner, didn't consider it a 'nice' thing for their sons to do. Social rules varied hugely from class to class and within each class, and were perhaps most finely honed among the working classes. So when these various factions were pushed together willy-nilly, in unfamiliar territory, there was bound to be trouble and misunderstanding. Or rather shock and horror, as the genteel middle classes saw it.

A prominent politician who had offered to accommodate ten evacuees in his country mansion ended up with thirty-one. He wrote priggishly, 'I got a shock. I had little dreamt that English children could be so completely ignorant of the simplest rules of hygiene.' As a politician, he might have known that in the late 1930s it was estimated that a high proportion of those living in cities were considered to be below the poverty line – and the majority of these were children. Coming from a city slum, with no running water and whatever outside toilets there were being shared, how could these children possibly be expected to know what 'hygiene' was? Living in the mean streets of London or Glasgow or Liverpool or any other major city, keeping alive was enough; staying clean, if it were possible, required enormous efforts. For children from this type of background, middle-class standards of food and table manners and lifestyle in general were as alien as life on the moon. This story, possibly apocryphal, has been repeated over and over: visiting mother of evacuee to her six-year-old child, who insisted on using his host's carpets as a toilet: 'You dirty thing, messing up the lady's carpets. Go and do it in the corner.' This type of behaviour did happen, but – as we shall see later – it was rare and exaggerated out of all proportion.

Even for children of very poor but decent homes, the social differences they were faced with must have been both confusing and frightening. And social differences cut both ways. Many children used to warm and well-lit city and suburban homes were horrified to find themselves stuck in primitive country cottages lacking water and electricity. Most children, even if they were fairly happily placed, were struggling to adjust. And for all the children, and the parents they had left behind, the future stretched ahead interminably. When would they be going home again? When would they see their parents? When would their family be reunited?

There are as many different stories of those wartime evacuations as there were evacuees – and those who took them into their homes –

but it seems that most evacuees have memories similar to these snap-shot recollections of

a kind word remembered, engulfing homesickness, a harsh and un-deserved punishment, the coldness of foster parents in withholding affection, taunts of village children, fear of walking down the dark and eerie garden path to a murky outdoor toilet, waiting outside the house to be let in by a foster parent, living above the Post Office-cum-sweet shop, strange, awful food . . .

. . . running free in the fields, picking cowslips, a new local friend, making dens, fishing along river banks, animals shrieking in the darkness at night, a bar mitzvah conducted in a sheeted church hall, milking a cow, learning to snare rabbits, entertainment in the village hall, digging pota-toes from frozen fields . . .

The evacuees' experiences runs the gamut from children who were so miserable that they either ran away or had to be returned to their homes to the occasional, joyful 'they treated me as their own' accolade awarded to foster parents that children grew fond of. Sixty-odd years later, partly for themselves, partly for their children and grandchildren, some have put down their memories in their own words.

One man wrote of his foster parents in Devon:

They seemed an old couple to my sister and me, but of course at our age then – I was twelve and my sister ten – everyone over twenty seemed old. The lady was plump and warm and friendly, and I never saw her without an apron pinafore. Her husband was a short and powerful man with an Edward Elgar moustache. He returned from the pub several times a week rather drunk . . .

The house, which was detached, had a large garden. It contained a walnut tree, which produced massive amounts of nuts, and space to grow all the vegetables they needed – potatoes, carrots, onions, beans, peas, cab-bages . . . But what I found most interesting was the asparagus, which he grew in trenches: mouth-watering and wonderful, and the most delicious thing I have ever tasted. I have never tasted asparagus like it since.

The house had no running water, no electricity and no flush lavatory.

The water came from a well in the garden, lighting was oil lamps, and the lavatory was in the yard – a seat over a bucket which was emptied daily in the garden somewhere.

I have often wondered if this was the reason for the luscious asparagus!

That boy and his sister were lucky. Others were not. May, aged nine, was evacuated slightly later on in the war, and recalled it vividly:

I was evacuated later than other children in my area because I had been very ill with diphtheria . . . My grandfather had been killed in the bombing . . . My mother coped with caring for a new baby and two members of the family who had been bombed out, and therefore I became superfluous to requirements . . . I was to go up to Liverpool and then on to a small village in the wilds of Lancashire, where my brother had a good billet. His foster parents recommended one of their neighbours, and everyone thought that I would be well cared for. After the long journey up north my Dad seemed pleased with the room I had been given, and he left me there, bewildered and tearful.

But this home did not turn out to be what her father had hoped and expected:

Once he had gone on his way . . . I was made to sleep in a cold attic with a camp bed and bare boards. Then I became aware of a lack of food. I stole some from the larder, and ate the crusts that were put out for the birds. I attended the village school and was given a thin soup at midday, which put a bit of nourishment into my stomach.

As winter set in, the conditions got worse:

I had to wear all my clothes at once to keep from freezing. I was plagued with chilblains, and suffered from bullying by the local children . . . When they taunted me for my London accent, I had to chant to myself the dialect of Lancashire. I could say 'oop' instead of 'up', and gradually enlarged my repertoire until nobody could suspect that I was not a native . . . On arriving home from school I would have to wait out in the freezing cold until the lady returned.

When her parents came to visit, although they were hardly left alone with her, they suspected all was not well and that she was miserable. 'Get packed – you're coming home with us,' her father told her. 'I grabbed my bits and pieces and rushed downstairs, ready to run if need be . . . thankful to return to the bombing.'

When she got home, her bad memories and insecurities turned into terrible nightmares, which persisted well into her middle age. And her Lancashire accent, which she had struggled so hard to acquire, was no longer appreciated: 'My main problem at first was making myself understood.'

Rose, aged nine, came from a large family in the teeming industrial area of Clydeside, and was evacuated to a remote village in the surrounding countryside. She found barely a roof over her head, was badly used by her foster mother, and had no proper care or affection for four years. Her first billet was with a woman whose husband worked on a local farm:

I had only been there a couple of days when she said she couldn't keep me. I walked around the village and a woman was shaking her mat. She asked me what was wrong, as I was very upset. She went to see the other woman and told her she would take me in and look after me . . . My father came one day to see me. My brother, who was evacuated near by, hid on the bus and went back home with him. He never came back to the village. There were no taps in the house I went to . . .

To go to the toilet was quite a walk round cottages up the path at the back. The toilet was wood with a hole in the middle. Once a week a horse and cart would come to empty it out . . .

I had to peel at least one bucket of potatoes a day . . . I was not allowed in the woman's house alone . . . She liked me to comb her hair, and I also had to cut her corns, which I hated . . . One Sunday I'd had my dinner and I thought, 'Now I'll have to do her hair and feet.'

Sometimes my dad visited and he gave me pocket money . . . I got my money out of the jar and left . . . I walked 2½ miles to the bus . . . I found my way back home . . . I had been away over four years.

My mother was surprised to see me and took me back to the police station for them to send me back. She would have too. We were both upset.

But the police got a message through to the lady saying I was home. And I stayed. So I won that time.

Undoubtedly, whatever their reasons, a few parents used evacuation as a way of getting rid of their parental responsibilities – at least for a while. The following is a strange, sad little story which has no ending, happy or otherwise. But it makes one wonder what lay behind it.

Waiting on the platform with a group being evacuated to the West Country, John and his mother, who was travelling with him, witnessed a tragic scene which he never forgot. Nearby were a brother and sister, both very young, complete with their gas mask and labels, neatly dressed, saying a 'tearful goodbye to their mother, who had attached them to a group of evacuees. When the authorities came to allocate them a railway carriage and destination, they found that their mother had pinned a note on one of them. She had recently heard news of her husband's death in action. Without a home, or much means, she intended to start a new life, unencumbered by what she saw as responsibilities – her children.'

John, a youngster of ten, could not get understand how a mother, no matter how grief-stricken and depressed, could do such a thing. Many years later he said, 'I have often thought of those children – the sadness and bewilderment they must have felt. In all my years, it is the worst social story I have ever heard. I have also thought that perhaps the authorities were able to trace the mother . . . I hoped that it was an isolated case, but I have heard since that it was not.'

The outcome might have been happier than John supposed, however. Records show that the number of evacuees not claimed by their parents at the end of the war was 'minuscule'.

Early in June 1940, a ten-year-old girl called Jennie was evacuated to a family in the West Country with her younger brother and sister:

The family was quite prominent . . . Their daughter Lizzie, only a few years older than I, was a beautiful girl with a very happy nature, and the odd thing is when we visit, as we have done all through the years, I never see her as an eighty-year-old but as she was . . . Her mother taught me milking, the care of calves, hens and ducks . . . We were free to wander the farm fields and copse. She showed me how to cook. We children had our first chicken and duck meals there, and I am sorry to say I could watch them being slaughtered without too much upset.

There were never any difficulties in our relationships with local children. We were all quite happy at school, but were encouraged to help the war effort. We were offered work picking up potatoes, taken to the fields by open lorries in the winter ... It was fun, and we were paid ... The highlight of the farm year was threshing. I would help take cold tea and bread and cheese at lunch, and when it was almost dark they would wash up outside on a bench and the dining room and living room would be filled with tired men and much laughter.

Unlike most children, these three were anything but happy to be taken home by their mother, particularly as there were still air raids over London. Their country evacuation of several years, which they had truly enjoyed, had a sad after-effect. Possibly because of personal resentment, or a division of loyalties, Jennie's relationship with her mother was badly fractured and took many years to heal.

Jill, evacuated aged eight to a village in Northampton where she stayed for five years, wrote of an equally happy evacuation, which informed the rest of her life. She came from a large family and was taken in by a couple who had no children, but many years later she glowingly described her time with them. 'It was a most wonderful childhood, and my foster parents moulded me into the person I am today. I saw my mother once in five years. I went away a Cinderella and was turned into a princess ... They had a niece next door who was a couple of years younger than I, and we are the best of friends to this day (sixty-five years on).'

Hilda, seven, was evacuated to a village in North Wales with her four siblings:

The journey was endless, but after we arrived at the village hall and had a meal the villagers came round and picked out the children they wanted ... I was one of the first selected and was whisked away in a car (the first car ride of my life) ... The lady I was with was very house-proud, and I was expected to help in the house and do the shopping while her daughter, a year younger that me, sat playing the piano. I had only one real complaint: it was that the daughter had strawberry jam for tea and I had plum jam – which I hated.

Later on in the war, Hilda and her two brothers were taken in by another villager, called Blodwin –

a lovely scatter-brained lady. She was the exact opposite of our mother; she swore like a trooper. Her husband was a gentleman, and when he went away – he was in the RAF – she would have a swear box, and try to mend her ways. But that didn't last long; she was broke in a couple of days! . . . We stayed for six years, and I cried and cried at leaving all my friends.

Her affection for this Welsh village and its inhabitants, who were unfailingly warm and welcoming, has been lifelong: 'Today, when I feel a bit nostalgic, I just get on a train and go back.'

Many children, dumped into rural areas, had to make very rapid adjustments to their usual standard of living. Outside lavatories – which they were not used to – were a daunting experience for many evacuees. Joan, then aged six, came from Leicester. She never took to either her foster parents or their rather eccentric ways: 'They had an outside toilet, which I wasn't used to, and I cried a lot if I had to go out to it . . . We had our baths in a tin tub in front of the living-room fire, because the lady's husband kept the proper bath full of yellow canaries.' Years later, perhaps remembering those scary walks to the lavatory in darkness, she wrote sympathetically that 'as a grand-mother, I often think of the worry, the sadness we experienced as children going to live with strangers for some unknown length of time.'

Alfie, aged nine, was evacuated from Hull to the wilds of Derbyshire and was billeted on a farm owned by a local landowner:

It was the Lower Farm. My foster parents were an elderly couple. He was a master ploughman – with many trophies to prove it. He spoke to his shire horses as if they were children. They seemed to understand. He had no time for tractors and such. He was very tall, and looked like the Hollywood actor C. Aubrey Smith. He was a very kindly man who gave me jobs to do about the farm.

Our school was a very small one: a Victorian school-house, a man and wife as teachers. They used to go to market on Wednesdays. I was left in charge, and school was always over very quickly on Wednesdays. These were happy days.

This, too, was a good evacuation, with interested foster parents and surroundings that he enjoyed – a childhood episode that genuinely broadened Alfie's knowledge.

The historian Angus Calder, allowing for exaggeration, claimed that 'certain evacuees were amazed to discover that apples grew on trees and not in boxes and that cows, which they had only seen in pictures, were bigger than dogs.' That is as may be – although he was describing a time without television, and without much social mobility, when most children led very narrow lives. But it seems clear that, once they had overcome the strangeness of it all, a lot of evacuated city children took eagerly to country life.

Ken, a confident ten-year-old, evacuated to Devon, soon found his way around the village, although he had lived in London all his life:

It all seemed like real-life adventure . . . I joined the local gang – welcomed for my tales of the big city, most of which were embroidered upon to suit the audience – . . . and I learned about keeping bottles of lemonade in the village well to keep them cool . . . that the local chalk pit was an exciting place to slide down on an old tin tray . . . about churning milk into butter and cheese . . . and to pick watercress from the river on the way home.

When his parents brought him back to London before the end of the war, the city seemed very grim and dirty. The mean little backyard of his home was a poor substitute for the open country. There was still enemy action from the skies, and, delivering groceries one Saturday, he was knocked off his bike by the outer blast from an exploding rocket. Although he soon picked up his old life, he wrote with real affection of his time in the village, the family he lived with, the friends he had made, and the minutiae of country living. As with many other children of his generation, evacuation had opened his eyes to the countryside and all it had to offer.

When Sue was evacuated, she became, and remained, a country girl at heart. Leaving the city with her school, she was billeted with foster parents who lived outside a village 'in a thatched cottage nestling under the South Downs. Idyllic? No electricity, no running water, privy in the garden, cold and damp in winter. But we became country kids, roaming pretty freely, gathering wild flowers (Oh, the cowslips in early summer!), building dens, snaring rabbits, chopping wood, working the fields at harvest time . . .'

After her father had joined the RAF, Wendy and her mother shared a rented cottage in North Wales with friends from Liverpool. She was then about six, and she later said that 'the experience of living in the cottage has stayed with me – no electricity or running water, make do and mend at every turn, water fetched from a spring in the field, loo down the garden, and such freedom! My love of the country was born then . . . I left the city at the first opportunity, and have lived in the country ever since.'

All over the country, parents in differing circumstances had wrestled with the problem of what to do for the best for their families. Sometimes people packed up their children and belongings and left to stay with relatives in areas deemed 'safe', and sometimes friends joined forces to rent a house for their families in such areas. It is estimated that there were some 2 million private evacuations, most involving children, over the late summer months of 1939.

Although they usually remained with at least one parent, children who were evacuated privately faced all the same difficulties as those evacuated through the government scheme: change of home, new school, missing friends. Young children parked on unknown or disliked cousins were sometimes just as miserable as in any random billet. Sent to stay with well-meaning relatives outside Carlisle, Sue, eight was made both unhappy and homesick. 'When I was alone with my distant girl cousin, she was deliberately nasty. Every night I waited until bedtime and cried myself to sleep. My mother came over once a month by train for a few hours – later I learned she cried all the way home too.'

Private family evacuation to 'safe' areas could also be uncomfortable, with none of the domestic amenities of home. One family, faced with primitive surroundings and even worse 'hosts', soon decided that air raids were preferable. 'My father was very short-sighted and worked in what was considered an essential business,' their daughter Ann recalled, most vividly.

We rented two rooms in a farmhouse which bore a strong resemblance to Cold Comfort Farm. There was only an outside toilet, some way down the garden. We had a bath in an enamel tub in front of the living-room fire, as the bath was used for curing the recently killed pig. The farmer only washed his hands and face during the week, doing a slightly more thorough job on Sundays, so he didn't need the bath himself! The farmer's wife used to scratch her back with the bread knife, then cut the bread with it. She also used to scuttle off to bed when she saw the electric meter running low, so that my parents had to put the money in it.

James was also evacuated privately, with his mother and older brother, but this turned out very satisfactorily. He was seven when they went to live in the Lake District at the beginning of the war. His father had served in the First World War, and his terrible experiences at the front had affected him greatly. 'He looked after the well-being of his family with great dedication, and was very apprehensive at the idea of any of us running into danger.' The boys and their mother ended up living in the home of a retired farmer. His brother went off to boarding school, and James was given some basic schooling by his mother.

We had no electricity or hot water, but my father equipped us with a rather newfangled Aladdin lamp, which was thought to be superior to the oil lamps and candles used in the rest of the house. There were no luxuries save for a portable radio, which was powered by an accumulator containing acid which had to be charged up once a week at the garage in the village over a mile away . . .

There were a great many characters, and I cannot recall any that I disliked. I was particularly fond of the cobbler . . . He worked in a tiny, cosy shed with superb views across the foothills to the lake, and he was completely content with his life – a tiny, rotund man who could have taken his place in *Snow White* without being out of place. His little stock of leather lay on the beams above his head, and he reached it by swinging rather dangerously on a rope . . .

At night I would play Chinese chequers and occasionally visit a whist drive in the village. Sometimes there would be concerts in the village hall, or a church, my mother playing the organ, which was powered by hand bellows pumped by my brother and me. The gentle folk of the village were good to us . . .

The war hardly touched these people, and I doubt if they worried about its outcome. It was a benign environment in which to spend a part of my childhood.

One positive outcome of extended families living together was that children got to know grandparents they normally saw perhaps only once or twice a year. One man remembered, 'I was taken to live with my grandparents in Norfolk, where I had a very happy time, surrounded by animals, the countryside and a family I had scarcely seen before . . . It was a tiny one-street village in the depths of the country. I thought it was absolutely wonderful.'

Six-year-old Robert had his horizons greatly expanded when he and his mother moved in on his grandparents near Glasgow. His grandmother, an extremely energetic lady, was 'very switched on politically and insisted that I join the family listening to Churchill's speeches. She ran the local WVS* with great determination, and threw herself into organizing a multitude of activities – the Red Cross, the Women's Guild . . . The billiard room filled up with "parcels for the boys", and the lawns were dug up and we all helped to plant vegetables.' Her large home, always full of people, was a lively place for a young boy with an active mind to grow up in wartime.

As October wore on, the continued lack of bombs, and eerily little war news, was playing on everyone's nerves. And many of the householders who now found themselves with the added responsibility of strange, unwanted children made no bones about disliking the interruption of their lives. Young and vulnerable, with little or no outside adult supervision, evacuees were frequently taken advantage of: being expected to do housework and domestic or farm chores on top of long walks to and from school was not unusual. Many also had to put up with teasing, snide remarks and generally supercilious attitudes from local people.

When Ella, a girl of eight, was evacuated with her sister and classmates to the large country house of a prominent politician, it was written up in the county press. Commenting on their arrival, the report noted that 'there were about twenty of them [evacuees] who

* Women's Voluntary Services, or Civil Defence.

had come from the slums.' To this day, Ella remembers the fury it caused her family. 'This was simply not true,' she said. 'I remember my mother was up in arms about the article, and soon telephoned the newspaper concerned and put them right.' It was especially galling as the children came from decent and caring homes and were already being treated unfairly in their elevated new surroundings, and having their skimpy butter rations withheld. (This was something many evacuees later reported of certain foster parents.)

The clash of backgrounds between evacuees and foster parents – of manners, speech, habits – was obvious, and went right up and down the social scale. In the haste to find billets, there was no time to match children with appropriate homes. Affluent home-owners, landed with evacuees who were quite unused to their new standard of living, were often forthright about what they considered were the children's shortcomings. While many were kind and understanding and did their best for the children, many were not.

Although only a small minority of the children came from seriously disadvantaged homes, those emerging from the most blighted city areas naturally lacked adequate clothing (particularly shoes), as well as any concept of middle-class living standards. Angus Calder, in his book *The People's War*, lists some of the comments received by the headquarters of a large number of Women's Institutes throughout England and Wales and referring to the 1939 influx of evacuees. They include:

- Condition of their boots and shoes – there was hardly a child with a whole pair and most of the children were walking on the ground – no soles, just uppers hanging together . . .
- The state of the children was such that the school had to be fumigated after the reception . . .
- Except for a small number, the children were filthy, and in this district we have never seen so many verminous children lacking any knowledge of clean and hygienic habits . . .

And so on.

These sad consequences of bad social conditions did occur among the more disadvantaged evacuees. But they were by no means widespread. At the time they were vastly exaggerated, both privately and by the press, and the bad feelings have lingered. A careful post-war survey estimated that between 5 to 10 per cent of evacuees may have been ignorant of decent toileting routine, and a further percentage – quite a high one – probably did lack adequate clothing. But for sections of the genteel British middle classes such numbers were enough, and tall stories of the horrors of taking an evacuee into a respectable home proliferated.

They soon spread quickly throughout the shires. The writer Mollie Panter-Downes unwittingly illustrates the kind of patronizing middle-class snobbery that was then considered respectable, even amusing. Her reports on the young mothers who had been evacuated with their babies, or very young children, to her area have a sarcastic edge that would be unthinkable today. She wrote in the *New Yorker* that 'the young mothers, cigarette smoke wafting above their pasty infants' heads, whiled away the time, bored out of their wits, longing for the vulgar amenities of Woolworths and such like which were alas unavailable in our beloved village.'

Given the gossip and the unpleasant rumours, it is hardly surprising that people felt increasingly disinclined to take in evacuees as the war progressed.

Miles, a senior schoolboy of seventeen, who had stayed on to take his Higher Certificate, experienced this resistance later in the war, in 1943. He was evacuated with his school, and because of the difficulty of keeping the more advanced classes together the boys moved foster homes frequently. One of his many billets was in a large country house. 'The billeting officer took me in his car, stood me with my case on the front doorstep, stuffed a compulsory billeting notice into my hand, instructed me to give it to whoever answered the door, ran to his car – and was away before the door was opened.'

It turned out that the home-owner was on active service, and the mansion was occupied solely by his haughty wife and their ten-year-old daughter, who still had several servants to look after them. So far she had managed to avoid having evacuees living there, and he was given a frosty welcome:

I was definitely not a popular visitor . . . Exams were near when the cook-housekeeper, who rarely spoke to me even though I lived with the servants, asked to see me. She looked at me sternly. 'Madam has asked me to make you a wonderful offer. Normally she wouldn't entertain anyone under five foot ten, and certainly anyone who wears glasses . . . but she understands you will be leaving school soon and she is willing, in the present circumstances, to employ you as an under-footman.'

I couldn't stop laughing. She was furious . . . I then explained that I would probably be called up fairly soon, and when I came out of the forces I was going to university. She had never heard of 'ordinary' people getting an education and entering the professions. I was obviously getting above myself . . . The other servants thought I was crazy to pass up such a wonderful opportunity.

Many years later, Miles looked back on this episode with amusement. He got his Higher Certificate, entered the services, and after the war went on to university and a successful professional career.

It is worth pointing out that, as we have seen, while many middle-class householders were dodging evacuees, and foster parents were wringing their hands over their charges' worn-out plimsolls and general shortcomings, many evacuees in rural areas were equally appalled at the backward living standards they found, and what seemed to them rough and uncouth ways.

Inevitably, most children's education suffered badly through evacuation. The school parties that had set out from London and Liverpool and Manchester and Leeds, and many other cities, early on those misty September mornings had a good many adventures before the war was over. (Schooling is dealt with fully in Chapter 6.) Some schools stayed together quite successfully and were found adequate, or even good, dormitories and classrooms wherever they were evacuated; a few, lucky enough to be housed in prime facilities, prospered; others amalgamated half-heartedly with local schools, with more or less success; some broke up altogether, resulting in the children learning little or nothing, sometimes for years at a time.

Although much of the schooling was chaotic, the education authorities put a gloss on the situation by noting that this was, after all, a very grim period of war. As long as the children stayed in country areas they were certainly safe, and it was vaguely assumed that a different, and broader, living experience at least partly made up for the lack of formal studies. And for some it may have done. For long or short periods throughout six grinding years of war, evacuated children were safe from the bombs falling on their home cities. They played and had fun and good things happened – and the schooling of some children did continue, and work well.

Will, aged seven, evacuated with his school to a Sussex village on 1 September 1939, was one such child. His was an evacuation that worked well on all sides and left good, enduring memories. Hearing the first siren of the war was Will's

very earliest memory – sitting by the pond, watching the swans, and wondering what the noise was . . . Moaning Millie, we called it . . . A local landowner had cleared out of her big house to make way for eleven evacuees, with two of the mothers to look after us . . . This wasn't bad, but it became even better for me when my parents came to live in the village too, my elderly father having poor nerves. A council-house tenant kindly found room with her family for us . . . The transition from manor house to crowded council house bothered me little, for I had never been so happy.

The village school, charmingly set on the green, nearly burst at the seams as the normal staff and pupils squeezed into half its premises to give us the other half. There was plenty of ocasion for friction – but I was not aware of it. In fact, to judge from other stories, both we and they were lucky. We tended to keep within our own groups, but I cannot remember any serious trouble.

During the autumn, while the evacuees were coming to terms with their new lives, the entire country was waiting. A journalist wrote that the mood was 'like a little boy who stuffs his fingers in his ears on the Fourth of July only to discover that the cannon cracker has not gone off after all'. There was a sense of unreality, almost of let-down. So much remained the same, yet so much had changed.

Under glorious blue skies, evacuees all over the countryside, whatever their problems and heartaches, learned to wander through lanes and make the acquaintance of farm animals and run freely through the fields. But a great many of these children were experiencing bouts of emotional disturbance: homesickness and bed-wetting.

Most evacuees, away from their families, from time to time suffered from acute homesickness – an engulfing emotional experience, closely mimicking depressive illness, which is sheer misery for the sufferer. Bill, nine, living in Dorset, spoke for thousands of other evacuees when he said that he and his schoolmates were 'often homesick, but it soon passed as long as we kept busy'. All agree that the nights, when there were no distractions and thoughts turned to the familiarity of home, were the hardest to bear. Some evacuees, unhappy almost beyond endurance, say that they often thought of fleeing home, and some did attempt it; many ran off for some hours, got lost or hungry, and turned back.

A thirteen-year-old boy called Tom, evacuated to a remote farm in Wales, later said ruefully that during a desperate attack of homesickness he had trekked off one afternoon with vague thoughts of getting a bus to the nearest station. But after about three hours, as it was getting dark, he returned to the farm. His foster parents, alarmed by his absence, seemed so relieved to see him that he broke down and told them where he had been. They amazed him by being concerned and sympathetic for the first time. Perhaps this act of sheer misery touched them, for their attitude towards him, which had been cold and uninterested, certainly changed. Tom stayed on until the end of the war. He ended up by getting thoroughly involved in life on the farm – milking the cows, doing odd jobs, and helping with the harvest. He and his foster parents became great friends. Sixty years later he wrote that he felt these five years were eventually among the happiest of his life.

Like most long-term evacuees, Tom overcame his homesickness. Some did not, and a few had to be sent back to their homes.

Visits by parents, although well intentioned, could also be emotionally difficult for evacuees. These frequently stiff and unnatural occasions often set off a new bout of homesickness just as the child was beginning to settle. Without telephone access, children took the opportunity to try to persuade parents to allow them to come home – which was sometimes successful. A boy of nine who was evacuated to a country area of the Midlands, unhappy with his foster parents, hid in the back of the bus his visiting father had just caught, and when he eventually surfaced his father hadn't the heart to send him back.

Making friends, joining in with a gang, and getting involved in school life eased the chronic ache for most children. Bill, the lad in Dorset who was frequently homesick, was befriended by a much older boy whom he hero-worshipped, and who took him under his wing:

The blacksmith opposite our cottage was young and unmarried, and I thought him a very strong man. When school was over I used to hang over the half stable door and watch every blow of the hammer as he constructed blank horseshoes from raw strips of steel . . . A warm brotherly relationship developed, and some Saturdays he used to take me out into the country to farms to shoe farmers' workhorses or to fix farm machinery.

As Bill got involved with his friends in village life, his homesickness vanished. As he looked back in later life he said, 'I really enjoyed those three years. I wouldn't have missed the experience for anything.'

Undoubtedly linked to the grief of homesickness was the occasional bed-wetting which many evacuees, whatever their circumstances, suffered from at some time. Given the levels of stress, disruption and unhappiness that all experienced to some degree, this wasn't in the least surprising. A sensible WVS leaflet, *Information for Householders Taking Evacuees*, offered good advice which was enlightened for the time: 'Some children may try your patience by wetting their beds, but do not scold or punish; as this will only make matters worse.'

A boy evacuated with his school, all of the children about nine or ten, said that 'We obviously had some disturbance. Many of us had periods of bed-wetting among other symptoms of unsettlement.' A girl made to share a bed with her much disliked cousin remembered that often in the mornings the bed was so wet 'I didn't know which of us had done it.' But most children suffered only brief spells, which disappeared with sympathetic handling.

It was said later that the authorities had been warned of these possible disturbances by the Royal Navy, where it had long been accepted that young recruits were apt to suffer bouts of both intense homesickness and bed-wetting. So it was unfortunate that the medical authorities had not given warnings, or guidelines, of any kind to the foster parents who had to deal with these difficulties. In later evacuations, foster parents were at least warned, and mackintosh sheets were handed out as a precaution.

In a few of the most desperate cases of bed-wetting, when the child had genuine psychological problems, he or she had to be sent home. But most evacuees appear to have managed the ups and downs of their new lives, bed-wetting and all, despite difficult patches – keeping up a cheerful front, and carrying on with a good deal of dignity. Looking back from a much later perspective, we would certainly describe them as brave.

Mortifying and unpleasant as bed-wetting must have been for the emotionally stressed evacuees, it is hard not to sympathize, too, with their country foster mothers. These women were already facing extra housework and cooking as well as stringent wartime conditions. With an enuretic evacuee in the house, no washing machines, and only a hand-turned mangle as an aid, they now had to slave away at yet more hand washing. This cannot have improved the often fractious relations between evacuee and foster parent. But the fact was that in some of the loveliest parts of the land, in that brilliantly sunny autumn of 1939, lines and lines of newly washed sheets billowed gently in the breeze.

With no bombs falling, and the majority of parents and children deeply unhappy about their separation, the move back to the cities began. The young mothers with babies, bored and anxious, were the first to leave, many taking off with their babies back to London or Bradford or Birmingham after only a few days – bombs or no bombs. Shortly after, dithering mothers began agitating to get their children back home. 'There was a phrase my mum used,' a twelve-year-old girl who had been evacuated to Wales said. ' "We're in this together," she used to say over and over. "We stick together, we stay together . . ." ' This was the attitude of many parents, and by December the headlong rush back to the cities was on.

Although this was a big relief to many evacuees and their parents, it was a big headache for the educational authorities. The government promptly took steps to prevent as many children as possible from returning. The meagre allowance given to householders for lodging evacuees was raised slightly; money was suddenly found for essential clothing needs, particularly shoes, in extreme cases; and parents were encouraged to visit evacuated children and were allocated money for train fares. But none of this helped much. Despite the high hopes for the scheme before war was declared, and the relatively successful way in which it was carried out, by the end of 1939 it had to be admitted that evacuation was not working well. The overriding pull of family life, combined with the lack of air attacks, meant that by the end of the year nearly half of the children who had been evacuated at the beginning of September were back in their homes in the cities. They left behind a minority of evacuees, reasonably well settled, many of whom stayed on with their foster parents for several years or, in some cases, the duration.

During the following five years, there were two more major evacuations, although throughout the war children were constantly being evacuated, brought home, and possibly evacuated once or twice more, both privately and through government-sponsored schemes. Richard Titmuss summed up the evacuation pattern succinctly: 'The great uprootings of human beings from their homes took place in three big waves of diminishing strength, each connected by a slender, continuing trickle.'

Over the spring and early summer of 1940, children were moved to safer districts from certain towns on the south coast, which were considered at risk from a German invasion. But the second major evacuation, which was considerably smaller than that of 1939, took place over a period of weeks and months after the bombing had started with the dramatic Blitz on London in September 1940. The fierceness and destruction of night after night of terrifying air raids, making sleep impossible, finally jolted many parents into the necessity of getting their children away. During that September, 25,000 unaccompanied children, in small, organized groups, were sent out of the Greater London area into the safety of the countryside. Some of these children had been evacuated the previous year. Having returned home – 'just in time for the Blitz', as many described it – they were now sent away again. But these evacuations were carried out on a much smaller scale than in 1939, with whatever transport could be mustered.

From October 1940, when heavy raids started on other large cities – including Coventry, Birmingham, Hull, Liverpool, Plymouth,

Southampton, Bristol and Cardiff – similar evacuations of children took place all over the country. Through trial and error, the schemes were now operating more smoothly, with children receiving proper medical check-ups and more strict supervision. And in the spring of 1941 the blitz raids on Glasgow and Clydeside precipitated Scotland's second, and last, large-scale evacuation.

In June 1944 the first V1 flying bomb fell on Greater London, and the ensuing panic caused many parents to send their children away. Over the following two months almost a million children, and some mothers, were evacuated with government help from London and the south-east. A further trickle took place after the first German V2 rocket landed on London on 8 September, but by then there was a growing feeling that the war was in its last phase, and thereafter most evacuation was carried out privately.

Despite homesickness, social differences and downright unhappiness, we have seen that plenty of positive, sometimes amusing, memories also emerged from the evacuations. Here are two more of them.

Imagine a Jewish woman living in the East End, not long arrived from Lithuania, not familiar with British ways, and not speaking much English. Her nine-year-old son was evacuated to the country with his school, and as he was a bright, good-looking lad his foster family grew fond of him. Told that he was settling well and taking part in village life by using his fine singing voice, his mother determined to go and see for herself. So she made the long, slow train journey to the West Country to visit his foster parents. We can only imagine her shock to find herself in the local church on Easter Sunday morning; and when the congregation rose and the procession entered, leading it – in the floor-length robes of a choirboy, cross held high – was her son.

Older boys of thirteen and fourteen, evacuated with their school to a Welsh mining community, found kindness – and a bracing new experience that they never forgot:

My friend and I were taken to live with a tall, gaunt coal-miner and his buxom wife . . . and living in a coal-mining town has left indelible memories . . . The constant thumping of a pump operating at the valley coal pit. An overhead rail system discharging slate on to an enormous slagheap.

The sounds of miners' boots and the miners clattering along the pavements as the shifts changed. Our foster father arriving home, and his wife filling the bath and then scrubbing the coal dust from his back.

Local children called us 'the vaccies'. Our history master – the image of Adolf Hitler, complete with moustache – was branded a German spy.

The removal of children from home and family at a young, malleable age, even for short periods, was bound to be a raw emotional experience. As in all human dealings, personal make-up played the biggest part. The success or failure of the evacuations of those wartime children depended on two crucial factors: luck, or otherwise, in the foster parents they were assigned and the innate personality of the child and his or her ability to make the best of things. Many evacuations were successful, greatly broadening a child's experience and setting up ties for life; the majority of children either rubbed along – or changed billets – or went home very early.

Evacuation was for a long time thought to have failed. But it did not. As official records show, there is no doubt that it did save children's lives. And, importantly, evacuation gave parents a safety net throughout the war. They knew that if things got too rough, or nerves too frayed, they could get the children out.

In general, the authorities had greatly underestimated the strength of family life – and overestimated, however wisely, the likely toll of enemy bombing. The seemingly limitless capacity of large cities to carry on, even with sustained raids, was also not anticipated. And all those involved in the evacuation scheme – especially the evacuees themselves – played their part in bringing about the changed, and much more equal and more inclusive, society that staggered into being at the end of the long grind of war.

Richard Titmuss concluded wisely, 'Without affection, life has little meaning for most people and none at all for children.' That being said, it makes sense to give a last, short memoir of a child whose warm and valuable evacuation had affection – on both sides – at its core. This was written, many years later, by a man who was evacuated from east London in September 1939, aged eight. His father had recently died, and he, his mother and his younger brother had few means and lived meagrely. After an unsatisfactory first billet, he was taken in by a couple who had no children, and stayed with them for several years. He wrote:

My foster father had a great knowledge of natural history, and through him I developed my lifelong interest in that subject. He was a natural and patient teacher who taught me to shoot, to catch rabbits with net and snare, to bud a rose, to graft an apple tree, and a thousand and one things that I retain to this day. He was a father to me.

I shall never forget their joy when I paid a surprise visit, years later, in the uniform of subaltern. The pride and affection on my foster mother's face is with me still.

The last contact was in 1977, when I received from their niece a small packet containing a letter and a pruning knife. She explained that she was disposing of his modest estate and she had come across the knife that he cherished because I had given it to him as a present for Christmas 1942. I have it now, in front of me, on my desk, as a letter-opener. It is a constant reminder of my happy years as an evacuee . . . and of the couple who opened up the horizon and stimulated the ambitions of a docklands boy.

4

UNDER ATTACK!
JULY 1940 TO MAY 1941

While their mother watches grimly, two eager children, the boy with his gas mask slung across his body, clamber into the family's Anderson shelter ready for a big adventure

Not until over three years had passed was it possible to say that the enemy had killed more soldiers than women and children.
R. Titmuss, *Problems of Social Policy* (1950)

We had a terrible, miserable time. We saw sights that no child should see.
A thirteen-year-old girl living in a heavily bombed working-class area of a large city

We lived every day as another time won.
A woman who was eight when the war began, looking back on her childhood near London

Spring 1940. Over six months into the war, life for most people in Great Britain was still only gradually shifting into the austerity of wartime. With Easter falling at the end of March, parents took the opportunity to give children a seaside break, and almost as many people poured into resorts on the coast as in peacetime.

It was never compulsory to carry gas masks and by now, lulled by the surface normality of everyday life, few people bothered, although schools attempted to maintain the rule that masks should be to hand at all times.

Popular music calmed the nerves and stiffened resolve; adults doted on the patriotic warhorse 'There'll Always be an England', and fervently hoped its message proved correct. The irreverent, spunky British humour, a big morale-booster, had kids up and down the land bawling (to the tune of the dwarfs' marching song in Walt Disney's *Snow White*):

Whistle while you work!
Hitler is a twerp.
Goering's barmy,
So's his army.
Whistle while you work!

The home-front spirit, which would soon be severely tested, had already started to give rise to odd alliances: people made contact with out-of-touch relatives and parked themselves on them; children from the back streets of Liverpool tried to make some sense of life in a Welsh mining village.

In the suburbs of a small Surrey town, Alan and his friends, all around sixteen and soon to start their sixth-form year at school, were uncomfortably aware that they were not far off the call-up age, which had been lowered to eighteen on the outbreak of war. As they watched the events of that ominous period they were excited, apprehensive – and increasingly patriotic. Alan remembered, 'We saw that now the war effort was put before everything else; it was our absolute priority. It completely changed our thinking about our immediate futures. There was no distinction between high and low, rich and poor, old and young, or those who were or weren't educated – all were totally committed to beating the Germans, and in particular the Nazis.'

Families who had ganged up for the duration settled in and made the best of rubbing along together, and bonds between friends and neighbours strengthened: people depended on each other now, and they knew it. Moira, who was twelve and lived on a small housing estate in Hull, well remembered this uneasy period of bonding. 'My grandmother lived with us . . . and her sister, who lived alone not far away, came to our house every night because she was very afraid . . . There were only fourteen houses on our road, and we all helped each other. It went on like that all through the bad times.'

During the previous bitter winter Britain's Atlantic convoys suffered terrible losses from Hitler's U-boats; petrol rationing had started three weeks after war was declared, and bacon, butter and sugar rationing began over the following months. Jenny, then a wise little girl of seven, quickly spotted that rationing became an instant test of character. 'With our tiny bit of butter every week, did you scrape or have an orgy? I was always an orgy person.'

Most evacuees had returned to their homes in the cities, and even after a comparatively short evacuation their reactions were surprisingly complex. While most children felt nothing but relief at being back, some missed their new friends and the open country surroundings which promised so much scope for adventure; others had been severely emotionally disturbed by the stress of leaving their families in the first place – a reaction that could have long-lasting effects.

A thoughtful girl of twelve called Mary, who was evacuated with her younger brother to the south coast, had experienced decent but harsh foster parents. She came to believe that 'after being evacuated even for a short time, those of us with loving families tended to appreciate them more when we got home'. However, Joe, a ten-year-old boy from London, who had had a fine time mucking about with the gang in a pretty Devon village, would always think of his return to London as disappointingly dreary. 'I remember our small, grimy back garden instead of my foster parents' big, green one . . . Nobody kept chickens . . . the people seemed sullen and watchful . . . and I had spotted the grotesque steel structure of the Morrison shelter* in the living room.'

Early in May 1940 Neville Chamberlain's weakened government fell, and to most people's relief – certainly his – Winston Churchill became Prime Minister of a wartime coalition government. It is a supreme paradox that Churchill – an aristocrat, a writer, a soldier, of profoundly romantic temperament, and someone who, according to his wife, had never been in a bus and only once on the London underground – found, retained and brilliantly exploited a unique ability to inspire the ordinary people of his country.

His great unifying power was felt right across the generations. A boy of twelve, standing in a labour exchange with his father, listened with the rest as Churchill's voice came thundering out of a

---

* Morrison shelters – indoor shelters with heavy wire-mesh sides and a steel plate on top – were widely distributed in November 1941. They were named after Herbert Morrison, the Minister of Home Security, and, like the outdoor Anderson shelters, proved most effective.

loudspeaker. This was one of the his most stirring broadcasts, and the effect was immediate. First one, then another, then a small group of men stepped out of queues and went straight to the line that had formed to enlist. Younger children, who could not have grasped the significance of what they were hearing, still recall listening – rapt – to the gravelly torrent emanating from the family radio. And a talkative five-year-old always remembered her uncle, who had fought on the Somme, sternly reprimanding her when she started to chatter in mid-speech.

On the 13 May the new premier, confident of fulfilling his personal destiny, addressed the House of Commons as Prime Minister for the first time. It was a period of great uncertainty for the country, and his electrifying performance that day would become part of British history. 'I have nothing to offer but blood, toil, tears and sweat,' he said. His goal was 'Victory at all costs, victory in spite of all terror, victory however long and hard the road may be.' 'Come, then,' he urged, 'let us go forward together with our united strength.' The resigning Neville Chamberlain received the standing ovation when he spoke in Parliament that day, but it was Churchill who touched the nation's soul.

However, Churchill's brave words soon acquired a bitterly ironic ring. By the end of May Belgium had fallen and the British Expeditionary Force in France, surrounded and isolated by the German army, had retreated to the coast at Dunkirk. Half a million British, French and Belgian troops – exhausted, chaotic, many wounded – massed on the beaches, forming easy targets for strafing German planes. With a combination of courage, skill, good luck and good weather, the Royal Navy, backed up by an assortment of fishing boats, private yachts and leaky old pleasure boats like the *Bournemouth Belle* (the 'shilling sickies', as J. B. Priestley called them), managed to evacuate some two-thirds of the men. The remainder were captured or killed. Given the appalling predicament of these troops, the desperate operation to save as many as possible was described as a 'miracle'.

Joan, twelve, who lived on the Kent coast and whose father was in the fishing trade, said that he took his boat out and went across to France and back three times, rescuing many Allied soldiers.

He and his mates were exhausted, and Mum was in a terrible state, beside herself with worry . . . My older brother was angry because she wouldn't let him go off in the small ships to help with the evacuation as well . . . There were hundreds of soldiers – Belgian, French and our men – and they were sitting on the roads and the pavements all through the town, because there was no transport to take them inland. All the women in the street were making tea and sandwiches for them.

Schoolboys at their desks in Sheerness watched the drama unfold. John, who was supposed to be studying for his School Certificate with the rest of the form, never forgot the sight. 'We were in our classrooms overlooking the Thames Estuary, where we could see the whole assortment of small ships going about their rescue duties. It was an amazing panorama.' Whatever they were officially learning, those boys were also watching history being made. Right along the coast, as the little ships landed, the beaches became 'scattered with weary, sand-covered soldiers – those who had made it back from Dunkirk'.

The country only gradually learned what was happening 20-odd miles across the Channel as snippets of grim news dribbled out in bulletins and the shattered survivors struggled back. Dunkirk would be etched for ever in the mind of a boy called Peter, aged eight, who was living just back from the coast in a village on the old Roman road between Dover and London. 'It was a beautiful spring day . . . The road by our house was completely blocked with vehicles unloading soldiers covered in dried mud and looking physically exhausted. I don't remember one that wasn't wearing some kind of bandage. The neighbours came out and invited them in for food – and a cup of tea – and heard their horrifying stories of survival.'

A few days later, Daphne (twelve) was sitting in her garden in Derbyshire with her mother, listening to her Uncle Tom – 'very handsome in his uniform' – telling them about his escape from Dunkirk. 'I remember feeling very important, and my mother telling me that what Uncle Tom was saying was part of history and I must pay attention . . . I do remember his telling us of his dash to the coast in some army vehicle, that there was so much broken glass in the village streets from the bombardment and the shelling that the fleeing British army drove over it for miles.'

Although total catastrophe at Dunkirk had been avoided, 'Wars are not won by evacuations,' Churchill thundered. With crack German troops digging in across the Channel the country was severely unnerved, and a German invasion was now considered a realistic possibility.

Seven-year-old Yvette, trapped with her brothers and sister and their English mother in their holiday home on the coast of Brittany near Saint-Nazaire, could never forget the ordeal of keeping their heads down as the German soldiers, of whom the children were terrified, moved in all around them.

We all spoke perfect French and passed as locals, although Mother's English (Yorkshire) background was once questioned by the German authorities, which was very frightening. It was too dangerous to speak English even among ourselves. Fortunately, with the four of us children, our house was too small to have a German soldier billeted, but all the soldiers seemed well disciplined and behaved very correctly.

They were convinced at that time that they would very soon be in England, and talked about it openly. One German officer who was billeted in a house near by boasted to my mother that as sure as he was sitting there, talking to her, he would be in London and having a drink at the Ritz by September.

Throughout southern England, fortifications along the beaches were strengthened, and conspiratorial plans – frequently somewhat eccentric – were made for a resistance movement. It was said that in the midst of making his powerful and patriotic speech anticipating a German invasion – 'We shall not fail or flag . . . we shall defend our island whatever the cost may be . . . we shall fight on the beaches, we shall fight on the landing grounds, we shall fight in the fields and in the streets, we shall fight in the hills . . .' – Churchill paused for refreshment and murmured, 'and beat the —s about the head with bottles: that's all we've got.'

Two resourceful young brothers of twelve and fourteen, living on a farm in the south-east and believing themselves in the front line should the Germans invade, decided to make their own preparations – closely modelled on their father's Home Guard activities:

Word had it that the invasion was expected hourly. The thought of sur-render never occurred to ordinary people . . . So my brother and I made a plan. We quickly learned a bit of basic German. When we came upon an invading German – probably a parachutist, we thought – we were to threaten him with our pitchforks: '*Hände hoch!*' He would of course be very frightened to see us, and promptly raise his hands and cry on cue, '*Kamerad, Kamerad . . .*'

We would then give him a cigarette and frogmarch him back to the farmhouse for a cup of tea. Meanwhile one of us would raise the alert, and eventually the village policeman would pedal up on his bike to take him away.

Perhaps fortunately for the boys, a handy German parachutist failed to appear.

Around this time the Luftwaffe started attacking convoys passing through the Strait of Dover; British fighters were scrambled to engage with the enemy so frequently that this neck of Kent coast was given the nickname 'Hellfire Corner'. This is where, and when, the Battle of Britain – generally agreed to be the pivotal event of the war – began. The date is officially put at 10 July 1940.

It was close to Hellfire Corner that a BBC correspondent, in mid-broadcast, spotted a German raider in air battle with a defending RAF fighter; enthralled by what he was watching, his exuberant commen-tary was likened to reporting a 'dogfight'. This vital, moment-by-moment radio technique caught on, and was used a good deal on different fronts throughout the war. It is fondly remembered by a generation of schoolboys, mainly in the Home Counties, who spent weeks that summer with their necks craned, picking out the feathery vapour trails arching and swooping high in the calm blue skies.

Kit, a mechanically minded youngster who later became a racing driver, was one of these boys, and has never for a moment forgotten the excitement of it all as seen through the eyes of an eager six-year-old. 'The Battle of Britain could have been laid on expressly for my gratification. Afternoons were spent studying aerial tactics and "spot-ting" the twenty or so different aircraft that filled our skies . . . My friends and I knew every one of them.'

Jonathan, aged eight, who lived in north London during the time of the Battle of Britain recalled, 'We all collected shrapnel after raids, and it was a point of honour to have a substantial collection . . . And I remember lying on my back and watching a fierce dogfight in which aircraft were destroyed and everyone cheered.' But Jonathan's mother, who came of a liberal, pacifist background, was also watching grimly, and she remonstrated firmly with her son. 'In the First World War she had seen a German airship destroyed. Everyone cheered then too. But her mother had said, "The poor men, they're burning." . . . She also hated military music, which encouraged men into death, she said. But nevertheless she too supported the war as being a dire necessity. Yet she wanted to indicate to me strongly that it was no sport.'

Indeed it was not – for either side. Clare, who was eight, had a dashing young uncle called Jamie, only ten years older, who was a newly trained fighter pilot. By the summer of 1940 Jamie was confident enough to show off his new flying skills to the family by casually 'buzzing' his parents' house and scaring them out of their wits. Because of the shortage of trained pilots, despite his lack of experience Jamie was frequently scrambled for Battle of Britain skirmishes. One morning Clare was in the garden with her mother and grandmother when a telegram boy knocked on the front door. 'I knew at once what it was,' Clare said sixty-odd years later. 'I wasn't told anything, but still I knew. My mother and Grannie went into the house at once and talked for a long time . . . but I could tell from the air of acute tension what had happened.' Jamie's plane had been shot down in action with the enemy. He did not survive. He would have been nineteen two days later.

Like most children at that time, Pam, a teenager, was fascinated by planes. Her parents were abroad during the early part of war, so she spent the holidays at her boarding school 'with eight or nine other girls in the same boat'. During the summer their housemistress took them out into the country for a picnic at the top of a hill somewhere in Surrey:

At this time I was mad keen on aircraft recognition (Dorniers, Heinkels etc.), and just as we were enjoying our meal two planes flew over. I announced that these were German planes, but was firmly told not to be silly and frighten the younger children. Two minutes later the siren went and we scrambled down the hill to the village, where we were ushered into a shelter. 'One of my pupils identified those planes, so we were just leaving to take cover,' the housemistress told the air-raid warden grandly. After that, whatever I said was gospel.

Charlie, then a boy of eight, has never forgotten those extraordinary months when he and his friends would scamper all over the countryside looking for trophies after deadly dogfights:

I used to stand in my father's back garden (in Sussex) during that long hot summer holding my grandmother's hand. My grandmother would wave to the Spits and Hurricanes and shout 'Good luck, boys', and we would watch as they shot at each other at low level. After the all-clear siren we would rush across the fields and pick up souvenirs – enemy cartridge cases, and occasionally much more dangerous debris.

Close by, a brother and sister of ten and twelve, evacuated from their home right on the coast, were living with relatives near Ashford in Kent. They too were captivated by the almost daily theatre of air warfare:

We watched endless dogfights take place over our heads . . . We children would stand outside and watch them, enthralled, until we were driven in by an irate Home Guard man in his tin helmet . . . We were shot at by a low-flying German aircraft on two occasions – once when we were biking along an open road and had to take refuge in a ditch. The German pilot waved at us as he took off, and I remember being intensely amazed.

An eleven-year-old boy called Douglas, about to go to boarding prep school for the first time, was staying with his widowed mother in Epsom. They had also been evacuated from the coast. 'We arrived just in time for the Battle of Britain. I recall rushing in from the garden to tell my mother that I could hear a band and kettledrums. She told me sharply to stay in: what I had heard was an aerial dogfight overhead in the hot July sky. Exciting to me, alarming for adults, who knew the implications.'

Liz was sent away to boarding school in the Home Counties when her father went to work at the War Office and her mother took up war work. She watched these desperate air battles with her heart in her mouth but 'with great pride, even then, at the bravery of our pilots – so few of them, and endless raiders…I remember it so clearly.' Doreen, a fourteen-year-old girl living on the outskirts of London, said that when the air battles became fierce her family retreated to their Anderson shelter. But her daring older brothers, exhilarated by the danger, refused to miss the action. 'During the Battle of Britain, my brothers used to frighten the life out of my mother by getting out of the shelter entrance to watch the dogfights overhead or picking up shrapnel from our anti-aircraft guns. They couldn't wait to be old enough to join the forces.'

Some of the children who watched these airborne duels with so much eagerness and excitement, not truly grasping the dangerous reality of the battle, were inevitably exposed to tragic sights. Just before the end of the summer term, late in July, an eight-year-old called Ned was in class in his village school not far from Dover:

About fifteen minutes before going-home time, a Merlin engine was heard circling overhead. Suddenly – silence. Then the big bang. We came running out of school and saw black oily smoke emanating from a hole in the ground a couple of fields away. On arriving breathless at the edge of the burning crater, Mr Brigham, the village policeman, came close by and laid down a piece of charred meat which was mangled up with some pieces of blue cloth with one sad brass button glinting in the sun. He turned to me and said, 'Go home, sonny.'

Deeply affected by what he had seen, Ned started having terrible nightmares and was kept away from school for several days. He never forgot the smallest detail of the downed RAF plane and its tragic young pilot, exactly as he had come upon them, lying smashed to smithereens in that quiet summer field.

The probing German raids were stinging national pride, but, galvanized by Churchill's dynamic leadership, the country was pulling together fast after the disaster of Dunkirk. Unless they had a very young child at home, more and more women, in all classes, were getting involved in war work, and soon experienced the confidence gained by doing valuable work, and being paid for it. Women who had never worked before in their lives now queued up to do their bit, and for many wives and mothers a second wage was a welcome boost to tight family budgets. Cynthia, an only child who lived in Kent and who was soon sent off to boarding school with her cousin in a safer area, remembered, amused, that 'Mother, who had never so much as lifted a finger before the war, wobbled off on an unaccustomed bike to do some factory work occasionally.'

In Stepney, east London, a cheerful but fatherless Jewish boy remembered this summer for getting himself 'bar-mitzvahed between Dunkirk and the Blitz', and for his mother, living on her 'widow's mite' of a pension, still managing to keep a good and welcoming home for her large family – two children still at school, and two about to enter the forces.

As summer wore on, there were more, and heavier, daylight raids, which encroached further and further on strategic targets. Ken, aged twelve, living in the inner London suburbs, unwittingly found himself with a bird's-eye view of a daring enemy raid – without knowing what he was watching:

One evening, during the summer the Battle of Britain was starting up, I was in my bedroom when I heard the whine of planes. I ran to the window to get a better view of the planes I could see swooping and diving in the sky in the direction of Croydon. I was completely unaware that they were actually attacking Croydon Aerodrome, only a few miles away. Shortly after, the air-raid siren went. Too late! Later we heard on the wireless that German fighter planes had got through our radar defences without being detected and had shot up almost all of our planes that had been on the tarmac at the time.

During August, Merseyside was badly knocked about, and Liverpool's city centre suffered extensive fire damage on the night of the 31st. Fighter Command, greatly helped by the warnings given by radar, fought a brave defensive battle. Although heavily outnumbered, the RAF had the advantage of faster, lighter planes – and superbly trained young pilots. On 8 August, 'the bloodiest day so far',

31 German planes were shot down and the RAF claimed to have incapacitated 60 more. Hitler, infuriated and outraged by these losses, ordered the total destruction of Fighter Command.

On 28 August the flying ace Richard Hillary, who would come to symbolize all those dashing young airmen, and who later in the war would write the classic memoir *The Last Enemy*, flew south with his colleagues. He had been training in Edinburgh with twenty-four other young pilots, all of whom now joined the desperate fight for Britain. 'Of those twenty-four, eight were to fly back,' he wrote sombrely, sometime after. The 'long-haired boys', as he called them, had good technical skills, personal courage and, on the surface at least, a raffish, devil-may-care style. Mostly university students, several were still in their teens, little more than boys. And when Churchill delivered a rather grandiloquent appreciation of their prowess in the House – 'Never in the field of human conflict was so much owed by so many to so few' – their typically schoolboy and self-deprecating response was 'The PM must be referring to our mess bills.'

Great moments in history frequently hang on some minor human frailty, and so it was in the summer of 1940. Accidentally losing their way on the dark and moonless night of 24 August, German pilots, undoubtedly terrified, probably young and inexperienced, mistakenly attacked central London – thus disobeying Hitler's specific orders. The bombs were the first to fall on the city since the Zeppelin raids of 1918, which had caused so much civilian panic, and Bomber Command was promptly dispatched to bomb Berlin in return.

Although this attack was feeble and largely unsuccessful, Hitler was furious. He had sworn that he would never allow Berlin to be bombed, and he decided on all-out retaliation with a massive and sustained attack on London. It can be said that the actual timing of the Blitz may well have been due to a combination of disorientated German pilots and Hitler's ungovernable rage. It was a combination that would change the UK for ever.

By all accounts, the afternoon of Saturday 7 September was exceptionally fine – clear and sunlit, and virtually cloudless. Despite the restrictions of wartime, family life continued: children played outside, and lawns were mown and tea was drunk in neat suburban gardens. It was around five in the afternoon when German bombers, so long expected, finally droned up the Thames towards London. These harbingers of destruction came out of the blue: as specks of shining silver approaching through pale azure skies.

Harry, aged twelve, spent that sunny afternoon kicking a ball with his friends in Streatham Vale in south London. About teatime, they heard a low, continuous sound that caused them to pause and look up. It soon became 'the distinctive drone which would become familiar to Londoners . . . The sky filled with German bombers, flying at high altitude in tight formation. Then came the Spitfires and Hurricanes, like mosquitoes weaving in and out of the tidy formations . . . Shell cases began to fall all around us. Of course we ran to collect these irresistible items, disregarding the calls from many houses offering us shelter.' By nightfall, Harry said, the docks and much of Stepney were ablaze. 'The brightness at night of the sheeting fires destroying the docks also remains with me.'

He stayed on in London with his family throughout the war, frequently stuck for hours in a cramped shelter, 'all eight of us, reasonably comfortably, with our dog – an amiable terrier, but who unfortunately suffered with wind'. And Harry was a lucky wartime Londoner: 'There were many tons of bombs dropped on Streatham, but neither my school nor my home and family ever suffered a direct hit.'

Guided by the destructive work of incendiary bombs, wave on wave of German bombers kept on coming until the following dawn. A seventeen-year-old girl called Joan, who had recently started her first office job, had gone with her friend that night to a performance at Sadler's Wells Theatre.

We could only afford 6d. (2½ p) to sit in the gallery. Halfway through the performance the manager came on stage and stopped the show. He announced that there was very heavy bombing, and people were offered their money back if they wanted to leave . . . People in the 'gods' could come down to the stalls. We jumped at the chance, and saw the show through to the end. When we emerged, all transport had stopped so we had to walk home from the Angel to Stoke Newington. On the way we watched the sky over the dock area all lit up . . . It was bright as daylight all over. We kept dodging into doorways for shelter. I shall never forget.

It is said that at midnight the light in Piccadilly was bright enough to read by. A young evacuee, an eight-year-old boy living in Pulborough in Sussex, some 30 miles from the East End, saw the red glow in the sky over London and wondered fearfully about the safety of the rest of his family, back in Camberwell.

For Londoners (especially the East Enders, who bore the initial brunt of the Blitz) – and later for Coventry, Birmingham, Manchester, Liverpool, Hull, Plymouth, Southampton and many other cities and their inhabitants – this was an experience of hell. On that first night of the London Blitz 437 civilians were killed; thousands were injured and left homeless, and an incalculable number were shattered by nervous prostration. Bombs came down 'with a tearing sound as well as a whistle: they did not fall, they rushed at enormous velocity, as though dragged down towards the earth.' The incendiaries danced and rattled as they hit the streets, and if they weren't extinguished immediately they caused leaping fires and much structural damage.

Batteries of anti-aircraft – or 'ack-ack' – guns throughout the city got going with an almighty racket in some sort of organized response. Seven-year-old Andrew, in north London, was mesmerized: 'Searchlights lit up the sky. The ack-ack was usually rapid-fire guns, with the occasional "crump" of a true anti-aircraft gun – a shell containing and producing "flak", into which curtain of steel it was hoped the raiding enemy aircraft would fly.'

Although they were not very effective, and the shrapnel falling back on the streets was a positive danger, ack-ack batteries were soon trusted like old friends, and the very fact that they were hitting back at the enemy somehow raised people's spirits. The firemen, wardens, policemen, nurses and rescue workers, all civilians, were at the pit face on the home front – as were the city householders and their children, frequently evacuees who had with unfortunate timing only recently returned home.

Many of these children were to be evacuated again, as the savage bombing of the Blitz set off a second, lesser, evacuation. It soon became apparent that the authorities had vastly overestimated the likely fatalities in bombing raids – and badly underestimated the amount of structural damage and the consequent homelessness of hundreds of families. But from that first night of the Blitz the Second World War became – as anticipated, and as the historian Angus Calder would rightly define it – 'The People's War'.

A substantial percentage of the 'people' on the new home front was, of course, children and babies. The mournful wailing of the air-raid alert, slowly rising and then falling back, lasted for two minutes. (The all-clear, also two minutes in duration, was a single note.) A woman who was no more than three at the time of the Blitz, living in Greater London, has never forgotten the sound of the siren and the fear that it precipitated. That threatening noise, whenever – wherever – she hears it, 'still makes my hair stand on end', she says. Another woman, also a very young child during the Blitz, remembered being carried down steps into the underground to shelter; she too was profoundly disturbed by the siren – for years after, its sinister notes haunted her with terrifying nightmares.

This profound aversion is echoed by most people who lived through the war, and who continued to associate any siren with imminent danger for the rest of their lives. But there were exceptions. Anna, aged eight at the time of the Blitz and living in the country just to the east of London, remembered her local siren with a quirky humour: 'The air-raid siren for our village was called Wheezy Annie. Everyone else's sirens swooped up and down in waves. Ours had lost the top part of the range and so wheezed defiantly. My younger brother and I thought this was quite funny, as our nanny panted too and it sounded just like her.'

Once the raids on London had started, they continued mercilessly. The sirens started up and clashed and surged as one after the other the different sections of the city warned their inhabitants of impending danger, destruction and possible death. Nerves tensed as the bombers throbbed into hearing, menacing, and growing ever louder. The writer Graham Greene felt that during every raid each bomber was seeking him out personally: 'Where are you? Where are you?' they all seemed to be saying. And once the bombs fell all hell broke loose and the noise rose to a cacophony: burglar alarms ringing, glass shattering, walls and buildings collapsing, gas pipes exploding, water gushing, terrified dogs – and the Heavy Rescue Services, in the thick of it, attempting to get the hoses and vehicles through. The stores along Oxford Street were badly knocked about and mostly window-less; John Lewis got a direct hit. 'More Open For Business Than Usual' was a notice in what had been shop windows that never failed to raise wry smiles.

Londoners of all ages gradually found their individual ways of dealing with their fears, and the profound disruption of their every-day lives. Constant sleep deprivation intensified already over-stretched nerves. An imaginative eight-year-old said that it was the wailing menace of air-raid sirens that terrified her most: 'the panic I felt as my throat/heart/whatever fell to somewhere below my stomach. Crammed into our horrid shelter, we cheered when our local ack-ack battery got going.'

The raids continued for seventy-six consecutive nights, and most parts of Greater London were badly hit. Chelsea, the West End, and the City and Westminster were bombed remorselessly at different times in the war, and historic landmarks like the Bank of England, the Tower and Westminster Abbey were all scarred or suffered serious damage. That St Paul's Cathedral escaped more or less unscathed was largely due to the bravery of firewatchers who managed to neutralize a major incendiary bomb which had landed on the roof before it ignited. In time, the magnificent, towering dome became such a symbol of national survival that the rescue ser-vices were under orders to save it at all costs, even at the expense of lesser edifices near by.

But it was the poorer areas of the East End that suffered the most widespread damage and homelessness. In these ethnically mixed, mostly deprived, districts the huddled rows of housing, small shops and businesses and gasworks were vulnerable targets and easily destroyed – through a combination of shoddy construction and inadequate foundations on marshy sites. Mosley's Fascists had won a considerable following in the area during the thirties, and the area seethed with political and social discontent. The MP and diarist Harold Nicolson wrote in his diary on 17 September, 'Everybody is worried about the feeling in the East End . . . There is much bitter-ness. It is said that even the King and Queen were booed the other day when they visited the destroyed areas.' Nerve held – just. But there was much bitter resentment at inadequate support by social services and too few rest centres for families who had been bombed out.

As part of a community under aerial attack, the children survived as best they could. Youthful resilience, and perhaps a lack of clear understanding of the full danger, was on their side, as was the nervy excitement of it all – as long as the terror did not come too close. But, despite the best efforts of parents and the ARP, children were exposed to dreadful sights and human suffering.

Many returned evacuees experienced the same ironical turn of events as Vera, ten, who had been evacuated to Norfolk the previous September. She had not been happy there, and her parents had brought her back home. These are some of her vivid memories of the raids that she and her family now endured:

Like many of my school friends, I returned just in time for the Battle of Britain – and spent most of my school days down the air-raid shelter and the evenings in the basement of the pub opposite, as we had no garden for a shelter. We played games and slept on old mattresses on the floor.

One night a baker's boy came in. He had just had his van machine-gunned. He was all right physically – just terribly shocked. The next morning we came out of the shelter to find landmines had been dropped and there wasn't a house left standing.

For other children, like Wendy, in the middle of the bombing with her family, it was the Blitz that finally convinced their parents to evacuate them, or to send them away for a second time. For this reason, Wendy remembered one very severe raid especially.

I think it was a Sunday. We trooped through the kitchen down to the shelter when the air-raid warning sounded. Our tea of salads, jellies and cakes was already laid out, and there was a bucket of pickled eggs. Within minutes there were bombs falling all round us. When the all-clear sounded and we picked our way through the rubble we found that all the houses at the back of us were on fire and our house, our tea, and our bucket of eggs were smashed to pieces.

The next thing I knew was that I was decked out with a large label, a gas mask and a small case and I was on my way to being evacuated.

A boy of fifteen, Eric, stayed with his mother in London through-out the war; he was an only child, and his father was away in the forces. Despite many near misses, and a landmine in the next street, they got through unscathed. 'The relief of still being alive and the family house still standing was immense,' he said, reliving that pro-found relief over sixty years later.

The countryside just to the east of London caught the edge of some of the heaviest bombing raids. Anna, who lived there throughout the war, recalled vivid snapshot memories of her family's life in their large and draughty country house at that time:

Early in the war, the time of the Blitz, there was often an air-raid during dinner. One time the bangs and crashes were closer than usual, and Mummy got down from her chair intending to take shelter. Father, eye-brows raised and looking over his glasses enquired.' 'What *are* you doing?'

'I was going under the table,' she admitted, and sat down again.

Later, when Father's coffee cup was raised, a tremendous explosion shook the house. His white shirt front was spattered, so Mummy got her own back and said loudly, 'What *are* you doing?'

Father took to wearing his dark-blue buttoned-up mess jacket for the rest of the war. Outwardly to save his shirt washings and starchings, it was also a clear message: standards are to be maintained, Hitler or no Hitler.

A young woman of eighteen, who had a job as a secretary in the City, never knew what new shock each morning would bring that autumn:

I used to cycle to work each day, and I'll never forget the absolute amaze-ment and disbelief cycling through the City after one particularly bad night and seeing all the solid City buildings reduced to rubble . . . One day as I was hurrying to my job I saw about a dozen soldiers waving cheerily and calling to passers-by from the windows of their billet above a train station at Holborn. The next day when I went past the building was a smoking ruin. A direct hit. I cried for days for all those soldiers who had been waving – just boys they looked.

She never heard what had happened to them, and she never forgot.

Iris, nearly fourteen, was in her last year at school in the north-east of London during the Blitz. Her family lived in a small terraced house in a working-class neighbourhood which was heavily bombed, night after night:

We spent over fifty nights in a row in the air-raid shelter in the backyard – brick built, about 6 foot by 9 – my parents, baby sister and myself. And the lady next door and her two children, back from evacuation, came in as well. We sat on hard chairs, upright. Then the raids slowed down a bit and we spent the occasional night in our beds – but more often than not the siren went and we had to get up and go.

Our next-door neighbour was an auxiliary fireman, too old to be called up. He built bunks in our shelter, supposedly for his daughter and me. When they were finished I was too big for them, so his daughter and my sister were able to lie flat instead of on their mothers' knees all night . . .

His wife was deaf, and it was my responsibility to go and knock at her door to get her and her daughter into the shelter in a raid . . . Sometimes I slept on her bed in case of a raid, and once I didn't hear the siren and we were all asleep and my mum rushed in and dragged us all out and hit me for not waking over and over again as she was getting us into the shelter. I was used to it, but I never was hit like that before.

We lived near King's Cross station, and the bombs seemed to follow the path of railway lines. Our house got blasted out three times. The first was when bombs fell in the next street and all our windows fell in – the frames as well. All the inside walls fell down. We all lent a hand and patched things up. That entitled us to £4 per adult and one blanket per child. So we all traipsed off to the town hall to collect our dues, and had a blow-out on the money.

The partially deaf neighbour whom Iris used to alert during the raids lived to a great age. Many years later she asked Iris whether she remembered the hiding her mother gave her that night. Iris, who was then nearly seventy, said that she did.

After each night of bombing, Londoners emerged into roads full of debris and broken glass. Gas, power and telephone lines hung off shattered walls. The emergency services struggled through roped off streets smelling of gas or chemicals or chocolate, depending on which plant or warehouse had been hit. There was little or no public transport. Worst of all was the death or injury of friends and neighbours.

For Iris 'It was shocking to come out of the shelter in the morning to see the air still thick with dust and the ground littered with inches of rubble and glass – but worst of all was to hear passers-by shouting that this building or that place was down and that Mr and Mrs So-and-so were still buried . . . and the deathly hush as they listened for sounds of survivors.'

For a girl of eight called Jean, the raids became almost normal, she said. Her family had a

a nightly ritual, getting the flask of tea, blankets, candles and sandwiches ready to take down to the Anderson – which incidentally was always swimming in 6 inches of water. We could tell by the sound of the engines of the planes whether they were friend or foe. It was a nightmare to go through the non-stop bombing night after night . . . My mother was praying continually with her rosary in her hands.

When we emerged each morning alive it was a miracle. It was better still if we could have a cup of tea and a wash to take the grime out of our eyes from the dusk and smoke of the fires and the buildings that had collapsed.

Dilys (seventeen), who was living in Clapham, had similar harrowing memories of appalling loss within the neighbourhood: 'There was the terrible experience of coming out of the air-raid shelter one morning to find that a landmine had dropped very near our house and buried a family who were sheltering in the cellar underneath their shop. We knew them well. They were all killed.'

Over Christmas 1940, Douglas, aged eleven, on holiday after his first term at a boarding prep school, went with his mother to stay with relatives in London. 'So we experienced the Blitz at first hand. I remember seeing a red sky over the burning city. The father of a friend I played with was a volunteer fireman. One morning he returned to his home, wet and filthy in his uniform. Ignoring everyone, he just flopped down on the sofa and fell asleep, staying that way for twelve hours.'

Pushed by the danger of the moment, families made the best of whatever sheltering facilities were on hand. People living in grand houses did the same – with surprising variations. Anna remembered clearly the early, rather eccentric, arrangements at her family's country estate near London:

At the start of the Blitz our air-raid shelter had not been dug out, so my brother and I slept on the shelves in the silver strongroom. Nanny, who was short and very round, was squeezed in too. Nanny's nerves were imperturbable. Father, having spent the First World War in the trenches, preferred to be above ground. When our shelter was ready he ceded his place to us, and we slept there – under the roses – for the duration.

The noisy nights and the blackouts, which were difficult for grown-ups, did not affect us much. One night there was a heftier than usual explosion, followed by crashes and rumblings and tinkles for quite a while. My brother said, 'Was that the house?' It was clearly my responsibility, as elder sister, to give some reassurance, so I said, 'I expect so. Go to sleep.'

Mummy came down to us later. The house was still there, but the windows weren't. They had to finish dinner in overcoats, she said. The conservatory or palm house was not there any more (the space became a swimming pool twenty-five years later).

The sheep had to be taken off the lawns so that they shouldn't eat glass shards. Poor sheep – they had a lot to put up with, what with bombs and packs of marauding dogs and us with our invasion games.

Lily, who was born and brought up in east London, spoke with heart-wrenching difficulty of her cousins; so many years later, it was clearly still an ordeal for her. Her aunt and uncle and five cousins lived two streets away from her own family, she said, and they were in and out of each other's houses all the time.

One night, during a raid, they were all in the shelter except for one of the girls, my cousin Josie, who wouldn't go and stayed in bed. There was a direct hit and they were all killed except – by a miracle – the girl in the house. But she was terribly burned. The oldest son was in the forces at the time, and when he came looking for her in the hospital where she was being treated he didn't recognize her, her face was so bad.

Lily said that it had been a long time before any of the remaining relatives could mention the tragedy in any way.

Every raid left new damage, both to the great national monuments and to familiar shops and streets. Nowhere, not even a corner shop, could be taken for granted. Like most boys of his age Dan, aged thirteen and living in Golders Green, later remembered the Blitz as both terrifying and exciting:

I was enjoying the Blitz most of the time – shelter-hopping during an air-raid warning on the way to school and watching the fighter planes high in a cloudless sky was a macho thing for young boys to do . . .

I went out one morning after a particularly heavy bombing, to inspect the damage, and discovered that my much patronized neighbourhood sweet shop had been almost totally destroyed. All that was left was the end of the wall shared with the adjoining property. On the shelves of that wall, miraculously untouched, were all the large jars of sweets from which, in those days, our twopenny orders were scooped into small brown-paper bags . . . The sun was shining, and a unique, dazzling and multicoloured display was on view to the whole street. Even to this day I have a strong visual memory of those exposed sweet jars.

Given the obvious temptation, with shortages and rationing, a policeman was already guarding the site when Dan came upon it.

Children who were living in cities all over the country still remember the pitiful debris of familiar, bombed-out shops. Shattered chemists' shops gave off a peculiar acrid, chemical smell from burnt medicinal compounds. A girl who lived in a central London square, which was badly bombed, said that after a direct hit on her local chemist's 'the railings all round the square were covered with bandages – like streamers – and the street and the pavements were white with powders.' Sue, aged seven and living on the outskirts of Newcastle, inspecting a demolished chemist's near her home, saw 'jars and jars of spilled, smashed Brylcreem all over the pavement'.

Anna retained an acute and telling memory of her dignified father as he stubbornly carried on as normally as possible and attempted to restore order to their world:

My first visual image that always comes to mind of 'bombing' is of my seventy-year-old father, with his dinner-jacket lapels folded up over his starched shirt front, shovelling snow from the stairs back through the shattered window frame and muttering about his soup . . . The incongruity of snow on the dark Victorian carpeting . . . My formal and distant father using a coal shovel competently . . .

The scale of importance weighted more on the side of his (cooling) soup on the dining-room table than of the destruction of the window. The danger of the situation was less important than staying immaculately dressed for dinner.

A six-year-old girl called Mary said that during the Blitz she and her younger brother had makeshift beds in a cupboard under the stairs in their house, her parents deciding that this was preferable to damp and smelly shelters. 'We suffered near misses from a landmine and from a marker flare (a tremendous thud, a bright-red flickering glow) which blew open our little cubbyhole. My brother whispered to me, "Have we died?" I was five, and I am told my reply was "I'm not sure – we'd better say our prayers again, just in case." '

During the twelve days following the beginning of the Blitz on London, the army was put on high alert for a German invasion, and Sunday 15 September was designated a national day of prayer. Londoners, stunned by attack after attack, night after night, and exhausted by lack of sleep, kept their wobbly morale going somehow by 'making a job of this business of living and working under fire', as Churchill put it. And the Prime Minister went to see the worst-hit areas for himself. Guided by his unfailing empathy with the working man and woman, he left his official vehicle and its convoy and toured the shattered East End streets on foot. As he moved through the smouldering debris, trademark cigar in hand, word spread quickly and the crowds gathered. 'Are we downhearted?' he bellowed at them, clearly relishing the buzz of being at the heart of it all. 'No!' the admiring Cockneys roared back, cheered by the sight of him. 'No, no, no . . .'

Hard by the City, a six-year-old girl called Meg spent many a night during the Blitz clutching her red Mickey Mouse gas mask for luck. She and her family and their neighbours were in a big underground shelter under the Fruit Exchange in Spitalfields Market. The bunks were in tiers, and I slept in the same bunk with my mother as I was very small. My father was too old for the forces, but he was part of the Heavy Rescue and went in right after the bombs had dropped.

I used to do my singing and dancing act there in the shelter with my friend – and the audience couldn't escape! But I remember that everyone was very kind and caring and made the best of it and tried to have a laugh . . .

After the bombing I remember seeing half a block of flats opened up as though someone had sliced through the rooms, exposing the fireplaces and wallpapers and an odd chair . . . These bomb sites were very familiar – they became our playgrounds.

In Hampstead, seventeen-year-old Charlotte, who had just left her private school and was about to take her first job, on a current-events magazine, remembered the early raids on London. 'At first, my two sisters and I came downstairs whenever we heard the siren. We all slept on the floor in our hall, near to the door, in case we had to escape if the house was bombed. One sister owned two very precious pairs of silk stockings, which she carefully brought down with her every night.'

As the attacks moved through other parts of the country, children spent hours in cramped, smelly Anderson shelters. 'I can summon up the smell of damp sandbags almost at will,' Dick, who lived in Wandsworth, said. 'But nights were exciting for a young boy . . . We had food, cards, games of ludo . . . Now of course I can understand what I could not know at the time – the enormous worry it must have been for my parents.'

Moira, who spent nights in a similar shelter in the north, said that her father 'kept some precious chocolate and gave us each a square as a treat in the shelter. He joked that it was an "anaesthetic" that would help us to sleep. The times I spent in that shelter left me with claustrophobia later in life.'

Anderson shelters withstood everything but a direct hit, and undoubtedly saved lives, but they were extremely uncomfortable – and frequently waterlogged. 'Ours was erected by a kind neighbour, but was never used for the simple reason that there was always a foot of water in it,' Jim, aged ten, who lived on a council estate in Hull, said later. 'We took shelter under the kitchen table when the air raid-warning sounded.' Many other families made their own makeshift arrangements too. In Newcastle, one heavy raid came when eight-year-old Sue had only just returned after a period of evacuation with distant relatives. 'Our Morrison – indoor – shelter hadn't been delivered. So Mother turned the armchairs upside down and we crouched underneath. A bomb came whistling down, and I was scared. A dull thud near by. It was in the field at the back of our house. My nearest squeak.'

Many adventurous youngsters, not able to grasp the danger, revelled in all the fuss and the commotion, long past their bedtimes. 'I was six in 1939, and I was disappointed when the war ended,' Joanna said. It was like a non-stop football match to many younger children. I felt guilty about feeling like this until I realized that others did too . . . We lived in the industrial Midlands and we quickly came to recognize the sounds of different fighter bombers – "theirs" and "ours". Poor Mum – Dad was off fire-watching. But to my younger brother and me, not properly aware of the danger, the war was a thrill. Being stuck in the shelter, top coats over our pyjamas, was a big adventure. As for the raids, the noisier the better. And a thermos of hot milk and biscuits too.'

Josh, a mischievous boy of five, off playing with his friends in north London after a close and heavy raid, and too young to be fully aware of the dangers of moving around damaged buildings, got up to tricks that would have made his parents' hair stand on end: 'We had some wonderful opportunities for adventure. The house that had taken the bomb blast, which had shredded our furniture with glass fragments, was only 100 yards away and it was the perfect adventure playground. My parents thought we were all harmlessly riding our bikes round the block while we were inside the house clambering up broken stairs.'

Rose, aged eight, whose father had taken over a house at Eton College in September 1939, was usually spared the Anderson shelter because her mother – an asthmatic – could not tolerate it. During one particularly noisy raid, she recalled, 'Mother, dressed for dinner, grabbed me and we retreated under the grand piano in the drawing room – where she proceeded to read poetry aloud to me above all the bangs and crashes . . . If we had been hit we would have been like gingerbread men, flat as pancakes.' The deafening ack-ack guns, she said, frightened her far more than the planes and the bombs.

And there was, too, a pervading sense of fear. I still react when I hear a siren, and I have never forgotten being woken from a nightmare – I was being pursued by motorcycles backfiring . . . I was also very aware of the sudden change of lifestyle as I watched my mother struggling to run the house and feed the boys.

Of course, tragedy soon intruded. I remember our deep sadness when the first old boy from my father's house was killed. It was very early in the war, he was no more than seventeen or eighteen. We children knew him particularly well, as his parents were abroad and he spent some holidays with us.

Over sixty years later, Rose's memory of him, and of the great sadness of his boyhood death, is undimmed.

It was the young people who had recently left school and started work who tended to put on a show of bravado during air raids. Also, a superstitious resignation quickly took hold: it was commonly believed that if a bomb had 'got your number on it' and you caught a direct hit it was fate, and short of spending every night in the underground, which was crowded and unpleasant, there wasn't much you could do about it. 'After a bit, I was determined not to go down to that smelly shelter – I said that if I was going I'd rather it was in my own bed,' recalled Jilly, then just seventeen, who had recently become a sales assistant at Swan & Edgar's well-known department store in Piccadilly. 'But one night I was sleeping in bed during a raid and a landmine landed near my home. I slept through it – covered in glass, as all the windows had blown in. My mother rushed to see if I was all right and, finding me still asleep, thought for a moment that I was dead.'

In the midst of danger and extreme discomfort, youngsters continued to find some fun. Peggy, who lived in Stoke Newington, was determined to enjoy whatever she could, despite the stress of wartime, and leaped at the chance to live a bit of normal life.

In 1940 I was sixteen, and near where I lived there were several public underground shelters where people would go after work each night – even before the siren sounded. One enterprising gentleman opened the cellar under his shop as a dance hall, and of course all the young people went there. I told my father that I was fed up with sleeping in the shelter and preferred to sleep at home.

Of course I didn't: I waited a while after they had left for the underground to shelter, and then went to the dance hall – which was fine until one night there was a very heavy bombardment and my father came back to take me to the shelter, but he didn't find me at home.

It didn't take him long to work out where I was – and that was the end of the dancing.

All over the country, during intense periods of bombing, desperate families left the inner cities at night for the country or the suburbs, even if it meant going on foot. They became known as 'the trekkers'. Alice's father, a London taxi-driver, hit on a novel way of getting his family out in some comfort during the worst of the night raids of the Blitz. He and his taxi-driver mate, both of whom had a young child, fixed up their cabs with boards across the back seats and mattresses laid on top. 'Then off we would all go into the countryside somewhere, taking the cabs in turn, and we would sleep in peace and quiet,' Alice recalled. 'When the Blitz was really bad, we went through this "holiday" routine about twice a week.'

For all the superhuman efforts of the local authorities, emergency services and ordinary citizens during the fierce bombing of the Blitz, one of the great problems – apart from shoddy and smelly public shelters – was providing food and shelter for families whose homes had been badly damaged. These excruciating problems were soon to be encountered in other cities as the attacks widened.

Paul, then a schoolboy of thirteen, was living with his parents and sister in suburban Greater London, where the family was in the front line of aerial attack. In November 1940 they were bombed out. This is his precise account of how it happened, his family's dealings with the emergency services, and how they all came through it – including the adopted family cat.

A little before the war my father decided to take down the dividing wall between the two reception rooms downstairs to make one big room. With the help of a builder friend the wall was removed and replaced with an RSJ or steel girder ...

When the Blitz began, my parents moved their bed to what was the dining room; the steel frame was covered with timbers, and a bed for my parents, my sister and myself was made up underneath. This was our home-made version of the Morrison shelter, which came along a little later.

The evening of 1 November 1940 was cold and wet, and we were all sitting round the fire with our cat, Smut – who had been bombed out from another house and we had taken in. Just before nine I stood up to turn on the wireless, as we wanted, as usual, to listen to the news. As I stood up I heard a very short whistling noise and shouted to everyone to take cover; in a situation like this we normally went to the cupboard under the stairs.

I woke up in pitch darkness breathing in a foul mixture of plaster dust and soot with a block of about six bricks on my lap and a huge bump on my head. Still dazed and completely deaf, I called to the family and started to make my way to the front door, but kept stumbling over bricks and rubble. When my eyes finally adjusted to the near darkness I realized there was no front door – just a space looking out to the road.

I was very relieved to see my parents and sister standing on the pavement, and the four of us crossed the road to knock at the door of a neighbour – but they didn't have a front door either.

Other neighbours appeared, and we all made for a brick-built street shelter. Hot sweet tea with a dash of whisky arrived at about the same time as the ambulances. My mother and sister were taken to hospital with cuts and bruises and shock, while someone tried to find me some shoes – mine were blown off, and the ground was covered with rubble and broken glass. I finished up with a pair of old high-heeled shoes to go round to the first-aid post for bandaging, then to the rest centre – a school hall.

The facilities at the rest centre were basic – a cloakroom with a hand basin, where I tried to get a few layers of dirt and soot off my face, and a selection of stretchers to sleep on. Next morning I went round to a friend's house, where his mother provided a bath and tried to get some of the soot out of my hair and gave me some old clothes to replace the tattered remnants I was wearing.

I stayed there for a few days until my mother and sister came out of hospital and we were moved to a large requisitioned house in Harrow, which we shared with another family.

Right: A girl helps her mother make wooden window battens for the blackout and to protect their home against air raids. Sticky tape is already in place, criss-crossing the windows

Below: A sign proclaiming 'Sandbags on toast' offers a cheeky welcome to customers outside a popular and heavily fortified London café

'Chin first!' An older boy dutifully instructs two younger children in the technique of putting on their rubbery gas masks

Holding hands, Jewish refugee children from Berlin waiting at Liverpool Street station after their journey across Europe in a special closed train, a *Kindertransport*, August 1939

Right: Three young evacuees, and a favourite stuffed toy, wave a cheerful goodbye to their parents from a train window as they set off for the country

Below: Close to tears, mothers watch from behind barricades at Waterloo station as their children leave with their schools for unknown destinations – and the care of strangers

Above: Winston Churchill makes his famous V sign to the residents of Bristol after heavy bombing. 'We shall let them have it back,' he thundered, raising the spirits of the homeless. Behind him stands the American ambassador, John G. Winant

If *you* can't go to the factory help the neighbour who *can*

How you can help

Arrange now with a neighbour to look after her children when she goes to her war-work—or give your name to

CARING FOR WAR WORKERS' CHILDREN IS A NATIONAL SERVIC

Issued by the Ministry of Health

Left: A 1943 Ministry of Health poster encouraging mothers to get out of the home to do factory war work – which, often with babysitting help from neighbours or older children, many did

Right: A mother and her young daughter, wrapped in a blanket and seated on a dining-room chair, guard the remains of their home after the second German air raid on Coventry, November 1940

Below: After a stint in the potato fields, a Devonshire farmer's wife scrubs the hair of one of her young evacuee helpers in a tin bathtub while the others await their turn, summer 1941

Digging for Victory! East End boys set about transforming blitzed areas into allotments, turning over the soil with tools provided by the Bethnal Green Bombed Sites Association

Evacuees from London being taught some basic Welsh words by their new teacher in a schoolroom in Wales

Above: A familiar sign for most children – echoing the popular wartime song – at a fruit-and-vegetable market stall

Right: Many school-leavers started their working lives doing urgent war work. Here, instructed by experienced women workers, girls learn to assemble fuses in a die-casting factory, 1942

Left: Making friends. An American GI, settling into the community in the run-up to D-Day, teaches a local lad the all-American game of baseball. The boy is wearing the GI's US Army cap

Below: A victory street party in London, May 1945, typical of the outdoor neighbourhood parties that were being held all over the country. This photograph was taken by the mother of the boy wearing a cap in the bottom left-hand corner. An only child, and very shy, he remembered feeling 'sad and forlorn' despite the festivity. Note the flag and the bunting, the partial window blackout, and the grimy buildings scarred by the wear and tear of war

Visiting the bomb site the next day, we could see the crater in the front garden of the next-door house, about 6 yards from where we had been sitting. Our neighbours had been in their Anderson shelter and were dug out unhurt. Across the road, three children had been in bed asleep when the bomb landed. The wall of the house had been blown away, but they were safe. It was little short of miraculous that there had been no fatalities. We had been saved by the RSJ – it had caught on the only piece of brick-work still standing, the chimney breast, and made a little cave in which we had been sitting.

The cat had vanished, but turned up a couple of weeks later – and stayed with us for years.

The most terrifying raid on London so far occurred on 29 December 1940, a Sunday night. The City was savagely targeted and, as many of the offices and factories and warehouses were unattended, there were few people about, including firewatchers, to raise the alarm. The incendiary bombs quickly created an inferno. The Thames was at an especially low ebb, which made the job of the Fire Brigade, struggling to get water for the hoses, all but impossible. It was on this atrocious night that the epic photograph of St Paul's was taken: the dome of the cathedral surrounded by raging fires and smoke, but still surviving, a symbol of the gritty determination of Londoners under fire.

London's wartime hell that December night brought to mind a similar catastrophe that had occurred in the capital nearly three centuries before: the Great Fire of London in 1666. It had spread like wildfire through the wooden shops and houses of the City, and, ironically, it was this first Great Fire that had caused St Paul's Cathedral, as we know it today, to be built. The previous cathedral perished, and it was Sir Christopher Wren's daring and innovative design that produced the spectacular dome which would outlast London's second Great Fire.

For a child living in the vicinity of the City, the fire raid of 29 December was a terrifying experience. In its intensity and brilliant fiery hell, that night came to symbolize the essence of London's wartime. It was a night that Jim, who lived in Islington, would remember as the heaviest air-raid of the Blitz – and it was an experience that stamped him for life:

I had been evacuated to Cornwall, but Mum came and got me back. My school was closed, so we kids larked about. Then came the Blitz. By Christmas it was into the shelter night after night, racing out into the smoke and rubble to pick up shrapnel the next morning – scary stuff, but exciting too . . . But that raid on 29th was different. I never heard such a racket. Bombers coming at us wave after wave. All the City was blazing, and it was fires and death and destruction all round us next day. I was thirteen. I can honestly say that that night made a pacifist out of me for life. No human being should have to live through horror like that – or visit it on his fellow man or woman.

And a small girl's memory of the same night:

It was the day after my fifth birthday and my father had bought me a doll – my pride and joy. She was called Henrietta. We spent the night in our cellar, wrapped in eiderdowns. Next morning I found Henrietta fallen from my bedside chair, smashed to smithereens. Years later my mother told me it was the night of the infamous fire raid of 29th December.

A small boy called Tim, who was five, also never forgot the drama of that night – mixed up with his personal, childish memory of war:

The single most impressionable incident of my wartime boyhood was the morning after the raid of 29 December. My father and I had gone for a ride – he on his bike, I on my tricycle. We were returning from our outing when he pointed out the red sky, even in the daytime. It was the City and the docks, ablaze from the night's air raid.

I was looking so hard at this amazing sight that my tricycle overturned – and some of the family's precious butter ration was used for the large bruise on my head.

For a while after the turn of the year the German bombers lessened their attacks on London and turned their attention elsewhere. But the following spring, early in 1941, the raiders returned. Anna, in the country on the fringe of the city, had a clear view of much of the action round London:

Looking east in the late evening the sunlit colours of an oak tree in spring were bright against a vast blue-black thundercloud behind it. Between the darkness and the tree, an aerobatic dogfight was taking place. Spitfires and Messerschmitts, diagonal lines of bright blue bullets, lightning, fire, and a stream of black smoke. One plane crashed two fields away from us.

Our tough, daring mother took my brother (four) and me (eight) to see the crashed Messerschmitt. Her idea was that we should know what was happening. I think she was wise . . .

I cannot abide the smell of burnt metal, and the sight of the blood-spattered Perspex of the cockpit has stayed in my memory . . . But my brother, who could not have understood very much, was fascinated by the mechanics.

Not long after the start of the Blitz on London, in the latter months of 1940 the Luftwaffe also began bombing major provincial cities. The pattern – that of 'an angry child', as the historian Richard Titmuss described it – was the same: causing great damage to the city centres through fire and destruction, and aiming for well-known landmarks and strategic targets such as war production centres. The initial attack was followed up with several more nights of intensive bombing. It was hoped that these massive raids would create mass panic among the civilian population, and a weakening of morale to the point of surrender. Though there were occasional bull's-eye hits on crucial targets – frequently more through luck than skill – none of this occurred.

Birmingham was heavily attacked in October and November of 1940, with terrible damage and loss of life. Between September 1940 and July 1941 there were 76 air attacks on the city; 2,000 inhabitants were killed, and some 3,000 were seriously injured; up to 20,000 houses and shops were either damaged or destroyed. As they had done in London, and would continue to do in towns all over the country, the civilians rallied. Young men who had just started work, and were too young to join up, played their part. Stan, then sixteen, and articled in a solicitor's office, was hastily given some training by the Fire Brigade and became part of the Auxiliary Fire Service. 'Within the year I became the deputy group fire-guard officer . . . The group officer was a friend, and we went from house to house recruiting as many volunteers as possible and passing on the techniques we had been taught – stirrup pumps, buckets, sandbags and sand . . . When the raids became intense, the strain of working all day and doing fire-guard duty all night became very exhausting.'

'Parts of the city were totally destroyed,' Brian, then attending school in the town centre, recalled.

My grandparents were bombed out, and next day there was an empty desk at school where a boy who was killed by a bomb sat.

Of course, being young boys we all rushed round collecting shrapnel and spent bullets . . . But it was bad, on and off, from November on . . .

All outside games were banned except for working on our Dig for Victory plots – parts of the playing fields that had been dug up. The school was hit in one raid, and for some time we had lessons in small groups in various homes.

Sixty years later Brian gave a talk – in that same school – on his wartime Birmingham childhood

For Kate, who was nearly four and lived on the outskirts of Birmingham, her earliest childhood memories are of this time:

I was wearing a fleecy blue siren suit, of which I was very fond. I remember being hurried down to the Anderson shelter in the night . . . then came a flash – a vivid white light in the sky . . . A searchlight or a plane being hit . . . whatever it was, it encapsulates the bombing raids for me . . .

As far as I was concerned, this spending nights in the shelter was fun. It was a cosy little living space, although I don't suppose the adults remembered it like that. Later on, as I got a bit older . . . it became less attractive: a dank concrete bunker with steps down to a wet floor, and full of spiders.

A slightly older girl, Ann (five) was living in a different Birmingham suburb. Her abiding memory is of how faulty house building turned out to be a wartime advantage for her family: 'We moved into our brand-new house at Easter 1939, when I was four. It appears the builders went bankrupt, and my father always complained that the windows were left loose and created a draught. What a blessing that was, because when a landmine dropped we were the only house to have its windows withstand the blast.'

This was fortunate, but in other ways Ann was fully exposed to dangerous wartime conditions. Her experiences show vividly the kind of stress that was put upon even quite young children at a time when dread and uncertainty were part of daily life.

A portion of my first school was made mostly of wood. To me, it looked very like a Swiss house. It certainly didn't survive when an incendiary bomb hit it. I can still remember the acrid smell and the black smouldering wood.

The school was about ten minutes' walk from home, and my mother said, 'If the sirens go, make for whatever is nearest – home or school.' I was nearly always halfway between, and it was quite a hard decision for a small child to make.

One day this happened when I was crossing the playground. A German plane literally swooped on me. I could see the pilot, the plane was so low. I imagine he had already dropped his bombs, because he didn't do anything.

Many wartime children, all over the country, have very clear memories of low-flying German planes – sometimes coming so near that the pilot's face was briefly visible. These were undoubtedly planes returning from missions, perhaps jettisoning remaining bombs – or looking for opportunities to machine-gun civilians. Clive, who lived in Birmingham, has retained an eerily dramatic memory of one heavy raid.

I suppose I must have been six or seven at the time. There was an air raid on a very bright moonlit night in summer. We went down the garden, lit by moonlight – practically as light as day – indeed I suppose dawn might have been breaking .. . and this enemy plane came over, flying extremely low.

I could see the rear gunner in the tail, and he seemed to be depressing his gun towards us. It was all over in a flash of course – and the noise was tremendous. I couldn't see the man's face clearly, because he had his helmet on.

Beyond our garden was a lane and then allotments. I was told later that two people walking along the road, just beyond the allotments, had been shot by this gunner.

Joan, who became a senior nurse and an executive in the profession, also had very clear memories of what she described as 'the rationing and gloom of wartime Birmingham'; she lived in the centre and, with her family, experienced the heaviest raids. The aftermath of one in particular has stuck in her mind – a childhood incident of acute menace and unpleasantness:

A line of shops had been gutted by incendiaries the previous night. Although quite young, I was expected to make my own way to school, and on that day I was terrified by the blackened ruins and the ghastly, sickly smell of water on burnt timber. I could not bring myself to walk past them, and ran home.

My mother wrote a letter explaining my absence for the day and nothing more was said. After that I used an alternative route.

Although neither she nor her home and family had been injured, Joan still faced the trauma in her everyday life that war puts upon civilian populations. In cities under attack, judgement and resilience were required even of young children like her.

After the onslaught of the London Blitz, perhaps the greatest bombing drama of the war was the attack on Coventry on 14 November 1940. Although Coventry had become an important area for wartime manufacturing, it was still quite a small town and relatively little known outside the country; no one had considered it a prime target, least of all the local authorities. The violent air attack which began in the evening came in waves and lasted for eleven hours; enemy firepower immediately gutted the medieval city centre, including its beautiful and ancient cathedral.

Almost a third of the houses in the oldest part of Coventry were left uninhabitable; half of all the buses were wrecked; the drinking water had to be boiled. Angus Calder wrote that, because of the city's relatively small size, the shock and the horror of its trauma were magnified. 'Nearly everyone had heard the fall of nearly every bomb.' The onslaught – with 554 people killed, more than 1,000 injured, and the beloved cathedral in ruins – left the entire country, as well as the beleaguered people of Coventry, profoundly shocked and depressed.

A fifteen-year-old boy called Jack never forgot the dreadful sight –

the raging inferno – that he and his family watched that night: 'Coventry was ablaze. We lived in the country, a little to the south. Our house had a flat roof, and I remember standing up there looking at the glow in the sky . . . From time to time great tongues of flame shot up, but mostly the brilliance was the light of the fires reflected on the clouds of rising smoke.'

Sam, aged eight, whose father worked for one of the city's major aircraft manufacturers and was also an auxiliary fireman, spent that night in the family's shelter in the garden of their house in Coventry:

Usually nothing much happened when the sirens went, and the all-clear sounded after couple of hours and we could come out of the shelter and go back to the house to bed. This night it didn't. At six o'clock the milkman came and told us that the raid was over but the siren had been bombed and didn't work any more. I can still picture the rectangle of sky where the shelter door (or the sheet of corrugated iron) was opened. The water on the shelter floor was almost over the top of our boots, mine and my younger brother's . . .

Back in the house we had no gas or electricity. My mother tried to cook us breakfast over the fire in the grate, but it wasn't a success. Then, at about midday, the cry went up: 'Here's Daddy . . .'

I rushed out to greet him. He was soaking wet and black from head to foot. He clumped past me and passed out, face down, on the settee.

In the space of eleven hours, Coventry, its smoking cathedral now a ruin, had had the heart blown right out of it. Mass-Observation, taking the pulse of the inhabitants a little while after, found that the phrase 'Coventry is finished' was a part of most of their conversations; morale was at a low ebb.

Sam, clearly a child who was sensitive to what was going on all around him, described the strange limbo the citizens of Coventry found themselves inhabiting.

'We had many relatives living in and around Coventry, and this was a big anxiety for my mother. Nobody had a telephone then, and in any case all the lines were down. Some days later we set out in the car to find them. Many roads in the town were blocked by wreckage and huge bomb craters, so we had to make a lot of detours. The fire engines were still in attendance, and some buildings had firemen lying spreadeagled on their slate roofs, still putting fires out.

Everybody we visited seemed all right, very shocked at what was happening, but getting on with it as best as possible.

To the nation's surprise, and despite the crippling damage the German bombers had inflicted, the people of Coventry fought back. Morale improved remarkably quickly, and in homes, offices and factories people pulled together. Within weeks, Coventry was up and running; factories – some without roofs, open to the sky – started up again, and the city got back to work. A stoical resignation had set in.

Sam, who was later evacuated to Cheltenham with his mother and brother, remembered the time very clearly.

After that awful night we didn't bother with the shelter when the siren went; we tried to sleep in the cupboard under the stairs instead. Once, after another bad raid, we found the house opposite had been hit. Our front windows had gone, and there was broken glass everywhere. But what upset my mother terribly was that her curtains were in shreds.

Our front door had a leaded window. The lead had stretched in the heat, and the individual pieces of glass now looked like squares in a bar of chocolate.

Given the natural British reliance on shipping, the naval ports were obvious targets, and they were viciously and repeatedly attacked throughout the war. Large parts of both Portsmouth and Southampton were completely destroyed, and the raiders came back again and again to deliver more punishment on weary citizens. Sally, the daughter of a naval officer, was living with her mother in the centre of Portsmouth during many of the worst raids. 'In one fierce incendiary raid, Portsmouth guildhall was in flames and we saw soldiers frantically trying to get water for hoses from pumps along the road. There were bodies of marines who had been caught in one terrible explosion strewn about. I know we had to queue for drinking water at standpipes.'

The heavy raids on Southampton began in November 1940. Tony, then aged eight, whose home was there, recalled the dreadful experiences that he and his family endured, the hellish sights they witnessed, and his own lucky escape from a notorious bombing incident that turned into one of the town's major wartime tragedies.

We were bombed out twice in the bad raids – we lived in the centre, and much of the area was flattened. All the places and buildings we knew simply weren't there any more. We used to come out of the shelter and walk past shattered and still burning or smouldering buildings, dragged along by Mum. I wanted to stop and pick up all the fascinating things which I could see, blown into the road . . . But Mum wouldn't let me. She said it was dangerous.

There was one really big raid, I remember. Mum had sent me to the corner shop for a tin of condensed milk – 6d. I got to the counter, just about my head height, reached up, put the coin on the counter, and asked for the milk. Simultaneously, the siren went. The shopkeeper told everyone to go down into the cellar, but I refused, saying that I was going home to Mum. I grabbed the 6d piece and ran.

A landmine fell directly on the building and killed everyone in the cellar outright. It was one of the worst local disasters of the war.

Once the huge scale of the bombing emerged, Portsmouth and Southampton, with several other centres, became eligible for the government's evacuation scheme. Soon after the incident from which Tony so miraculously escaped, his family was helped to evacuate to the surrounding countryside. 'Our nerves were terrible by then – even us children's,' Tony said.

The raids on Cardiff began soon after the end of that dreadful year, just into 1941. They arrived, as had become the pattern, in sudden, fierce bursts. Jim, fourteen, a bright and motivated schoolboy who lived a little way outside the city, remembered that the sirens sounded and ack-ack guns were fired early on in the war. But he said it was not until January 1941 that Cardiff was targeted at full strength.

Cardiff received its first massive raid that January. We were in the shelter built by one of the neighbours. My father and his brother, who was home on leave from the air force, immediately returned to their vigil of looking for fires and damage. That night many people were killed, rows of houses were destroyed, a church at Llandaff North was burnt out, and Llandaff Cathedral was severely damaged. We were all in great fear.

When the all-clear sounded in the early hours we were told to find some other accommodation, as a landmine had fallen in the nearby school fields.

My father, as a Civil Servant, was directed to supervise a rest centre in a badly bombed part of Cardiff – for the homeless and injured – and had to attend to people who had lost family members. We did not see him for a week. He returned home drained and deeply disturbed from his ordeal, and never forgot those days of horror and the sights that confronted him.

The following day my uncle took me into Cardiff centre to see the damage. Buildings were continuing to smoulder, and the water used to quell the flames was freezing into icicles.

Tom, who also lived and went to school in Cardiff, said that, of the many bad raids at that time, one in particular remained very clear to him: 'During one fire-bomb raid, an incendiary fell on my school – but the vicar's son, who lived near by, extinguished this. He was then a school hero and suitably lauded . . . We kids got on with our lives and made our own fun. And I remember that, when it wasn't being used, the Morrison shelter, erected in the living room, acted as a super table-tennis table!'

The raiders moved north, to Merseyside, Manchester, Sheffield and Leicester. Most of the attacks again came in sudden, unexpected bursts, often followed by an eerie lull which left unnerved civilians in dread of what was to follow.

Jill was living on the outskirts of Manchester and watched, her heart in her mouth, as the city centre went up in flames. 'When Manchester was bombed you could see the huge fires from our house. The air-raid sirens went regularly, and most nights we would rush out to the Anderson shelter clutching a birdcage with our budgie in it – and also the cat, who wasn't very happy at having to stay in a constricted area like an air-raid shelter.'

Shirley, a teenager who lived in Sheffield, remembered hearing that 'After an incendiary raid which caused huge fires in the town centre, one department store remained standing with a broken sign "Orchestra Playing Daily in Restaurant" hanging crazily from one wall.' When she visited relatives in London very soon after, she said, she took a sad walk down Oxford Street, 'spotting the well-known shops, Selfridge's and the like, and seeing the space, like a newly extracted tooth, that denoted one well-known name that had "bought it" – a popular expression then – and been reduced to a pile of rubble'.

The constant anxiety of being at some sort of risk of attack from the air caused untold stress to the country at large. For the five years from 1940 to 1945 there were few places, however remote, which were entirely free from the menace of droning planes or random bombing and strafing.

A boy called John who was evacuated to a pretty village in Devon was severely shocked when his local school was badly damaged by a German plane, presumably dumping unused explosives after bombing one of the nearby coastal ports. In a quiet corner of East Anglia early one evening Alf, aged ten, was walking with his father across the family farm. Father and son were suddenly plunged into active warfare when a damaged German plane limped into sight, began losing height and started sputtering above their heads. Within seconds it had crashed into a field of cows, turning the peaceful green pasture into a bloody quagmire. Running terrified back to the farm to call for help, Alf stumbled upon an airman's boot: a human foot, and part of a leg, were still inside it.

Carol, whose family lived on a farm in a remote area of Yorkshire, recalled her patriotic father's extreme irritation when a stray German plane, with the RAF on its tail, flew over his land. 'Dad was stomping up and down the landing in the middle of the night ranting "How dare they, how dare they", because a German bomber had released its bombs to escape pursuit – over the hills of the Yorkshire Dales, right on our property, killing two sheep and leaving a hole in the track!'

Even an isolated hillside in North Wales wasn't safe from the long reach of German raiders. Hilda, evacuated from the south coast, later wrote rather wistfully that the only excitement in the village during the four years she lived there was a stray bomb that 'landed on the mountainside and killed two cows and a bull'.

Sheila, living with her mother and sister in a small town near the Clyde, though a good way from major target areas, was also constantly aware of planes droning overhead – British as well as enemy raiders.

We were far enough away from Greenock and Port Glasgow, with their docks and shipbuilding, not to receive much bombing, but the bombers seemed to go over very frequently on their way there. We did not have an air-raid shelter, but as soon as the siren went my mother would hustle my sister and me into a room on the ground floor of our house which had a large wall outside, presumably to protect us if there was a blast. Very young and unfrightened, I used to say 'Damn Hitler' and go straight off to sleep.

Few bombs were dropped where she and her family were living. And when one was jettisoned in the market square, much to the surprise of the local inhabitants, very little damage was done. The jagged hole left by the bomb also delivered a very hopeful postscript, which was carefully recorded by Sheila and her sister: 'On the edge of the bomb crater was a tree with a blackbird's nest in it. The mother bird stayed put, and I am happy to say the baby birds all hatched and eventually took to the wing. A miracle, we thought.'

In March 1941 there were major raids on London and Clydebank, and raids of lesser intensity on Bristol, Cardiff and Portsmouth. On Clydeside itself the people suffered extremely heavy bombing. Inadequate precautions had been made by the local authorities, and the brick public shelters offered poor protection. Acres of flimsy and overcrowded housing made a vulnerable target, as during the Blitz in London. There was more unrest in this area than in the other cities under attack, and a great many people 'trekked' out into the countryside each night, either on foot or by any means available.

Robert, living at his grandparents' house quite near by, well remembered the thud and drone of heavy bombers night after night as they flew inexorably towards their shipping and industrial targets. 'The air-raids started in earnest then. Nights became interrupted as the sirens sang their mournful refrain. I was bundled downstairs to sleep in a quilt while the planes droned overhead . . . "Why can't I go up on the roof with grandpa to look for fires? I've got an old tin hat too." Somehow, the answer was always "No!"'

Every city rightly took pride in its ability to 'take it', and there was a certain amount of grumbling that London, and the initial Blitz, got more than its fair share of the limelight. Possibly it did, but this in no way lessens the stoicism and bravery displayed by men, women and children living in the other great cities which were also heavily attacked.

It is a fact that London, as the capital city and prime target, was on duty every day during the war: the sirens sounded in Greater London 1,224 times, first to last, and the historian Richard Titmuss estimated that during the entire war Londoners were in some way threatened by the enemy once every thirty-six hours over five years. Of the approximately 60,000 civilian bombing deaths during the war, about half occurred in the Greater London area.

From a strategic point of view, the whole of the east coast and East Anglia were easy, accessible targets for the Luftwaffe. Hull, a vital port, suffered appallingly with repeated bombing. Outside London, the cities which experienced the heaviest raids of the war are thought to be Plymouth, Birmingham and Liverpool. But, together with Portsmouth, Hull was under constant threat and endured sustained and heavy enemy attack. Home Secretary Herbert Morrison went on record as saying that he believed Hull had (just) earned the accolade of being the most bombed provincial city.

The citizens of Hull have not always felt that their courage was fully appreciated – or given its due praise. Margaret, who was evacuated briefly in 1939 and returned to spend the rest of the war at her home in Hull, wrote:

I grew up in Hull, which for its size and population was the most bombed city in the UK. My poor daughter was brought up never to say 'Coventry' in my presence . . . Just because our cathedral wasn't hit (we haven't one) no one knows about us. We were always called a north-east coast town in every news bulletin – and we knew very well who we were.

I didn't mind the blackout at all. What I really minded was being woken up several times a night by the sirens . . . This happened a lot, as we were in the flight path to Leeds, Manchester, Liverpool etc.

I got so that I ignored the sirens and waited until I thought the enemy was definitely overhead, and then made a mad dash for the shelter. I was a big trial to my mother.

Our dad was an air-raid warden, patrolling the street. When things got bad we used to call out, 'Daddy, Daddy, come into the shelter.' Occasionally he did.

In 1941 Andy was an apprentice bricklayer of seventeen who lived on the outskirts of Hull. At the time he was working at a major, well-fortified aerodrome some miles away, and it was here that he watched a daring German raider make a lightning strike.

I was walking towards the perimeter of the drome when three twin-engined aircraft approached to land. Two were ours; the third was an Me 110 German fighter-bomber. The German pilot then proceeded to shoot the place up. My mate and I just stood there rooted to the spot.

The raider took off, but our boys got him – with Lewis guns they said – as he was heading back out to sea.

He and his crew are buried in the military section of a nearby village cemetery. His name, Hafter, is on the grave.

When you think . . . like me and my mate did . . . although he was the enemy, that pilot was a brave man.

It was an astonishing scene for a young man to watch in wartime. And it says a lot for young Andy that he could see the bravery and the futility of war on both sides.

Nowhere in the Hull area was safe, as Peter, who was eight when the war began, and who lived there throughout, said with feeling:

Hull and its docks were the target, with Bridlington – near by – getting the strays. It was said at the time that the German pilots headed for the white cliffs near Bempton and did a circle round Hull to avoid some of the gun batteries in east Hull.

As the war progressed, air raids became more frequent. In 1941 many were daylight raids – which changed to night raids as the Luftwaffe suffered considerable losses. My first sighting of a German plane was while standing at the window of our house. Turning to Mum I said, 'Look, there's a British plane.' It soon became clear it was German when three explosions took place . . .

The only time I came near to being a casualty was when I was walking down the main street of town and a German plane flew low overhead and actually machine-gunned the street. Fortunately for me, a shopkeeper waved me in and I soon found myself in a Morrison shelter with wire caging – like an animal in the zoo, I thought!

Felixstowe, another east-coast port, also suffered frequent raids. Mary, aged three, and her family lived in a neat, detached suburban house on a quiet, leafy street there. But in the spring of 1941 their world was suddenly ripped violently apart when the terror of war intruded:

There were many raids on and off . . . but the one I remember so vividly was on 12 May 1941. My mother grabbed me up from the couch when the siren went. She had also persuaded my grandmother to come down when the raid started – although she always said she was prepared to die in her bed! We all squeezed into the cupboard under the stairs.

My father was standing beside the open kitchen door, as he did on such nights. My mother called, 'Come in, George, they're getting close!'

Thank goodness he did. The next instant there was an horrendous bang as a bomb dropped just behind our house. All our doors and windows were blown out by the blast. The ceilings collapsed, and a huge hole appeared in the wall, just over the couch where I had been sleeping.

When the all-clear sounded, my father went to the hole where the back door had been. I can hear him now saying, 'Good God, the neighbour's house has gone!'

Eight houses had been demolished, four people had been killed, and ten injured seriously.

Our house was boarded up. It was three months before we were able to return.

Towards the end of March 1941 there were major raids on several large towns, and the enemy bombers returned to London. Barely recovered from the pasting of the Blitz, exhausted Londoners rallied for more punishment. And it was hard: more fatalities; more families bombed out; more buildings reduced to smoking ruins.

It was at this time that Faith – then aged about fifteen – witnessed an episode of acute personal loss that would affect her for the rest of her life. Outside her family's house in a wide, pleasant street in central London she experienced a scene of stark human tragedy. During the previous night there had been a major bombing incident very close by. The following morning Faith was standing in front of the house, waiting apprehensively to see what had been hit. She said quietly:

I literally watched a man being driven to madness . . .

It turned out that there had been a direct hit by a landmine on a row of houses at the top of our street. It was one of the worst incidents we had in the neighbourhood throughout the war. I was standing outside watching the rescuers. This was March 1941, the day after the Café de Paris, a fashionable underground nightclub near Piccadilly, was bombed – with many deaths and terrible injuries.

Then I saw a man, who I recognized, come up out of the underground at the bottom of our road. My family knew him slightly, and we knew that he was a musician, living around here, who was a member of the orchestra then playing at the Café de Paris. He had survived, clearly, but he was a pathetic sight that day – dishevelled, almost a Charlie Chaplin figure, his black dinner suit covered in dust and cut to ribbons. And, oddly, wearing a hat.

I saw him start up the street towards where the landmine had hit the row of houses, but the road was cordoned off by the police and he was stopped.

Suddenly he must have understood what had happened and where, because he began shrieking and wailing in grief, loudly, uncontrollably, gone clear out of his mind by the unendurable pain . . . The terrible sounds he made are with me still . . .

His wife and baby son had been in one of the bombed houses, their home. Their bodies were never recovered.

That spring the Home Counties were also being fiercely attacked. A brother and sister of eight and twelve were living near Deal, where their grandfather was in charge of the cross-Channel guns ('Winnie', 'Pooh' and 'Ratty'). The children were occasionally allowed to watch the mammoth guns being fired, and remembered hearing 'the German shells whizzing across, knowing that our guns would reply'. During one terrifying raid their house suffered a frighteningly near miss.

A landmine attached to a parachute sailed over our house only to explode in a nearby field – leaving a huge crater. The night it fell my younger brother was crying out for attention from his bedroom near mine, so I rather crossly got out of bed and asked him, irritably, what he wanted.

I was standing in his doorway when there came this truly overpowering crash that shook the whole house and we could hear the tinkle of glass as the windows blew in.

The doors of the stables were open, and the dogs came rushing and barking into the house. My bed was covered in broken glass . . . We had had a miraculous escape. I've never forgotten that bang. After this we got a shelter . . .

May 1941 brought yet more grim, sustained bombing, with London and the ports again taking a pasting. Early in the month Liverpool and the surrounding areas of Bootle, Birkenhead and Wallasey suffered eight successive nights of heavy attack; this terrible and prolonged episode of air warfare has become known as Merseyside's 'May Week'. In the Bootle district, only one house in ten remained undamaged, and overall some 70,000 people were left homeless.

Throughout the previous months the area had been targeted heavily, but sporadically, so the fierce attacks were expected. Yet the precautions taken by the local authorities in providing decent public shelters and emergency help for the homeless were quite inadequate, and this severely undermined morale. In 'May Week', with the Blitz raining down and virtually no proper protection, there was bitter condemnation and a good deal of social unrest.

It was an appalling time for the Liverpool area. 'Trekkers' fled the city in droves, and rumour and gossip multiplied, breeding more fears. After the war, it was estimated that about 2,000 people were killed during the Merseyside Blitz, and slightly fewer were seriously injured. The docks carried on somehow, but with activities reduced to a quarter.

It was during the 'May Week' bombardment that one of Britain's worst single civilian bombing incidents occurred. This has gone down in the annals of Liverpool as the Durning Road Disaster; its horror is still spoken of, in tones of tragic disbelief, nearly seventy years later.

During heavy raids, the extensive cellars of a local college on Durning Road, close to the centre of Liverpool, were routinely used by several hundred families as a nightly shelter. Maureen, who was taken there as a child of seven, remembered what had become her mother's regular routine: 'Seven or eight o'clock, Mum gets the flask out, puts the tea in it, takes three cups, makes sandwiches . . . and she used to have army blankets . . . one for myself, one for Jimmy (brother) . . . kiddies there laughing and joking.'

One night during that week in May 1941 the college received a direct hit from incendiary bombs intended for the adjacent, and strategically vital, railway yards. The structural damage was extensive, but even more crucial were the main boilers. These were pierced, burst, and flooded into the cellars, where several hundred people were sheltering. Maureen was there that night with her family as usual. 'I thought it was a bomb, but it wasn't – it was a boiler that burst . . . We weren't very far away from the place.' A young man of twenty-one, a neighbour she knew well, was blown to pieces in front of her. 'All I seen was horrible, just horrible.'

Because of what Maureen later described as a 'premonition' by her mother, she and her brother were still sitting up that night, awake, not sleeping on their blankets on the floor as they usually did. Alert to the instant and terrible danger of flooding and falling masonry, the three of them fought through the choking dust and hanging steel girders and were helped out. 'I remember somebody getting me out of this hole . . . then putting me on his shoulder,' Maureen said. 'Our hair was just white, coughing . . . coughing . . .' Along with the few other survivors, they struggled to the nearby police station. They were badly bruised, and their feet were cut to ribbons. 'All you could get out of me was 'My shoes are gone.' . . . Two days before, Mum bought me a pair of shoes . . . with black ankle bands . . . Now, with me not having any shoes on, they put sacks round our feet.'

Over 200 people were killed in that shelter, many of them drowned. Some bodies were unidentifiable. One poor woman, who had kept her two young babies home that night because they had had whooping cough and cried and disturbed other people, lost her four older children, aged seven, nine, eleven and seventeen. The seventeen-year-old – a girl – had been told to take the younger children down to the shelter as usual and look after them. That tragic mother did not speak a word for months after.

Many of the victims were buried in a mass grave. After the war, the college was razed and a new school was built on the site. Maureen, who suffered lifelong emotional effects from the tragedy, says that she still finds it impossible to walk down Durning Road.

At that same time in early May, London underwent yet another night of horror; many who were there throughout the raids are convinced that the air raid on the night of 10 May 1941 was the worst of the war. It was certainly the night on which the most fatalities were recorded: 1,436 people killed, and nearly 2,000 seriously injured.

It was a still, clear night; there was a 'bomber's moon', and again the Thames was at a low ebb, adding to the immense difficulties the fire services faced. Paula, aged ten, who would soon leave London with her mother and spend several happy and relatively peaceful years in a cottage in the countryside, remembers it clearly – 'The throb of engines from the enemy aeroplanes, the whistle of the bombs as they fell, and the sound of impact as they hit the buildings and then the falling masonry. The memory is as though it was yesterday.'

The following morning the air over London was thick with clouds of gritty, choking dust and swirling fragments of charred paper. The sun was obscured, and a third of the city's streets were impassable. Westminster Abbey, the Tower of London, and the British Museum (where a quarter of a million books went up in smoke) were among the targets hit on that terrible night. Churchill, deeply emotional and supremely patriotic, was seen openly weeping over the damage sustained by the House of Commons.

But, although no one in the country knew it at the time, the heaviest of the German raids were drawing to an end. Secretly, the Luftwaffe was starting to regroup in preparation for opening a new eastern front – a consolidated attack by the German army on Russia. So, while the inhabitants of Britain's badly hit cities set about picking up their lives and carrying on, the raids, while they did not stop, became somewhat lighter and more random.

Nevertheless, for all the welcome respite, a residue of fear and dread remained. As well it might have, for three long, hard years later – just as it looked as though the end of the war might at last be in sight – Germany would begin hurling ever more lethal weaponry across the Channel towards London.

5

FOOD AND RATIONING, CLOTHES AND COUPONS: 1940 ON

The contents of an emergency store cupboard permitted for a family of four, 1942. Note the smart Harrods labels on the breakfast oats and coffee

Pat-a-loaf, pat-a-loaf
Baker's man,
Bake me some Wheatmeal
As fast as you can:
It builds up my health
And its taste is so good
I find that I **like**
Eating just what I should.

Ministry of Food advertisement aimed at getting children to eat
National Wheatmeal Bread – 1943

Everything that children love stopped early in the war.
A young girl living in Scotland and remembering happier times

As a treat I was given an OXO cube to suck.
A boy evacuated from London to a farm in Devon

As soon as war was declared and the Anderson shelter dug in, all over the UK families with gardens or allotments got down to the serious business of preparing to feed themselves.

Many parents and householders had been youngsters during the First World War, and they retained bitter childhood memories of severe shortages of even such staples as potatoes and margarine – shortages made worse by an inadequate rationing system. In 1939 Britain – an island nation, overdependent on cheap imported food from a vast empire – was again under threat. The German navy and its fleet of deadly U-boats prowled the Atlantic, intent on cutting off supplies, and the shipping lanes that were still open were urgently needed for military purposes.

Despite the government's stern disapproval, hoarding – largely of tinned food – was inevitable at first. Someone who lived in Dorset as a four-year-old girl said that one of her earliest childhood memories was of seeing tins piled high in the larder around that time, and being puzzled by this. Throughout the country, householders who could afford to were buying up non-perishable food against hard times ahead. But these goods would not last long, and late in the autumn of 1939 food prices were already rising and goods were disappearing fast from the shops.

In October, the Ministry of Agriculture grasped the initiative and declared, in the patronizing manner of the time, 'We want not only the big man with his plough, but the little man with his spade to get busy this autumn . . . Let "Dig for Victory" be the motto of everyone with a garden.' As instructed, the 'little man' and his family set to work. In fact the Dig for Victory was to range from humble plot to public park, to sports field and to walled ancestral acres. Six-year old Andrew in north London saw it happening in front of his eyes:

My walk to school was across some open ground that was a large play area at the beginning of the war, but in no time it had been dug up by tens of families into allotments. After a year of this activity a walk to school became more like a walk through a season-long vegetable market.

This activity was taken surprisingly seriously, it was practical and there were strong moral pressures too, from the government's vital Dig for Victory campaign.

Those lucky enough not to live in flats or the inner cities began to look with new zeal on familiar apple and plum trees in their back gardens, netted soft fruit bushes, and rows of vegetables and salad greens; even the homely hen and the common or garden chicken were suddenly perceived to be valuable family assets. Home-grown produce was to hand, and it became, and remained throughout the war, the mainstay of many family meals, bulking out an increasingly restricted diet.

An eleven-year-old schoolboy called David, living in a village near Cardiff, where his father worked as a Civil Servant, clearly recalled that wartime burst of frantic horticultural activity:

All over the country gardens and parks were being dug up. The catch phrase (one of the many) was 'Dig for Victory'. Father rallied to the call and provided us with all the vegetables we needed, and gave large quantities away to neighbours, family and friends.

He was a member of the local allotment association, and through this association he received the occasional gift parcel of seeds from America . . . so we were grateful to our unknown American benefactors for their generosity.

Myra, seven, went with her family to live in Manchester, where her father – who was above call-up age – took a job. He became a fire-watcher several nights a week, while her mother, who was unused to cooking and housework, struggled with all the domestic work – as well as painful chilblains from inadequate home heating. In this household too, growing food was taken very seriously:

My parents were very concerned that my brother and I should be well nourished, and my father established a garden producing large quantities of fruit and vegetables and we also kept chickens at the bottom of the garden. These were kept for a year or two and when the rate of lay decreased they were killed (by the butcher, not my parents!) and we ate them.

New chickens were bought . . . and I remember the horrid smell of 'mash' cooking. The hens also were given grit, bought in bags, to ensure that they laid eggs with strong shells. The taste of eggs from these free range birds was very different even from organic eggs today . . . When I grew up I never wanted to eat battery eggs, or chickens, and never did if I could avoid it.

Later, as food shortages and rationing started to bite, and precious fresh eggs in the shops were down to one per person per fortnight, chickens became increasingly important to many families, even those who had paid scant attention to the birds previously. This could produce some odd results.

Besides feeding, and shutting up, chickens, even quite small children were expected to do their bit on the home-grown-food production front. This is young Andrew again, in Palmer's Green: 'We didn't need an allotment as we had a small garden in front and a larger garden in the back, both of which we pressed into vegetable-growing service – especially tomatoes. I was put in charge of these, which included the manure patrol, standing by with a bucket and a coal shovel after the milk cart or other horse-drawn vehicle had passed by, with luck leaving a suitable offering for fertilizing.'

It was frequently, but not always, the case that children evacuated to the country had healthier lives and better food than those who stayed on in the cities, and, although most evacuees were delighted to return home as soon as possible, some of the city children left behind viewed the bounty of the countryside quite enviously.

Iris was eleven in 1939, and she stayed on in east London through-out the war because her mother felt that she needed her help with her new baby sister. Soon after her fourteenth birthday, in October 1941, Iris went to work in a factory scheduled to make aircraft instruments. Many of the children in her neighbourhood were evacuated with their schools at various times in the war, and Iris deeply resented what she saw as their unfair advantages.

In London, we kids never had enough to eat. The children who had been evacuated started filtering back from the country, and I was envious of the stories they told of cows and sheep and farmer's butter and milk and fresh vegetables.

I longed for the day when I could join the Land Army, as they took you at 17½. Because I was an older child I missed out on some things: under-fives got three eggs a week, concentrated orange juice and cod-liver oil . . . Whenever we saw a queue we joined it, even though we didn't know what it was for.

During the bitter winter of 1939–40, when little was happening on the land-war front and for month after month the merchant navy suffered continuing heavy losses from German U-boats, the first food rationing began. Petrol had been rationed almost immediately after the declaration of war, as expected, and the public knew that food rationing was inevitable – and imminent. The first three items to be rationed were bacon or ham (4 oz per person per week), butter (4 oz) and sugar (12 oz). With commendable efficiency, everyone was issued with a ration book: green (in addition to a regular one) for pregnant women; green for the under-fives; blue for children of school age. The monthly quota of rationed food had to be bought where the ration-book holder was registered – the local grocery store and/or butcher. A large north-London family was quick off the mark: 'We immediately registered at Sainsbury's – rather enthusiastically,' one of the children, then ten, recalled. And on a Monday morning, 8 January 1940, housewives set off for the shops with ration books in hand for the first time.

Michael, then nearly five, who had been evacuated from Birmingham to Cheltenham with his mother and brother, remembered the occasion well: 'My mother takes me into Cavendish House in the grand main street in the centre of town to register for rations. It is the biggest shop I have ever seen, with tall stacks of tins in the grocery department. I accidentally send one flying, but they are very understanding.'

Faced with the modest amounts available of foods that were an accepted part of most people's diet, the nation received a short, sharp shock. At a stroke, the war was no longer a matter of anxiously waiting for enemy bombers or hanging on each word of the BBC bulletins, or waving goodbye to Daddy – it was present in every home, in every kitchen, affecting every meal: from the comforting teaspoon of sugar stirred into a cup of tea or cocoa to the family's favourite Sunday roast, which was abruptly curtailed. Over the following years of wartime and beyond, the consumption of meat would fall by more than 20 per cent, poultry and fish by 40 per cent, sugar and syrup products by 30 per cent, and tomatoes and citrus fruits by 50 per cent – while consumption of that all-purpose wartime mainstay the potato rose by 40 per cent.

Michael, who had happily trotted by his mother to register the family ration books in Cheltenham, was soon beginning to make out letters, and by the following year he could grasp the meaning of some words. 'I am quite quick at learning to read, and can manage "Western National" on the side of the bus rather successfully. But there is a word on a faded picture in the window of our greengrocer's shop that is beyond me – "Fyffes".' As the popular ditty of the time put it:

> *Yes, we have no bananas,*
> *We have no bananas today . . .*

Indeed, the length and breadth of the country, greengrocers did *not*. And Michael's early reading puzzle must spark a thousand memories for the children of that wartime.

Bananas quickly disappeared for the duration, and there are stories of children being given a banana later in the war – possibly by a relative returned from serving overseas – and being so baffled that they promptly started eating it skin and all. Oranges, while extremely scarce, were occasionally available and were distributed in a strict order: pregnant mums, under-fives, and then schoolchildren. Susie, who went to live with her mother and brother in an old rented cottage in Gloucestershire, near relatives, after her father was sent overseas in 1942, has a vivid childhood memory of this treat. When her mother managed to get hold of a precious orange she insisted that Susie eat it in her bath, so that she could devour it as greedily and as messily as she liked. Much later in life, Susie said wryly that she remembered the occasion perfectly – and fancied that no fruit since had tasted quite so delicious.

Once the first jolt had passed, on the whole rationing was tolerated well – albeit with much grumbling. It has been said that Britain was a healthier nation then because of the shortage of fat (butter etc.) and sugar, and this is correct. But it was no accident: it was the result of careful planning. The Ministry of Food – motto: 'We Not Only Cope, We Care' – had done its homework thoroughly. Before rationing began, a committee of nutritionists had been appointed to work out the dietary essentials needed to keep the civilian population in good health, with particular attention paid to the requirements of children and babies, and for all the shortages – and the long, dreary queues for nothing very much – and the petty deprivations – their efforts helped to put the distribution of food in the UK in the Second World War on a sound and successful basis.

Snapshot after family snapshot of children in those wartime summers (taken despite the near impossibility of obtaining new films for a camera) shows skinny brown legs between cotton frocks or shorts and scuffed sandals or plimsolls as children pick fruit or pose with bucket and spade on a rare seaside outing. Slim, fit and well-nourished youngsters they look too – not an overweight child to be seen. A man who spent his wartime boyhood in a country town in

Surrey wondered whether those early habits of lean, good eating, without waste, instilled in many wartime children habits of thrift and health sense that lasted through a lifetime. He wrote, 'I can't think of many of my wartime contemporaries, male or female, who are noticeably overweight. Perhaps some of our consumption habits have followed us over the years.'

Rationing brought particular benefits to the underprivileged. The Beveridge Report (which would provide the blueprint for the future Welfare State) was published in 1942 and pointed the way to a more equitable post-war society. But ironically, as a by-product of wartime austerity, sweeping social changes were already under way before then. Over the course of six years of war, thanks to full employment and a far better quota of decent food through rationing than they were accustomed to, the ill-fed, pale urchins from the inner cities seen on every urban street corner before the war – and who, as evac-uees, had so appalled the genteel middle classes in 1939 – ceased to exist.

Marguerite Patten OBE is a well-known home economist, lecturer and broadcaster who worked for the Ministry of Food in the war. Spritely, energetic and pleasantly direct in manner, she wrote several wartime cookbooks, including the wittily titled *We'll Eat Again*, as well as giving impromptu cookery demonstrations wherever she felt she was needed and had an audience. The venues ranged from the market place in Cambridge, where she battled to be heard above the stallholders, to the Ministry of Food Advice Bureau in Harrod's, which she ran from 1943. Her sensible, imaginative recipes, attract-ively presented, sought to overcome the shortage of vital ingredients and make the most of whatever was available. She built up a huge fol-lowing, and did much to lift the morale of women who were faced with the wearisome daily task of feeding their families on very limited supplies.

Years later she wrote of those years:

Food was severely rationed from 1940 . . . and the population had to manage without many of the ingredients they had taken for granted in pre-war days, but they managed. The fact that adults kept fit and children grew strong and healthy must prove that the British at home won their battle, just as the Forces overseas were victorious. In fact, our diet during rationing years was very much in keeping with the advice on healthy eating given today.

It was during the war that the concept of school dinners was expanded from being a service available only to the very poor to providing all schoolchildren who wanted it with at least one hot meal a day. This was of great benefit to many mothers who were working long hours in factories or performing other war work. In 1936 it had been estimated that almost a quarter of low-income children had an inadequate diet; by 1945, one child in three was being fed at school either free or for a nominal charge. Schools also delivered food supplements to very young children. A woman who was no more than four at the time remembered, 'We used to queue up every morning for our daily dose of cod-liver oil and malt, or Virol.'

Colin was evacuated with his school to an idyllic village in Surrey, where his parents later joined him, moving in with a hospitable local family. His class combined with the village school, and, apart from slight overcrowding, the two groups of children got along very well. Colin's recollection of the well-meaning, but very amateur, provision of school dinners is a fond childhood memory:

Our school dinners were cooked and served in a separate building by the Ladies of the village. Yes, capital L. Some of them were titled personages doing their patriotic bit by feeding evacuees. No doubt they had servants to do the cooking at home, because the food was awful.

The main course always seemed to be tasteless mince with potatoes in every stage of composition from raw to dissolved. The puddings (we called them 'afters') were even worse. To this day I have a loathing for bread-and-butter pudding, and their tapioca, I swear, was derived from the nearby pond. I used to give most of my meal to a boy from Kent who always seemed to be hungry. He needed to be.

I didn't care. At home, there were pilchards and Marmite and Spam, all of which I loved, and still do.

Although most people who lived through the war would afterwards groan at the very mention of 'rationing', the public did recognize the need for these restrictions, and by and large accepted the justice of the scheme. Those who were children then particularly remember being deprived of all sweets and chocolate, which were strictly rationed from 1942. But, 'The pathetic sliver of butter', as Sarah, living in Scotland, remembered it, seems to have been what children recall most clearly of the initial rationing during those depressing winter months of 1940, and Sarah remained adamant that the food she yearned for most throughout the war was not sweets but butter. 'I hated the primrose-yellow woolly margarine that tasted like sawdust that was available everywhere, even at school. I longed for the shiny, unmistakable, beautiful slice of butter – a couple of ounces – that we were allowed once a week. I still have an insatiable desire for butter. My great aunt, after the war, used to eat half a pound of butter a day. She lived till she was ninety-seven.'

Rose, privately educated in Windsor, where her father was a housemaster in a public school, always had 'a feast', scoffing her butter ration in one go. Sally, a teenager, keen on sport and long bike rides, was not much bothered by the lack of sweets and other shortages, 'but butter was another matter. I adored butter, and pre-war would eat butter balls whenever I could get at them.'

The introduction of food rationing, which was later extended to clothing, was well managed from the beginning. It was the responsibility of Lord Woolton, whose name may bring a wry smile to those who remember it from their childhood – perhaps associated with the famous 'Woolton Pie'. Rightly or wrongly, this simple vegetable dish has become such a symbol of British wartime cooking, that Marguerite Patten's recipe is well worth reading.

When he was made Minister of Food in 1940, few – least of all Churchill, who appointed him – believed that Woolton had either the flair or the ability to bring off the difficult and delicate task of feeding the nation in wartime. But they were proved wrong. Much of the system's success was due to his insistence on thorough planning, fairness and good presentation. Although at times he came close to becoming a figure of fun, he was both trusted and respected. He had a real knack for getting his message across in a friendly manner, and he became perhaps the most popular wartime minister.

Born and educated in Manchester, Woolton had an unusually

Woolton Pie

COOKING TIME: ABOUT 1 HOUR   QUANTITY: 4 HELPINGS

This recipe is named after the Minister of Food – Lord Woolton. It is an adaptable recipe that you can change according to the ingredients you have available.

Dice and cook about 1 lb (450 g) of each of the following in salted water: potatoes (you could use parsnips if topping the pie with mashed potatoes), cauliflower, swedes, carrots – you could add turnips too. Strain but keep ¾ pint (450 ml) of the vegetable water.

Arrange the vegetables in a large pie dish or casserole. Add a little vegetable extract and about 1 oz (25 g) rolled oats or oatmeal to the vegetable liquid. Cook until thickened and pour over the vegetables; add 3–4 chopped spring onions.

Top with Potato Pastry* or with mashed potatoes and a very little grated cheese and heat in the centre of a moderately hot oven until golden brown. Serve with brown gravy.

This is at its best with tender young vegetables.

---

varied background for a top administrator of that era. After years of outstanding social work (partly in the most deprived areas of Liverpool), he moved into business management, running one of Manchester's famous department stores, John Lewis.

Woolton knew that he had to make allies of the housewife and her family, and in his first wireless broadcast as minister he struck just the right note. The hallmarks of rationing on the home front in this new war were to be moderation, good sense, and a cheerful attitude. Raising the sacred subject of the national drink, tea, Woolton cosily suggested, 'One teaspoon per person, and none for the pot . . .' But there was never any doubt that dietary restrictions would be severe,

---

* Blend 8 tablespoons of national flour with 4 tablespoons of mashed potato. Slightly soften 2 oz (50 g) of fat and blend with the potato mixture. It is rarely necessary to add any water to bind. Roll out thinly.

or that he did not mean business. In a broadcast on 8 July 1940 he barked, 'I am issuing an order prohibiting the use of sugar for the icing of cakes' – which promptly put a damper on children's wartime birthday parties and Christmases.

Another of his clever decisions was to give his support to the BBC's fifteen-minute radio programme, broadcast every weekday morning at 8.15, called *The Kitchen Front*. The programme was soon attracting some 14 million listeners, and the expression 'The Kitchen Front' became a stock phrase, used everywhere. Marguerite Patten was a frequent contributor, providing recipes and useful household hints. A sample tip, particularly appealing to children, was 'To bring a sparkle to a wartime Christmas or a birthday party, dip greenery, or holly, in a strong solution of Epsom salts. When dry it will be beautifully frosted.' She was also straightforward in acknowledging the problems every housewife faced on the food front, writing later:

Many of the ingredients available, such as dried egg and wartime (National) flour, were a challenge to any cook, but it was surprising how we learnt to cope with these and produce edible dishes . . . Virtually every cook in Britain behaved like a zealous squirrel – we bottled and/or dried fresh fruits; we salted beans; we prepared economical chutneys and pickles; we made the very best use of every available ingredient.

A girl in her teens growing up in Manchester always remembered that the family had to keep totally silent during *The Kitchen Front* as her mother frantically attempted to scribble down one of the rationing-friendly recipes. Among many, she might well have collected Marguerite Patten's recipe for fudge, a great favourite with wartime children, and well worth repeating here – perhaps with a caution to brush teeth very thoroughly after eating.

'The Radio Doctor' (Dr Charles Hill), was another memorable contributor to *The Kitchen Front*. His earthy comments, robustly delivered, undoubtedly influenced thousands of youngsters as they half listened during the early-morning rush to finish breakfast and get to school on time. Some of the good doctor's wise words, unconsciously absorbed, might have included, 'Don't come over all superior at the mention of fish and chips . . . it's first-class grub. That's true

---

Vanilla Fudge

ECONOMICAL RECIPE

1 lb (450 g) granulated sugar
½ pt (300 ml) milk
2 oz (50 g) butter
½ – 1 teaspoon vanilla essence

Put the ingredients into a strong saucepan. Stir over a low heat until the sugar has dissolved. Boil steadily, stirring only occasionally (to prevent the mixture burning), until the fudge reaches 'soft ball' stage or 114 °C/238 °F. Remove the pan from the heat and beat the mixture until it just begins to thicken and becomes opaque (cloudy) in appearance. This is very important in making fudge.

Grease an 8 in (20 cm) square sandwich tin with a little melted butter or oil. Pour in the fudge and leave until almost set; cut into neat pieces with a sharp knife. Leave in the tin until quite firm. Fudge does not need wrapping in waxed paper although this can be done if preferred.

---

whether it's dished up with dignity to a duke . . . or scoffed by the nipper from a newspaper spread out on his knees.' Sugar in food was dismissed as 'a menace', and liver and kidneys – classed as offal and never rationed – were described as 'very solid organs stuffed full of food'. Salad greens – including Dr Hill's favourite dandelion leaves – were recommended as an excellent source of vitamins.

Betty, ten, living in East Anglia, said, 'We grew a lot of fruit and vegetables in the garden, and gathered nettles and dandelion leaves and any other edible greens.' Dr Hill would have approved, and may even have influenced her family in their wide choice of salad ingredients.

The onset of rationing began a period of more than five years when the stamina and resourcefulness of the British housewife would be tested relentlessly. While the men were fighting on the battle front, wives and mothers on the home front faced their own daily struggle – gritty, dreary hard work, almost entirely unsung – and came through with flying colours. Gillian, then fifteen, wrote much later:

I remember my mother working for weeks in the summer to make jams and jellies and to bottle fruit with the surplus. I used to help her if she was still working at it when I came back from school. I remember the pride with which she looked at her rows of provisions for the winter months. It was worth all that hard work ... The rations were very small ... but I honestly think we ate a great deal better than many children today.

It was fortunate that rationing was introduced gradually and had built-in flexibility to alter amounts slightly, depending on availability, throughout the war. A points system, covering such items as tinned goods, biscuits and cereals, was added in December 1941: points were allocated to particular items, and everyone was allowed sixteen points per month (later raised to twenty) and allowed to use them as they wished to select from among these items in any shop of choice. This meant a fair deal for all, and it immediately brought back to the shops such treats as tinned meat and fruit – on points – which had by then either disappeared or become too expensive for the average family.

The country's food supplies dipped to their lowest level early in 1942, when imports from the Far East were severely curtailed by Japan's aggression. The rationing (points) noose tightened at roughly three-monthly intervals: cheese, fresh eggs, margarine and cooking fats, and milk were the first to be affected, then dried fruit, mince-meat, rice, sago, tapioca and pulses; tinned fruit, tomatoes and peas; condensed milk and breakfast cereals; jam, marmalade, syrup and treacle; biscuits, lemon curd, honey; oat flakes and rolled oats; and finally chocolate and sweets (8 oz per four weeks, which was soon raised to 12 oz).

Wartime children did not take kindly to sweet-rationing, but many found ways round the system through donations from parents and other relatives – and even the occasional non-sweet-eater. Dinah and her brother, who lived close to the south coast, had the good fortune to have soldiers billeted on their parents' land. 'They were encamped in our orchard and paddocks and took pity on us – I think we must have been awful scroungers – and gave us their sweet rations.'

Some children could never eke out their ration over four long weeks. Three sisters who all doted on sweets remembered that 'Sweets went on ration, and of course we soon used up our monthly amount of ¾ lb within the first week. And as soon as the next month's ration was available – which was the first Sunday of the month – we would all rush off to buy some more.' Carrie and her brother, aged eight and ten, were more provident: 'As we could not buy sweets, and used our ration carefully, we used to eat raw carrots . . . You could buy Victory Lozenges unrationed, so we had those and used to suck them when we went down to the air-raid shelter during raids . . . We were told they would keep out the cold and the dampness.' Another brother and sister, in Derbyshire, experimented with whatever was available when the precious rations ran out: 'I remember the village shop had some revolting things called "Herbal Tablets", which were off ration, and we were sometimes reduced to buying those.'

Decades later, the wartime children still marvel at their mothers' ingenuity in coping in so many different ways and with so many different demands. Pat, speaking of those years recently, was still amazed at how well her mother managed the family's food demands. In 1939 Pat herself was at school in Surrey, where she lived with her parents and older sister. Her father was away on active service for most of the war. She left school in 1941, did a short secretarial course, and went straight into an office job, taking singing lessons when she could fit them in. After the war she trained as a singer. She gives a clear account of some of her wartime experiences of food and rationing:

Food was not too bad at the beginning of the war, but as rationing became more stringent we lived on a very meagre diet of vegetables and a bit of meat and, later on, Spam from America. This was to bulk up on the restricted meat, which was only a few ounces a week. My mother would buy lamb chops or minced beef – or in the winter a little bit of beef. If the butcher favoured you, he might occasionally save you some offal such as liver . . . Horsemeat was available, and my aunt would make a very good meat pie out of it by soaking the meat in vinegar first.

We had a neighbour who kept rabbits. They were beautiful creatures, and I could not bear to think of them as alive and running round, but we were so hungry I'm ashamed to say we stifled our feelings! We could also get tinned fish such as herrings and pilchards and made an evening meal of them, usually in a fish pie.

'How my Mum managed to pack our lunch up every day was amazing,' a man who was then an apprentice electrician in Hull said, looking back at a time of extreme food shortages and youthful, ravenous appetites. 'Rations was meagre . . . We had cold whale-meat sausages – not too bad to eat, but they left an awful oily smell round the house after cooking. Then there was Spam in many forms – cold sliced or cooked in batter. We had a greengage tree in the garden, so nothing but greengage jam for years! The one fresh egg we had was best scrambled – it looked more that way.'

Millie, who left school in 1943 and went straight into war work, remembered her own simple packed lunches: 'Sandwiches for school or – later – work were usually beetroot and salad, with an occasional delicious egg. I don't remember much ham being available . . . Of course there were the occasional field days such as when we were given a piece of freshly caught salmon.'

With supplies cut off from the Channel Islands and Brittany, even the zesty onion was rare until home-grown varieties became available. Faith, living in a large house in London, recalled that when her mother was given a supply (packed in a shoebox) by a friend in the country she immediately stashed it on top of a wardrobe. Dried herbs were not always obtainable, but fresh ones were invaluable. Rationing of cheese, a valuable source of protein and providing some taste in the uniformly bland cooking, hit families hard. The allowance was minuscule – 1 oz per week – although as stocks improved this was doubled. Young Michael, in Cheltenham, sometimes watched their weekly sliver as it disappeared rapidly: 'Our rations are delivered every week, neat little parcels wrapped in white paper and tied with string. My mother sometimes absent-mindedly eats the (minute) cheese ration while she is unwrapping something else.'

After leaving school, Ron, sixteen, worked as an errand boy in a grocery shop. He later well remembered preparing some of those meagre rations:

I used to weigh up the sugar once weekly into its blue bags in accordance with the RULES PER FAMILY . . . and I remember skinning a 56 lb round Cheddar cheese and cutting it into the required amounts per family – not very much of it either when you think . . .

In those days, everything essential appeared to be rationed. On my way to and from work, if something had 'come in' in one of the shops it didn't matter what it was . . . if you saw a queue, you joined it!

Daphne, who was eleven when the war began and lived with her mother and brother in the Midlands, truly admired her mother's ability to feed them all – and very well too:

At the beginning of the war, many 'upper-class' wives had hardly ever been into the kitchen and could barely boil an egg! Luckily, my grandfather had insisted that his daughters should go to a cookery course when they left school, so my mother was an excellent cook and very imaginative. She performed minor miracles . . . I remember that during the most difficult times she produced 'battered sprouts' and 'Lucky Dip' – whatever that was! I don't ever remember feeling really hungry.

Halfway through the war, Dick, who was ten, said that his mother baked something that was known as 'The Nothing Cake'; it consisted of flour, custard powder and dried egg – 'and my sister and I thought it was very good.' Sheila, aged eleven and living in Devon, her father overseas, anxiously watched her mother's daily battle with the meat ration – 'all the same, day in and day out. And although my mother was not a fancy cook she still managed to produce some very tasty meals with cheap cuts of meat.'

It was generally thought that larger families with several ration books fared better than people living alone, or a couple. And it was widely accepted that, although rationed like everyone else, the well-off had access to a much wider variety of food – particularly meat. Harry, a sixth-former at boarding school in 1942, and soon to be called up into the army, said that his parents had frequent gifts of pheasants and rabbits from country relatives: 'The upper crust fared a lot better than most as they could get hold of game, either from certain shops or from friends.' However, a family from London visiting relatives who lived in the country, close to a farm and surrounded by fertile fields, found to their surprise that much the same food restrictions and shortages were in place as in the city. The son, then a youngster of fourteen, remembered, 'The war was a great leveller, and, as we were all so clearly in the same boat, few thought or expected that they should have preference.'

Fish was never rationed, but it was hard to come by and the queues outside the fishmongers were long, and could become bad tempered as frustration set in. Snoek, a long, slender fish caught in the seas around Africa, was often available, but never became really popular. Salted cod was relatively plentiful at times. Home economists recommended that it be soaked in water for forty-eight hours before cooking and then be treated as fresh fish; but it was considered tasteless, and was usually cooked only if nothing else was available. Whalemeat, frequently turned to in desperation, was loathed – 'tough and fishy', 'like fishy liver' and 'smelling of stale oil' were some of the wartime children's kinder descriptions of it. Jenny, then aged ten and at school in Wales, remembered all her life the sheer revulsion of being faced by a plate of 'great purple slabs of whalemeat'.

Sausages were never rationed but, like good-quality fish, were very scarce and the objects of much queuing. Jimmy, fifteen, said that when his mother managed to get hold of a few from a friendly butcher he and his siblings learned to be cautious about their taste. No one was quite sure about the sausage fillings, which, apart from hefty amounts of bread, were of unknown composition – and probably a good thing too. His older brother, home on leave from the RAF, teased his mother mercilessly, referring to her prized sausages as one of the 'sweet mysteries of life'.

It is worth remembering that, if humans found rationing a hard and dreary business – as they did – much-loved domestic pets had an even more difficult war. Dogs and cats got by with scraps from the family eked out with unpalatable vegetables, and were often found raiding local bins and even pig swills. Feeding bread to wild birds, officially forbidden, was done meagrely and surreptitiously – a few stale crumbs scattered after dark.

In 1941, with stocks in Britain seriously depleted, vital shipments of badly needed food from the USA began reaching the country. This was part of the Anglo-American Lend-Lease Treaty: in exchange for Britain granting long leases on certain of its Caribbean and western Atlantic territories, basic food supplies would be shipped regularly to the UK – among them dried egg, lard, evaporated milk, bacon, beans and tinned meat. The meat introduced the population to the notorious Spam, which rapidly became an object of either great love or extreme dislike, as it has remained. Once these stocks were well distributed and accepted, splurging many points on a large tin of American meat, perhaps enough ham for three substantial family meals, became the housewife's big treat and was considered a clever food investment.

Lend-Lease also introduced the British public to dried egg and 'household' (powdered) milk.* While most people loathed dried egg (one packet per person every four weeks), young children sometimes thought differently and were ready to give it the benefit of the doubt. Ruth, whose mother was a clever cook, was not alone in secretly enjoying the taste: 'I always thought that an omelette made with this substitute tasted better than with a real egg.' Dinah, nine, who lived in a large household in Sussex, remembered rationing as severe and monotonous. And, although the family had access to some fresh eggs, she too preferred them dried: 'We managed on a rather restricted diet like everyone else . . . An uncle living in America once sent us a parcel of dried bananas, which were quite strange. But what I really loved was dried eggs!'

Milk was restricted, but evaporated (household) dried milk – said by many wartime children to have tasted vile in tea – was a ready back-up. Michael, in Cheltenham, grew fond of the local milkman and appeared unaware of any shortage:

Our milk is delivered by a dapper little man called Bill who drives a horse and trap which carries a sign 'Gloucestershire Dairy'. The milk is carried in a churn, and Bill scoops our allowance out with a sort of tin can on a stick and pours it into a jug which my mother leaves at the top of the front steps outside our front door.

* 1 tablespoon dried egg powder + 2 tablespoons of water = 1 egg
4 tablespoons milk powder + 1 pint lukewarm water = 1 pint skimmed milk

Bill wears riding breeches and shiny brown boots with gaiters. We are at the end of his delivery run, so he rarely arrives before noon, but there is always enough milk left. We can usually get more if we want it.

Tea rationing, at a meagre 2 oz per week, was imposed in July 1942 and cast a pall of gloom over a country where a 'cuppa' has long been a mainstay of life. An American journalist, downing a pint at a country pub the night tea became rationed, thought it very strange that the conversation of his fellow drinkers was confined to 'what "my old woman" had said about the government as a result', – while the war, then at its lowest point for Britain, was ignored. Further bad news on the tea-drinking front came when it was ruled that no tea ration for children, which adults had counted on, would be allowed. Bread was never rationed, but white bread became a luxury, and from April 1942 the government tried hard to popularize the mud-brown and dreaded National Loaf, which was universally described as 'nasty, dirty, dark, coarse and indigestible'. Griffin, ten, who lived in Wales, swore he remembered his grandmother contemptuously cutting it in pieces, and after much soaking, feeding it to the family pig. It might have been apocryphal, or an effort to cheer people up, but it was put about that the dreaded loaf had rare aphrodisiac properties – the rumour, it was whispered, was spread by none other than the good Minister himself.

A woman living in the Midlands, who had been a wartime child – she was four in 1939 – made some perceptive comments on rationing and shortages, putting the hardships into perspective:

It is easy to look back . . . and say, 'We had it tough' . . . but for us young kids there was little remembrance of groaning tables and a vast choice of foodstuffs . . . The 'points' system for many items like biscuits and cereals and tinned fruit was fairer, and reduced the 'under the counter' practice somewhat. Queuing when there were rumours of a sausage supply became a natural way of life. So was improvising, making do . . .

Still, the list of what was *not* rationed is longer than many people appreciate. All vegetables – including of course the ever useful potato – plus fish, bread, milk, fruit . . . True, we didn't have bananas or oranges, but we had tomatoes, apples, pears, all the summer fruits – including some extra sugar allowed for jam-making. And flour and pickles and potted meats. Many people today in famine-stricken areas of the world would marvel at how well we were fed!

As well as feeling the deprivation of not being able to buy sweets when they felt like it, most children also missed out on the childhood pleasure of licking an ice cream on a hot summer's afternoon. Sarah, quite enjoying her wartime in Scotland with her mother and sister, apart from feeling constantly cold, clearly longed for her favourite pre-war ice. 'The last ones to go were Lyons, – the ones I liked best. They looked like cylinders with paper round the outside that was removed and they were put in a cone. Even my adored comic, *Magic*, vanished.'

Even when rationing and shortages were at their most stringent, few children went hungry. 'I remember Mum using just a few vegetables from the garden and a stock cube to make dinner,' June, in East Anglia, said cheerfully enough. There was no excess; nothing was wasted, and even the younger children understood that such food as there was had to be used sparingly and well. Second helpings of relished food were rare. Andrew, living in north London, was frequently aware that he could happily have eaten a bit more, especially when it came to his favourite tinned peaches. 'Those were the days of rumbling tummies,' he said.

Yet these discomforts were minor compared to those of the British children who were trapped in the Channel Islands, under German occupation. Tony, who lived in Jersey with his family throughout the war, remembered, 'Towards the end of the war, after D-Day, the islands were cut off from all supplies. My dad, brother and I went down to a rocky bit of the seashore to collect limpets. Six yards away from us was a party of German sailors, who were also approaching starvation, intent on the same task. We ignored one another. Thank God, just in time, the International Red Cross arrived with food.'

Yvette, trapped in Brittany with her English mother and sibling when France fell in 1940, found living for five years under German occupation hard. Her family, too, was not far from starvation:

Rationing started and was strict. Fortunately our cousins were farmers and there was also a flour mill in the family, so we had help with butter and flour. The black market and bartering started to flourish . . . We started to keep rabbits and chickens. Milk was fetched daily from a farm 1 kilometre away . . .

But towards the end of the war all food was very scarce and there was no electricity. Bread was a brown sticky mess with maggots . . . One day we thought the Germans had left their camp near by, so we raided their stores for food. We found very little . . . Then they came back, angry, and started searching all the houses. The Germans had spotted our chickens and rabbits, and stole them a few days before Christmas. We had literally no food left – we lived on turnips.

With fresh fruits and vegetables unrationed throughout, there was no lack of bulk or vitamins. The Ministry of Food tirelessly encouraged children to eat their home-grown vegetables, especially carrots and potatoes. Taking a leaf from the popular kids' comics, a cartoon character in the shape of a potato, with a beaming face and spidery legs and known as 'Potato Pete', was soon plastered over newspapers and magazines, pumping up good will. He even had his own 'Song of Potato Pete':

> *Potatoes new, potatoes old*
> *Potatoes (in a salad) cold*
> *Potatoes baked or mashed or fried*
> *Potatoes whole, potato pied*
> *Enjoy them all, including chips*
> *Remembering spuds don't come in ships!*

Potatoes were one thing, and there was little choice for active, famished children but to eat them up. However, most people did draw the line at the Ministry's other bee in its bonnet: weird and fanciful uses for carrots – or 'Bright treasures dug from good British earth', as it rather absurdly described them. Children were encouraged to believe that carrots had magic properties, including helping people see in the dark or the blackout, for which purpose they were devoured by night-fighter pilots – which was definitely not the case. Certainly they were useful, and available, but the Ministry's 1941 recipe for 'Carrot Flan . . . reminds you of Apricot Flan – but has a deliciousness all its own' met with a resounding thumbs down. Other over-imaginative carrot recipes fared little better. A brother and sister in Birmingham never forgot their father's reaction to the carrot marmalade that their mother, with no oranges available, had struggled to make. 'After a single mouthful, he simply picked up the pot, walked out into the garden, and dumped it on the compost heap.' The hilarity this caused has become a family legend.

It was the monotony of meals – the lack of variety – and the absence of small pleasures that depressed people. Except for the very young, who knew nothing else, children longed for a change, excitement, something new. Whatever was on hand, whether in the garden or from nearly empty shops, had to be used again and again and again. One schoolboy in Dorset later recalled that 'We had to utilize whatever fruit we could get for jams and puddings and so on. So one summer Mother really went to town with damsons, which we grew and had a glut of, and every meal featured this fruit for months on end.' Sam, evacuated to Wales for three years, was put off sandwiches for life when faced with unappetizing examples day after day: 'The woman I was billeted with had absolutely no imagination concerning food variety. Every day, without exception, my brother and I were given dry white-bread-and-cheese sandwiches for supper.'

Fortunately, most mothers and housewives had the energy and the spirit to work wonders with whatever ingredients were to hand. As she later looked back to, say, the summer of 1943 or 1944, Marguerite Patten chose a simple, tasty family supper menu from one of her wartime cookery books – one she might well have cooked for her own family (see pages 203–5). The first course was optional; the main course was very popular and one of her personal favourites. Children, she said, found all these recipes appealing.

It is impossible to exaggerate the pleasure of 'treats' in the dreary wartime diet: a tin of fruit salad or tinned salmon bought with saved points, or some liver or sausages put aside by a well-disposed butcher, made for a red-letter day, and lifted the whole family's spirits. Such harmless bits of favouritism – which could in no way be described as the expensive, and rather sinister, black market – gave rise to the term 'under the counter'. This, literally, was where the treats came from. Christopher, a teenager who described himself as 'the family queuer',

Bortsch

COOKING TIME: 2HRS 5 MINUTES
QUANTITY: 4 HELPINGS

1 oz (25 g) dripping or margarine
1 large raw beetroot, peeled and grated
2 potatoes, peeled and chopped or grated
1 carrot, peeled and chopped or grated
1 onion, peeled and chopped or grated
12 oz (350 g) cabbage, chopped or grated
2 tomatoes, chopped
2 bay leaves
Stock or water
Salt and pepper
Pinch mixed herbs
Chopped parsley

Melt the dripping or margarine in a pan and fry the beetroot for about 5 minutes. Put all the vegetables and bay leaves in a saucepan, together with the beetroot. Completely cover with water or stock and bring to the boil. Remove any scum. Put on the lid and simmer slowly for 2 hours. Add seasoning and a pinch of mixed herbs. Serve garnished with parsley.

(Note: All things Russian, particularly food and recipes, came into vogue when the Soviet Union became Britain's ally.)

said that 'If you went to the butcher's shop and managed to get a few slices of corned beef, something extra he had saved under the counter, it was a real treat . . . The same thing with a precious tin of fruit, or liver, or a couple of oranges.'

Lots of sharp-eyed schoolchildren were on the hunt for anything special, or an unexpected queue, spotted after the school day. Mavis, living in Birmingham, remembered this well, and went off in the mornings well prepared to take advantage of a lucky windfall: 'Mum gave me some money every day when I went to school, so that as I

Cheese, Tomato and Potato Loaf

PREPARATION TIME: 30 MINUTES
COOKING TIME: 35 MINUTES   QUANTITY: 4 HELPINGS

1 lb (450 g) cooked new potatoes
12 oz (350 g) tomatoes
1 oz (25 g) margarine
1 oz (25 g) flour
7 ½ fl. oz (225 ml) milk, or milk and vegetable stock
3 oz (75 g) cheese, grated
Salt and pepper
To coat the tin: ½ oz (15 g) margarine,
1 oz (25 g) crisp fine breadcrumbs

Cut the potatoes into slices about ½ inch (1 cm) thick. Cut the tomatoes into slightly thicker slices. Heat the margarine in a saucepan, add the flour, then the milk or the milk and vegetable water. Stir or whisk briskly as the sauce comes to the boil and thickens. Remove from the heat, add the cheese and seasoning.

Grease a 2 lb (900 g) loaf tin or use an oval casserole and coat with the breadcrumbs. Preheat the oven to 180 ºC (350 ºF), Gas Mark 4.

Arrange about a third of the potatoes in a neat layer in the container, cover with a little sauce and half the tomatoes. Put in half the remaining potatoes, with the rest of the sauce and tomatoes. Add a final layer of potatoes. Cover the dish with margarine paper and bake in the preheated oven for 30–35 minutes. Turn out and serve hot with a salad.

passed the shops on the way home I could join the queues for any tasty treat that might be available without coupons.'

Sally, in East Anglia, had left school and was working in a local bank. A couple of times the greengrocer managed to get hold of bananas, which were as scarce as gold dust. 'When we got wind of this

Fruit Amber

This is a very good way to make a special pudding with a relatively small amount of fruit. If you can spare a fresh egg then the pudding can have a meringue on top.

12 oz (350 g) fruit
Little water
1–2 oz (25–50 g) sugar, or to taste
2 oz (50 g) soft breadcrumbs
2 reconstituted dried eggs
¼ pint (150 ml) milk

Heat the oven to 160 °C (325 °F), Gas Mark 3. Prepare the fruit. Apples should be peeled, cored and sliced; plums can be halved and stoned.

If using very firm fruit, such as apples or plums, pre-cook them for a short time in a saucepan with 2–3 tablespoons water and sugar to taste. The fruit should be almost, but not quite, cooked, then it should be mashed to make a purée.

With soft fruit all you need to do is mash this, without pre-cooking, to make a purée.

Blend the sugar with the fruit, if this has not been used in cooking, add the breadcrumbs and mix well. Whisk the eggs and milk together and add to the other ingredients.

Grease a 1½ pint (900 ml) pie dish, add the fruit mixture and bake in the preheated oven for 35 minutes, or until firm. Serve as soon as possible after baking.

on the grapevine we hurried to the shop, and sure enough there was a bunch of cardboard bananas hanging on the door window and this meant he had obtained a few bananas for sale.'

Treats came in many circumstances. Tommy, who lived on a farm in the middle of Yorkshire, was handed one on a plate while biking home from school with his friends: 'A vanload of biscuits had been thrown all over the place after the van had skidded on a bit of rough road over the moors and the driver had left the scene to get help . . . And as you can imagine, this was a paradise for little boys!'

Young as she was, Helena, living with her mother and aunt above the small family grocery shop in a suburb of Birmingham, saw the points and rationing system from the other side of the counter. Her mother, who was running the shop while her father was in the forces, found managing the rationing and dispensing the occasional goodies extremely stressful:

There was no hope of selling the shop during the war, and handling the complexities of the rationing system was a truly demanding job . . . Rationing really was the bane of my mother's life. It wasn't so much the staples which she had to apportion to her customers; that depended strictly, at least in her shop, on what coupons one had. She was rightly hostile to the 'black market'. But every now and then deliveries of a few cans of 'extras' would arrive – pineapple say. Then she had to decide whose turn it was to have a treat, and of course face the complaints of those who didn't get one.

We ourselves got only our fair share, and my mother was strict about doling out the few goodies she had. I was deeply hurt as a small child to hear a boy in the queue in our shop for (almost unobtainable) ice cream say, 'Bet *she* gets all she wants.' Of course I didn't.

Eating out was a rare experience for most children. Anna, who left school during the war and commuted to her office job in London from Surrey every day, made good use of what inexpensive restaurants there were, going out occasionally with friends for a meal.

You could eat in restaurants, and we did sometimes, and Lyons' Corner House was much frequented. The salad bar gave excellent value for money – about 2 shillings for as much as you liked. The meal included a bowl of soup, salad and bread . . .

A favourite meal of the time was Vienna steak. I really don't know what it consisted of – probably bread and some kind of meat mixed with herbs. It was usually tasty and it made a pleasant change.

By late in 1943, there were other changes afoot. Following Japan's attack on the American fleet at Pearl Harbor on 7 December 1941 –

that 'day of infamy' as President Roosevelt so bitterly denounced it – America had entered the war as a full Allied partner. Now, as the build-up to D-Day got going, increasing numbers of American servicemen established themselves in communities all over the UK. To Michael, then nearly eight, their presence in Cheltenham was miraculous; so picture his eyes, big as saucers:

The house next door has become a billet for American army officers. Their cooks, stewards and batmen all seem to be war heroes with rows of medals, badges, chevrons, flashes etc. and have taken over the basement level and turned it into a palace of unbelievable luxury, with a shower room, a fridge the size of a bus, full of help-yourself Coca-Cola, great big armchairs, comic supplements – you name it.

My friends and I are the most shameless scroungers you ever met – and they are very generous to us. They eat 'chow', which a jeep brings in a big urn with a lid on, and they are happy to let us eat with them sometimes. They have enormous tins of fruit salad too – far bigger than anything my mother could ever get on points. They know that, while we have just enough food, we do appreciate treats.

They have adopted a couple of semi-wild dogs, and I am quite frightened of them. One day the dogs raid our front doorstep and steal our milk from its jug. I tell the Americans what happened, and later on two GIs come round and apologize profusely to my mother, bringing with them as a gift the biggest tin of powdered milk you ever saw.

From the beginning, as part of the government's recognition of the vital importance of keeping the nation healthy on the home front, as well as in the forces, the physical well-being of all Britain's children – especially the babies and the very young – was seriously addressed for the first time in history. Emergency maternity homes, set up in requisitioned premises, went a long way towards making provision of prenatal and delivery care more equitable, and pregnant women were given a high priority in evacuation from cities under attack.

During the war, the status of babies – and their mothers – rose suddenly and dramatically, and in the grimness of 1942, after years of decline, the nation's birth rate began to climb – through either desperation or innate optimism. It continued to climb until the end of the war and beyond. 'I took the risk of bringing a baby into the world while there was a war on . . . as I wanted to have something if my husband did not come back' was the comment of one woman whose husband was entering the forces at that dangerous time. Such sentiments must have been present in the minds of many young women, and their menfolk, as they snatched at suddenly granted leaves and faced the real possibility that it might be their last time together.

During the six years of war, more than 4½ million babies were born in the UK, and, at a time of strict rationing and shortages, enlightened efforts were made to ensure their healthy start in life. Young men and women had taken a gamble on parenthood, and their own futures, and it was successful. An experienced maternity nurse, when asked about the condition of wartime babies, declared stoutly that they were 'As good – and better!' than those born in peacetime. Ironically, except during the early chaotic months, the war years were a fine time to be either a pregnant mum or a baby – for all mums and all babies, but particularly for the underprivileged.

Except when air raids on major cities fractured all basic services, decent maternity care for mothers and infants was available either free or at a nominal cost. Extra milk, free concentrated orange juice and cod-liver oil were recommended during pregnancy and were obtained via the blessed green ration book. Whatever toll the wartime stresses of family separation and anxiety may have taken, the country produced healthier infants than ever before, and the mortality rate among newborns declined.

However, all these chipper babies stuffed with the government's orange juice, and their mums, were also subject to the punitive lack of goods of all kinds on the domestic market. Babies' basic necessities – cots and prams, clothes and nappies – were hard or impossible to obtain, and new mothers had to make do with what they had, or borrow or swap what they could.

Goods of all kinds – from handy torches (and batteries) used for navigating in the blackout to make-up, to bicycles and lavatory paper – quickly became scarce or unobtainable. Soon after the beginning of the war, with synthetic materials all going into vital war production, the manufacture of toys virtually ceased. By 1944 the only toys available were of poor quality and extremely expensive, and few parents thought them worth buying. With no balloons, candles or paper hats, older children had to make do with whatever they could create for themselves for birthday-party decorations. A popular way round the lack of candles for the birthday cake (which might well have been made without eggs or icing of any kind) was a single utilitarian candle which the child blew out as many times as their age. The production of bicycles, which were widely used by both children and adults, was cut by two-thirds; and with skilled workers now in factories it was hard to get anything repaired, even a cherished wireless.

With all production for the home front drastically scaled down, and most available manpower and factory space given over to the war effort, there was little variety in tinned foods, biscuits, cereals, cleaning materials and so on. Brand names had disappeared. Soft drinks, plentiful before the war, were whittled down to a handful: 'Orange Squash, S.W. 153' was a typical drab label on a row of plain bottles in a food store. And the notice in the window of a chemist's shop in Southampton in 1941 gives a graphic idea of how hard it would become to maintain decent standards in everyday domestic family life:

WE REGRET WE ARE UNABLE TO SUPPLY:

Vacuum flasks
Saccharines
Lipsticks
Rouges
All tubes of vanishing cream
Rolls razors
Rolls razor blades
Gillette razor blades
Brushless shaving cream
Nivea cream
Barley Sugar

Until Further Notice

Once food rationing had begun, the public assumed that clothes rationing would follow and that, whatever the tribulations, it would make for a fairer distribution of such stocks as were available. Yet clothes rationing was considered a political minefield: Churchill, more than anyone, was strongly opposed, and grumpily outspoken in his views. He stuck firmly to the formal and highly individualistic dress code to which he was accustomed, and expected everyone else to do the same. According to a Civil Servant who saw him frequently, the Prime Minister's usual attire was 'short black coat, striped trousers, a blue bow tie with white spots and impeccably clean linen'. His occasional sartorial eccentricities included his famous siren suits, which were always immaculately tailored, and which he referred to as his 'rompers'.

A fastidious dresser, born and bred to aristocratic Victorian standards, he would have no truck with the idea of clothing restrictions, and peevishly accused the unfortunate Minister of Trade, Oliver Lyttelton, of wishing to reduce the population to going about in 'rags and tatters'. However, Lyttelton stuck to his guns, won his point, and carried the scheme through very successfully and largely with the support of the public.

Clothes rationing started on 1 June 1941. Everyone was issued with sixty-six coupons for a twelve-month period, and items of clothing were apportioned points: coat or blazer, 13; two handkerchiefs, 1; a dress, 11; underwear, 3 per item; stockings, 2. Hats and caps did not require coupons and therefore attracted a good deal of wartime attention. Children's clothes needed fewer coupons, allowing for growth.

Just as when points were put on desirable foodstuffs, items that had become expensive and were bought largely by the better off now became available to everyone, in all price ranges, on a more equitable basis. After the rigid clothing protocol of the 1930s, many men claimed to find clothes rationing, and the consequent informality, rather a blessing; scruffy little boys, used to being nagged at to be neat, must have felt the same. Boarding schools were sympathetic to uniform problems, and attempted to keep up their usual standards by encouraging a large pool of second-hand clothes of all kinds, including sports gear. At Cheltenham Ladies' College, hand-me-down regulation green overcoats, skirts and frocks were regarded as normal, a sensible practice that continued long after the end of the war. Only

Eton attempted to maintain strict sartorial standards, though boys were excused from carrying top hats into the shelters.

Although very much aware of the make-do-and-mend spirit, the frequently darned socks and home-knitted jumpers, and the occasional overcoat made out of blankets, younger children took these shortages in their stride. Elizabeth, living in Scotland with her mother and sister, said, 'My mother was always knitting jumpers and making skirts – out of anything she could obtain with our coupons. She even made us dresses out of rather exotic dusters that did not require any coupons. We had to have very long boots up to our thighs, because of the depth of the snow in winter. But nevertheless I was always cold, and the thing I can remember most about those war years was the cold – and how I hated it.'

Coal shortages (each household was allowed 1 ton per month) meant that open fires were luxuries to be carefully tended, hot water was at a premium, and baths were shallow and tepid. Chilblains were common among adults and children alike, and, with few buses and no cars, weatherproof clothes were essential, particularly for long walks to and from school. Warm clothing of all kinds was patched and mended and often made at home from whatever fabric was to hand. Evelyn, in Ipswich, said:

My mother often would make clothes for me from old clothes we no longer wore, using the reverse side of the cloth because the pattern was brighter and the material not plucked. She would also unpick old jumpers that had holes in the elbows, wind the wool round a thick book, tie up the skeins, and wash them. We had lots of jumpers made from oddments – different coloured stripes, which looked quite attractive. (We thought so anyway!)

I saw on television recently that a factory in Norfolk was producing 'distressed' woollens for export. These were knitwear items with holes made in them deliberately, and gloves with frayed cuffs etc. How the tables can turn in over half a century!

Jim, growing up in a large family in Yorkshire, said that 'make do and mend' became a way of life – clothes being handed round from one sibling to another as a matter of course. 'Clothes and shoes were passed down in families, or even to and from friends. Shoes were a bit of a problem: they were hard to come by, and required, I think, seven coupons . . . Sometimes the top leather was cut from the toe of a shoe or sandal to make it fit a bit longer. Or a thick cardboard sock was made for the inside of a shoe . . . We had no dressing gowns because of the coupons, and used to wear our overcoats instead.'

Even for children, overcoats were heavy on coupons and had to be conserved for as long as possible. Sheila, in her teens, remembered hers, and her mother's ingenuity in making it, with affection. 'The kind of topcoats we wore then took an enormous number of coupons, so you had to save for years to buy a new one. So my mother found some checked blankets which were either coupon-free or low on coupons and made me a coat from two of them. It was very smart: a dark blue background with a slightly shaggy check – plain, but very warm.'

Tony, living in the Channel Islands under German occupation, had a hard time keeping himself respectably clothed:

When I was about thirteen, my only surviving pair of (short) pants were more patches than pants. So my elder brother had to take me to some local government office where I was 'inspected' by a lady behind a desk who issued a permit to buy what were my first long trousers – French. I must have been an interesting sight: long skinny legs, tiny patchwork pants, and wooden-sole shoes! Incidentally, even with a pair of long pants, I still had to wait until I was fourteen before I got my ID card and was then allowed to go to a cinema.

Inevitably, the sad lack of pretty clothes, make-up and accessories fell hardest on young girls when they left school for their first jobs and started to take an interest in their appearance. A girl who left school at seventeen in 1941 said that she believed 'teenage girls then were about three or four years less mature than they are now, so at about seventeen I was younger in many ways than a thirteen-year-old is now. We didn't wear make-up or high heels or silk stockings until after we had left school.'

Starting a university course in Southampton in 1944, Gillian said that all the clothing she owned, in addition to some underwear and shoes, consisted of two dresses, one skirt, one blouse, one jumper and an overcoat. Pat who worked in an office for the last three years of the war, and later trained as a professional singer, also found getting the right clothes very difficult, but made the most of the occasional glorious splurge.

For me, clothes were always a bit of a problem as I started work without an adult wardrobe, so I was always looking round – hopefully – for bits and pieces. Underwear was difficult, and stockings even more so – I had long legs and stockings seemed to be made for short people. It became hilarious when skirts were made shorter so as to be cut out of about 3 yards of material. If you were tall, as I was, the skirt ended just above the knee and the stockings ended just above the skirt hem . . . so that when you sat down you were forever fidgeting to make the ends meet.

We all wore our underwear until it was ribbons – it was patched and mended, and had lace bits added to cover the darns, and was dyed again and again. Elastic was very hard to get, so we had to make do with buttons.

Later, I bought a second-hand coat from my friend's sister – a very drab khaki colour, but with a warm quilted lining. I did manage to save up and bought a very dashing red crêpe dress in a sale. I had only had it a few weeks when our house was bombed and it was blown out of the wardrobe, right into the street. It was returned none the worse for wear. I was lucky!

Shoes were another problem – particularly for children, who regularly and quickly outgrew them. At the time, one mother wrote despairingly that she had searched every shop in Oxford Street for a pair of sought-after 'Startrite' shoes for her son, without success. Shoes were also difficult for young women trying to put an attractive outfit together. Sally, who was thirteen when the war began, said, 'Leather shoes were hard to come by, expensive and seven coupons. I only remember buying three pairs of shoes during the entire war. But I do remember buying a pair of summer clogs. These had a sole and heel carved out of wood, with a rubber sole and heel stuck on. They were made of red leather, and were very comfortable. Only two coupons.'

As ever more of the country's manufacturing base was put to use for war purposes, production of all other goods shrank still further, and clothing coupons were slightly reduced by extending the yearly period to fifteen months. In 1942 the dreaded word 'austerity' entered the vocabulary, and soon after a range of plain, cheap goods and clothes, government-controlled and marked 'Utility', came on to the market. They ranged from household goods, to furniture, to clothing. At the time, they were considered unbearably drab and unimaginative, but their classic design has in many cases survived the decades, and changing tastes and styles, remarkably well. Certainly in 1943 the ordinary housewife was hugely relieved to find a simple coat or a dress or a pair of shoes for her child marked 'Utility' and costing a lot less, in money and coupons, than any non-Utility alternatives. Some customers were a lot less satisfied, however, and the very word 'Utility' came to be regarded as denoting something second rate and boring. A boy of seventeen, being fitted for his first suit, was sadly disappointed when the only one that fit was 'Utility' and – worst of all – the trousers had no turn-ups.

An enterprising spirit is hard to keep down, war or no war, and plenty of feisty young women worked their way round the shortages and managed to look smart and attractive. A group of girls, all about eighteen and starting their first year at Oxford, would use sheets and old curtain material for ballgowns, and one girl wore her mother's old black chiffon nightgown over a long pink petticoat 'most successfully'. Parachute silk left lying abandoned in fields by pilots who had baled out of planes was considered real bounty and was made up into all kinds of creations, including very pretty wedding dresses. Bunty, living in Kent, left school in 1943 and went to work in a local bank. She too made use of what was available and enjoyed her wartime youth:

We made earrings from big buttons and a hairpin. As a teenager then, I thought they looked great . . . Stockings were always a problem, and I partly solved it by knitting lacy stockings in fine rayon – and in the summer we used to use tea, left in the pot, to stain our legs and make a pencil mark like a seam down the back. I remember my mum bought a man's cap (no coupons needed, and it was cheap), cut the peak off – and she had a warm beret.

But for all people's ingenuity, Christmas in wartime was a muted affair at best, with a chicken substituted for the traditional turkey – if a family was lucky. One ten-year-old schoolgirl recorded her meagre Christmas morning in 1941: 'I woke early . . . made sure the blackout curtains were over the windows and . . . had a little peep at my presents . . . I had a pair of slacks, Mummy made them out of a blanket . . . a bar of chocolate, a whole orange.'

Michael, who was in his teens, had memories of better times, but, with a long war on, he was sensible enough to count his blessings:

We were lucky as we still had a house to live in – and we were all together. But Christmas during the war was vastly different from the 1930s, when I was a small boy. We had an abundance of chocolates, sweets, puddings with 3d. and 6d. pieces in them, cakes, and a large assortment of presents from parents and relative . . . What a change from 1940 onwards! There was little to buy in the shops, special Christmas fare was at a premium, and we made things as presents . . . One year, when shortages were at their worst, my Christmas presents from my mother and father were a tie and a coat hanger.

Try as a parent might, a special present was almost impossible to get, as this seven-year-old girl, who had set her heart on a fountain pen, discovered:

Pens were virtually impossible to buy, although second-hand ones were advertised regularly in the personal columns of *The Times*. I didn't fancy this so my parents put my name down with W.H. Smith and were told that there would be approximately a six months' wait, with no choice of make or colour. When my longed for pen eventually arrived – a Conway Stewart – it was a hideous shade of pink. I was bitterly disappointed!

All over the country, families made the best of it, with improvisatory cooking skills pushed to the limit. A girl remembered that her enterprising mother, determined to do her festive best for the children, 'made marzipan every wartime Christmas using soya flour and almond essence. We all still love that strong almond flavour!' And there were no fripperies such as Christmas trees. In Wales, a family yearning for the usual evergreens made do with 'a branch off a fir tree in the corner – decorations made from bits of silver paper saved from Dad's pipe tobacco.'

For the privileged few, good food was still obtainable – although restricted – in luxurious surroundings, and Molly's father decided to give his wife 'a rest from the worries of wartime catering at Christmas. So we went to the Savoy Hotel. The menu for Christmas of 1943 makes interesting reading. The Dîner de Noël of three courses, with choices, included 'La Dinde du Norfolk farcie aux Marrons du Dorset' despite the price restrictions of the order passed in 1942. How did they produce such a meal with a maximum cost of 5 shillings – 25p in today's money?'

By the time the last Christmas of the war came round, shortages were more stringent than ever. A nine-year-old boy, typical of very many children on that day, wrote gloomily in his diary, 'Christmas 1944. I awoke to find in my stocking – 1 Rough Plain Paper Blank Book, 1 Paintbrush, 6 small pots of water paint. 1 orange.' (Adding to the disappointment, he had queued for the orange himself a few days earlier.)

But by the early summer of 1944, with the solid success of the Normandy landings, the country had experienced a surge of optimism. The Allies were advancing steadily towards Berlin, and when at the end of August Paris was joyously liberated the end of the long war was at last in sight. But progress on the fighting front was not matched by any easing of restrictions at home. Rationing and shortages continued just as tightly, and would last until the end of the 1940s and beyond. The constant daily grind took its toll, and when Victory in Europe came in May 1945 the country that had been through so much was in every way shabby: from grimy city streets and wind-blown bomb sites to coats and jumpers and skirts worn threadbare.

Undoubtedly, those who had given most on the home front, tirelessly and generally unsung, were the housewives and mothers. It is worth mentioning, as a lot of wartime children do, that many a mother did without a new garment for herself when coupons were required for a daughter's party frock to go dancing or a son's first grown-up tweed jacket. One mother, who was certainly not alone in this, freely admitted as much. In the summer of 1945, when her husband returned after three years fighting overseas, she had saved up the family coupons for months and intended to buy herself a much needed smart new outfit. But it was not to be. 'In the end I rigged out the children instead, because of course, after those three long, hard years, I wanted their dad to see them looking as nice as possible.'

6

SCHOOLING AND
STARTING OUT

Schoolboys are taught to recognize the silhouettes of planes in flight. 'Plane spotting', of Allied and enemy aircraft, became a favourite wartime hobby of both boys and girls

Education, it was often said, was the first casualty of war, and . . .
an unfortunate minority bear the scars of wartime conditions
to this day.
Norman Longmate, *How We Lived Then* (1971)

Once the war started, I can honestly say I never learned a thing.
A girl, evacuated twice, who left school in 1943, age fourteen,
and started work

One advantage of being at school in wartime was that you never
started an exam or test convinced that you would have to finish.
Sirens were sometimes well timed. One much appreciated bomb
removed the school gymnasium. Thank you, Luftwaffe!
A schoolgirl, tongue in cheek, who heartily who disliked PE

I had just begun school when war was declared. By the time it
finished, I had attended five junior schools.
A pupil who lived in the thick of the Southampton bombing, was
evacuated to a nearby village, and, aged seventeen, won an open
scholarship to Oxford

Given the monumental upheaval of war on the home front, the constant ebb and flow of children's evacuation, the raids on cities, the teachers who disappeared into the forces, the make-do premises, and the shortage of all supplies, from books to pencils and paper, it is astonishing that any school-age child in the country learned anything at all for six years. Yet they did – after a fashion.

While a very small minority of children flourished academically despite the difficulties, most got through their wartime schooling

221

with what one girl would later describe as 'whole "blocks" missing – especially maths in my case'. Many, squeezed into strange new schools with unfamiliar teachers, found that they were ahead in some subjects, far behind in others. 'Decimals? But I was already well on to fractions,' a boy of twelve evacuated to Wales later recalled chirpily. Less fortunate children, shunted from pillar to post, and frequently in overcrowded classrooms of mixed ages, admit to having learned next to nothing.

Educational authorities, forced to improvise under the exceptional circumstances of wartime, did their best. Shelters were put in hand, and schools in the receiving areas made what arrangements they could to accommodate the flood of newcomers from the cities. And, apart from inner-city areas, by mid-September 1939 most children in the UK were getting some schooling, much of it part-time.

During those early months of war a desperate optimism prevailed, and it was put about that a child's experience of evacuation alone would partially compensate for fractured, or non-existent, formal education. As the historian Angus Calder wrote, 'It was often argued at the time . . . [that] town children had their horizons broadened while country children picked up new ideas and new ambitions . . . The Board of Education had rubbed its hands enthusiastically over the opportunities which evacuation would offer for fruitful changes in school curricula – local surveys and nature rambles for instance.'

Although the idea of 'nature rambles' as solid education might seem fanciful, many children evacuated during the war enjoyed their early experiences of rural life – getting to recognize the different trees and flowers, learning about crops and their rotation, and helping to care for farmyard animals. For Sarah, most happily evacuated aged nine to a farm in Cornwall, the joy of discovering animal life has never dimmed. 'Auntie (as I called my foster mother) taught me milking and the care of calves . . . and I looked after the day-old chicks, I was totally responsible for placing them under the incubator and lighting the oil lamp in it. I never lost one.' A woman of about Sarah's age, evacuated to Sussex, still spoke nostalgically of the magical nature walks with her new class, the teacher pointing out the different trees and wild flowers.

Ken, a canny Londoner, found a different way of adapting: chatting up the local gang in a village deep in the countryside, swapping stories, and learning to make new friends.

This gentler, happier side of evacuation, with adults and children from a wide range of city and country backgrounds rubbing along together, must have broadened horizons all round. In many children it undoubtedly inspired a deep appreciation of nature and the countryside, and may well have influenced later choice of lifestyles. 'I never really settled back in the city,' a man who had been evacuated to Sussex for four years said. Instead of staying close to his family in London, he eventually chose to live and work in the rural Midlands.

Possibly these new experiences did help to compensate for the basic education that was being so severely disrupted for so many. This disruption began immediately, and affected most school children in some way. Right after the declaration of war, twelve-year-old Bill living in Surrey noted gleefully that

One bright spot, so far as pupils were concerned, was that the school summer holidays had to be extended by three weeks while air-raid shelters were constructed in the school playground . . . although some of this free time was used in appropriately helpful tasks such as filling sandbags.

Those early months of war were relatively quiet and uneventful for us at our familiar school, but there was an ever present feeling of uncertainty and anxiety about the future.

Even very young children, longing for their first satchel and pencil case, were caught up in the nation's predicament. Kate was five, just starting school in Kent, and her mother was determined that the war should not interfere with her early education:

At first all the schools were closed, but Mum made sure that all of my mornings were spent with the three Rs. Later she volunteered to make a room in our house available to the class of first-year mixed infants and our teacher. Tiny desks were installed, and every a.m. there was the babble of tiny voices reciting their ABC – and every p.m. Mum went in to mop up the lino, after the inevitable tiny 'accidents'.

Did she get paid? No, it was her war work.

Right across the land, older children, fully aware of the political situation with many of their fathers entering the forces, were quick to notice change in their schools. That autumn term, Philip, fourteen, entered grammar school in east Yorkshire. He modestly described himself as a 'backward student'.

The first thing I noticed once the war started was the disappearance of the younger male staff, who were called up to join one or other of the services. They were replaced by old male and young female teachers. Unfortunately the change was not good for discipline, and my education went from bad to worse.

One of the young male staff to be moved out quickly – but not to the front – was a teacher who came in one morning wearing a swastika armband. He was one of Mosley's men. We were shocked. It was the first time I had seen a swastika, which was to mean so much to so many during the war.

Early in September 1939, Pamela, a talented girl of twelve who later trained as a musician, was evacuated with her school from London to a town on the south coast. Her parents, she said later, had agonized over sending her away, but decided that it was best for her welfare.

Our teachers vanished into a first-class carriage on the way down, and we were left to our own devices. The train was packed, and I had to stand for the whole journey. Late in the afternoon we reached our destination and were then touted round the town seeking people who would take us in. I ended up quite near the Downs with a man who ran a hotel and his wife . . . They were very kind people . . .

There was no school big enough to accommodate us all, and we were spread around the town. Eventually some classes were held in various churches and halls – including the gas showroom. Other girls got together with teachers in small groups.

Clearly, this was not a satisfactory arrangement, and after a few months, with no bombs falling, Pamela's mother came down and took her home. Like so many of the returning children whose parents had done the same, Pamela then found that she had nowhere to go, as her school had been requisitioned. But she was luckier than most:

I found that my school had become a fire station but that classes were being held in the infants school . . . They were being run by teachers I did not know . . . but I enjoyed being asked to work on my own projects and not being constantly told what I had to read . . . Quite soon I heard that one of the local grammar schools was offering bursaries and holding examinations. I decided to go in for it with a couple of my friends, and, although my arithmetic was appalling, I managed top marks in English. To my surprise I was awarded one of the bursaries.

The main problem for all schools was complying with ARP shelter requirements, even in 'neutral' areas. Many city schools were immediately shut and requisitioned, usually for Civil Defence purposes; in London around two-thirds of schools were taken over, and more than half in Manchester. Attempting to make up for lost lessons, the London County Council kept schools open during the summer of 1940, but any gains were lost in the mayhem of the Blitz, when schooling again became minimal. Small wonder that in all this confusion, and while more and more teachers went into the forces, between 1939 and 1941 there was a notable increase in juvenile delinquency.

All the teachers who remained, not only those struggling in the cities, faced continual problems and added responsibilities all through the war. Evacuated with their classes, they were forced into the role of all-round carer and adviser in addition to teaching in strange classrooms or unsuitable premises, frequently short of supplies. Many were brought back from retirement to face classes of perhaps fifty or more children of different ages and abilities, who were often exhausted by broken nights. With both his parents being schoolteachers in north London, Andrew was aware of such problems from early on:

From family conversation, I heard and understood a great deal about the difficulties of carrying on as normal a teaching curriculum as possible while being regularly interrupted by war activities – not always air raids and sirens (although these were extremely disrupting and anxious) but extra meetings and assemblies and drills and practices. Trying to keep up standards and give extra coaching when they could, they were both working nearly all the time.

Andrew also remembered the 'blast walls' that were installed for safety in many schools, and which sadly prohibited the high-spirited racing beloved by young children. 'These were built into the existing fabric at regular intervals down the main corridor. If the corridor was, say, 6 feet wide, then there would be a 4 foot wide floor-to-ceiling wall, about 18 inches thick, protruding from one wall, followed 3 feet further on by another from the opposite wall. This formed an inconvenient and narrow chicane, preventing hitherto breakneck speeds down the corridor.'

In 1939, of children educated in the state sector – 90 per cent of the overall school-age population – most attended secondary schools until the leaving age of fourteen. If passed, an exam taken at age eleven to twelve provided a ladder to further education in better-equipped and -funded grammar and vocational schools. But by no means all the children who passed this 'eleven-plus' could take up an offer: even if a child received an educational grant, the strict uniform requirements were beyond the means of many parents.

'I had just passed my eleven-plus so I wasn't doing too badly,' a woman whose subsequent schooling was severely affected by the war recalled, looking back regretfully. She left school at fourteen and started quite menial work, missing out on any better opportunity she might have had. There was no way of making up for this lost education except by night school, which was made much more widely available in wartime.

Many young school-leavers were able to take advantage of these extra-curricular classes, which were held all over the country out of working hours. Moira, a bright young woman who was born and raised in Inverness, refused to be beaten by the rigid system of schooling, and was able to make use of local night-school courses to further her own education. In doing so, she stumbled on a rich new world of the intellect:

My education could be said to have suffered in the war (depending on how you look at it), inasmuch as I was not given the opportunity of sitting the eleven-plus. It had something to do with when my birthday fell. Two other girls and I were top of the class, but we were told that despite not having the eleven-plus we could sit an exam for places at the grammar school when we were fourteen.

So we were sent to a technical high school and given a 'commercial' course in shorthand, typing and bookkeeping. We never did sit for the grammar school. However, because of the war, night-school classes continued all through the year. I immediately enrolled in night school to complete my secretarial course, and also to sit the Royal Society of Arts English examination. Members of the forces were also encouraged to attend – we had several in my classes, including a Canadian lumberjack.

I enjoyed every minute of it – especially the English, where I was introduced to the major nineteenth-century classics and I developed an appetite for challenging reading. I completed the course when I was seventeen. I honestly think it was much more stimulating than day school!

Ironically, the school-leaving age had been set to rise from fourteen to fifteen on 1 September 1939 for all except for those who were going into what was oddly described as 'beneficient employment' (which would have boiled down to the poor, who most needed to work). This was cancelled, but was eventually introduced for all children after the war, in 1947.

City schools, while often far from well equipped, usually had somewhat better premises and facilities than most of their counterparts in the country. Now, many of these rural schools – some no more than single rooms – were being asked to accommodate whole classes of city children of differing ages and standards into their premises, or whatever space could be found in the vicinity. This might have been a large country house, a pub, a village hall, a school that had previously been declared derelict, or a Salvation Army citadel. 'We ended up being taught in very small groups in people's houses,' Arthur, evacuated to deepest Somerset, remembered. 'It must have been terrible for the teachers, but we quite enjoyed it. Eventually, when things got more settled, we were absorbed by the local school – or went back home.'

The simplest way of coping with shortages of shelters and schools being combined through evacuation, was to stagger classes. During the previous war, many schools had been kept running with two, or even three, sessions per day. This was rarely satisfactory, and in 1939, and after, great efforts were made to keep to no more than two sessions. But, however carefully it was managed, this was rough and ready schooling which produced very mixed results. Sam, living in south London, had a typical experience of that early war period in his local school district:

An arrangement was made for girls and boys – whose school was without shelters and still closed – to use the senior girls school on alternate weeks. This proved fairly successful, and further arrangements were made for older pupils, five or six to a group, to go two days a week to private homes to meet up with a teacher to get homework etc. This too proved successful up to a point, and lasted for about six months – until the shelters were built.

Then, soon after, the air raids began, with more disruption of lessons and constant tiredness from sheltering that seriously affected our schoolwork.

All over the country, in urban and rural areas, other schools – like Sam's – teamed up, got on with the job, and made the best of it. Some larger schools with extra space were able to take in entire schools of similar size. With good organization this dual schooling worked well over several years – and some public schools also teamed up with other independent schools for the duration. However, the sharing of classrooms and facilities did put a good deal of strain on both teachers and pupils. David had vivid memories of this combined wartime education, which in his case worked quite successfully:

I was a pupil at our town's one local-authority-run secondary school, which had been due to move into a brand-new building . . . But from the start of the autumn term in 1939 the premises were, so to speak, doublebooked. A counterpart school had been evacuated from Southampton and was to share all the facilities. For five and a half years the two communities coexisted yet seldom met, thanks to a lengthened day, a shift system, and some hiring of church halls.

It was a successful operation, but wearing; when finally our own school regained sole possession, a sense of release could be felt daily.

Nearly every schoolchild experienced a unique blend of social experimentation and traditional education, which so often overlapped in wartime. Whether these experiences were lucky or unlucky or mixed depended to some extent upon a child's age, outlook, and ability to adapt.

Matthew was living in a village outside Cardiff, and attending a nearby grammar school. His school received a limited number of evacuees, who assimilated easily and did well scholastically. He was fortunate, because the war broadened, rather than limited, his schooling and brought about unexpected and enduring friendships:

We had a number of pupils who had been evacuated from London – few enough so that they could be absorbed into the class numbers. One of them became a lifelong friend . . . We also had a several boys who had come to this country from Germany . . . oppressed by the Nazi regime. They integrated perfectly with us, could speak fluent English, and without exception were brilliant in academic achievement. We were a mixed bunch, but got on well.

Hilda, who was seven when the war began, was evacuated from the south coast, with her siblings, to a village in North Wales. The children were well looked after, stayed for the duration, and thoroughly enjoyed life with their beloved foster mother, called 'Blod'. Schooling was basic, but none the worse for that. 'We only went to school half-day to begin with, but it settled down to having classes in the school in the morning and in the church hall in the afternoon – which worked quite well.'

This could not be said for Dorothy, who struggled along in a different village school. Evacuated for the second time to Devon, she made little progress even though she had already passed her eleven-plus exam. 'We weren't accepted at this school, even though one of our own teachers was there. We were blamed for everything that went wrong. The headmaster treated the evacuees very badly.' The day after she turned fourteen Dorothy set off back to London and her family, bombs and sirens notwithstanding.

May – evacuated to a remote village in Lancashire, where she was mocked for her southern accent and unable to understand the locals, said, 'Truly, my stay "oop North" was the most horrific time of my life. The school treated me like a leper, and I was taught nothing. My teacher was a woman with a peculiar temperament. She would fly into the most dreadful rages without any provocation, so I kept quiet at the back of the room so she hardly knew I was there . . . I would daydream my time away and long for my release.'

One class of strapping thirteen- and fourteen-year-old lads, on what one described as 'a big adventure', evacuated from Essex to a mining town in South Wales, took to their new lives and flourished. They were given a friendly welcome by carers and townspeople, assimilated well in the local schools, and tolerated good-natured teasing without fuss. Like many evacuees who landed up in districts that must have seemed to them a foreign country, these older boys made the most of their surroundings, eager to grasp any new opportunities available: 'The lovely summer that year continued until late in the autumn – and there were mountains to explore all around, which was a wonderful experience . . . The curate created a successful youth club in the church crypt, which opened every evening and provided games, a gramophone and records. And the miners let us use their institute, which housed billiard tables and a library.'

John, from Liverpool, was also evacuated to a mining district in South Wales with his school. The boys in his class got on fairly well despite the disrupted teaching and the varied standards of the children.

We were allocated part of an old school built in 1892 and situated up on a mountain – a long uphill walk. Once we were settled in our billets, our schooling continued with our own teachers for a while. I stayed on right through the war, and eventually older students were integrated into the senior schools in the locality and our teachers returned home.

I found that in arithmetic I was further advanced than my new class-mates . . . So there was I, as they were copying decimals from the black-board, carrying on with the teacher's handbook of fractions (which had the answers in the back).

Despite the many difficulties and educational lapses rightly associated with wartime schooling, it is heartening to know that there were some occasional good outcomes too. The wife of a leading academic believed that if her husband had not been evacuated from his school in a poor district of a great northern city, his gifts as a writer and teacher would not have been recognized. It was the sensitive school-master in a small rural schoolroom who first spotted his ability, and guided and encouraged his early education.

Young Robin's experience was equally good when, aged nine, he was evacuated with his younger brother to the West Country. The boys lived in east London, where their mother – a widow – struggled to make ends meet. Although his brother was somewhat less fortu-nate, Robin, intelligent and eager to get on in life, was lucky in his foster parents and his change of schools; in both vital areas of his life, away from home, he was looked after by caring people whom he came to love and admire – and to emulate:

I found myself in a clean, decent working-class home with loving guardians who treated me as their own. My 'uncle', as I called him, was a father to me, and his wife was equally affectionate . . . At the local Church of England school which I attended, the head teacher, although quite strict, was another father figure . . .

It was at school that I had my first experience of financial responsibil-ity. Because I was a bright child and excelled at arithmetic, I was given the task, every Monday morning, of collecting the National Savings deposits from the other children. This meant sitting importantly at a desk in the hall, taking the money, entering the sum in the depositor's pass book and the register, and reconciling the cash in the box with the end balance in the register.

We didn't appreciate it at the time, but the headmaster was skilled at picking boys and giving them responsibilities which developed their talents.

It was a proud moment for Robin, as well as his foster parents, when, some years later, he turned up on their doorstep while doing his National Service in the army – wearing his smart, newly achieved officer's uniform.

Evacuation, whether private or government-assisted, meant that children from varying schools and backgrounds were flung together willy-nilly and left to get along. Sarah, who was born in Edinburgh and evacuated to Glasgow with her family – 'to the Gorbals, where we had air-raid sirens day and night, while Edinburgh was never bombed' – had learned to write on slates. She said that the sudden transition to pen and paper in a new school was hard, and probably affected her writing ability for life.

Robert, living with his grandparents in Scotland in a large house and in some style, became quickly aware of social differences when he was sent off to the local school: 'Most of my classmates came from the council houses that had sprung up in the thirties. Being relatively privileged did not endear me to my peers, and I spent a fair amount of break time fighting! Discipline was maintained by use of "the belt", a thick 24-inch leather strap administered to the hand for various offences – including getting more than three mistakes in spelling or arithmetic. I learned quickly!'

In all schools, this type of basic discipline was swiftly administered with no questions asked – and was accepted. Mary, who was evacuated from Newcastle several times to various relatives in country districts, used her learning skills to keep out of the limelight – and the teacher's reach. 'School No. 4 . . . Classes of fifty were usual. If one could read, as I could, one was put to sit at the back of the class. Times tables had to be recited every day first thing. Miss X would whack those in the front row over their heads if they faltered. I felt sorry for one ungainly red-haired boy – he got more whacks than anyone.'

In the muddle of war – the comings and goings, the pandemonium of raids and their aftermath – youthful enterprise flourished. Finding life far too absorbing to be wasted on education, two enterprising twin boys, Londoners through and through, entered into the wartime spirit with gusto. Returning from a brief period of evacuation at the beginning of the war, aged eleven, they were sent to the local school, which had reopened to accommodate former evacuees. 'Schooling was spasmodic, very fractured,' one of the twins remembered.

Some of the teachers were very old and bad-tempered. We never did any homework. We did not learn to read until we were fourteen. By this time we had devoted our time to the Army Cadets and Air Training Corps . . . We went up in a glider, and were flying over the dockland area when above us we spotted a German Heinkel. We were so small that the pilot had been able to take us both up together. We were very scared!

232

When the bombing intensified, we were again evacuated, briefly, to Edinburgh, Teignmouth and Nottingham. In each place we campaigned to come back to our beloved London as soon as possible . . . and at 13½ we became service messengers (pretending to be 15¼). Often we stayed all night on duty and then had to attend school the next day. Small wonder that we were expelled from school for being ineducable.

Despite their school's exasperation, their adventurous wartime of extra-curricular education did them no harm. Quite the contrary: one became a university professor, the other a Member of Parliament.

Education, as always, came in many guises. Some of the well-to-do were able to continue the slightly eccentric private schooling methods with which their daughters, at least, had been brought up for generations. Annabel was eight and her younger brother Harry four at the beginning of the war, and they were taught throughout, at home, by their governess. Annabel, who became a successful academic, looked back at her early learning experiences with a good deal of affection – and much respect.

Miss E was a surrogate mother, an adventuresome companion, a sympathetic aunt and an artistic soulmate who went by the uncharitable title of governess. She didn't much go for complicated arithmetic either. A good thing altogether. The schooling was very basic, but so it was in most places then.

We made a large plasticine relief map of Europe and marked with flags the movements of armies in France. We learned first-aiding. We mended things. I knitted (painfully) mittens for soldiers. We helped with the hospital supplies that were stored in the larger rooms of the house. We made rather grey biscuits for the troops that were billeted near by. They were Polish at the beginning of the war, then Canadian. They could do and make all sorts of things that nobody in the village had any idea of.

Harry and I began to understand that there was a whole big world out there beyond our village imaginings.

Petronella, ten, was already happily exploring a world that was then quite new to her. After living in the middle of paved roads and neat fields in suburban Kent, the family had evacuated to Dorset when the children's father went to work at the War Office. She and her younger brother and sister revelled in the freedom of woods and fields, biking all over the district, and buying boiled sweets in the village shop with 'a jangling door'. However, she was soon briskly packed off to boarding school, some 6 miles away.

It was a very smart day school which had been evacuated from London to a stately home. The two ladies who ran the school had no idea about a boarding school, which it had become, so girls were able to bring their nannies or French governesses. I suppose there were about five of these, and they slept with the younger girls and looked after their clothes and their health. A few girls brought their ponies too!

The education was really very good. It included Picture Study, I remember, and this was my first introduction to art. Occasionally we would venture through the village to paint – I can remember sitting in a meadow covered in golden buttercups. On Sundays we walked to church, where the lord of the manor worshipped. He was very High Church, and we girls fainted at the smell of incense flung about (or we thought we did).

There was very little danger in east Dorset from the war, but occasionally a plane returning from Bristol would offload its bombs, or a pilot would parachute out. This happened on our golf course, and a girl of fourteen gained great notoriety by calmly giving the German airman a cup of tea while sending her brother for help.

Two sisters, aged five and seven, from a Jewish background, had a much darker experience of wartime boarding-school life. Once the London Blitz started, their parents decided that it was no longer safe to remain in the city, especially for their children.

But you can imagine how hard it must have been to send us away, still so young – and how hard it was for us to go. The school was a Jewish boarding school which was originally based in Brighton but which was evacuated to a village in North Wales.

The place where we stayed had been a farm, and I and about four other girls were allocated sleeping quarters in the attic. All night long we were disturbed by the sound of mice scurrying around, and on telling the teacher about this in the morning we were told to clap our hands and they would go away. This did not work and traps were set, and we took great delight each morning to see what had been caught . . .

A few months later we moved into better accommodation some distance away . . . Food was in short supply, and I remember going to the village to buy tins of Cadbury's drinking chocolate (not on ration) and we used to have midnight feasts spooning the powder straight from the tin. And the porridge . . . To this day I cannot eat porridge. It was solid and full of husks, and we all fought for a seat by an open window at breakfast time so that this bowl of disgusting stuff could be thrown out into the garden . . .

The two ladies who ran the school made sure their own comforts were not neglected. I can still smell the paraffin stove in their comfortable sitting room – when we children used to go to bed with all our clothes on in the winter because it was so cold.

Fortunately, the girls' parents visited as often as they could, and, despite the many discomforts, the girls were competently taught and did well scholastically.

Children in boarding schools benefited from the continuity that was so often lacking in wartime day schools, but they faced many of the same difficulties as the others: replacement teachers, icy class-rooms (and dormitories), poor food, and hours spent in shelters. Eccentric masters had long been accepted as a part of prep-school life. Alan, who attended a boarding prep school during the first three years of the war, found that this tradition, at least, had not changed: 'The school was run by a veteran of the Great War, who spent far too much of his time at the bar of the British Legion. The staff were either decrepit or young wets, one of whom confided to his class of nine-year-olds, "Don't tell anyone, but I think we're going to lose this war." ' When Alan moved on to Bedford School in September 1943, aged thirteen, he found that great efforts were made to continue the school's record of excellence, despite the constraints of wartime.

To the headmaster, the war was a challenge to be met. Somehow, good staff were brought out of retirement and good standards of conduct and work were maintained. The school had had an excellent hall and was chosen by the BBC as a venue for the rehearsal and recording of the BBC Symphony Orchestra under Sir Adrian Boult. He was charming to the boys and the

staff and we were sometimes allowed to sit in and listen to the music ...
This put me at ease with classical music from an early age ... Our art education was a bonus also, as we were taught by a talented Austrian refugee.

I was fortunate in my wartime schooling.

Adrian, who lived on the Sussex coast, attended a City of London-
supported boarding school of 800 boys in the Home Counties
throughout the war years; this school also had a reputation for main-
taining high standards. His clear memories of those wartime schooldays stayed with him long after:

At night the younger boys were evacuated into a service tunnel that ran
below the eight large boarding blocks. Even without alerts, sleeping was
difficult: I heard a senior master later saying that the boys got very tired
and their schoolwork suffered ... I remember a background of insufficient
sleep, limited and unexciting food ... [and] disruptive blackout arrangements in the winters, which were cold. Radiators were lukewarm, baths
infrequent, and water rarely hot. Even so we managed to enjoy ourselves,
with older boys keen radio listeners who followed the war's progress on
wall maps.

A serious effect was the quality of teachers, especially in science, maths
and languages. Retired teachers returned, women volunteered, and some
unqualified staff were employed. They did their best, but discipline and
academic standards deteriorated. I remember the senior science master
returning and telling us (sixth-formers by then) that we were so far behind
the usual exam standards that he would have to let us sink or swim while
he did his best to salvage the form below us.

Adrian, who later had a distinguished career in medicine, came to
realize that, though somewhat harsh at times, overall his schooling
was a good experience with plenty of fun; despite the stressful conditions of the time, he received a sound educational grounding which
stood him in good stead in his later studies and his life's work.

After living for two years in a remote part of the Lake District, fully
absorbed into its peaceful rural life and having forged close ties with
many of the locals, James was pitched into a large public school in
wartime with little preparation:

After the tranquillity of the Lake District, where I had been evacuated with my mother and brother, being plunged into public-school life was something of a shock. I was the youngest boy in the school, and the life seemed very strange to me . . .

Many masters went away to war – many were killed – and were replaced by a motley group which included several brilliant teachers. In that we were lucky, and somehow we received a rather good education.

The headmaster was legendary, and knew every boy by name. It was his custom to read out a list of casualties, masters and boys, in chapel on Armistice Sunday. In my first year, 1941, it was comparatively short; as time went by it became dreadfully long, and he clearly had the greatest difficulty getting through it without being overcome by the sheer sorrow of remembering boys he had known well and for whom he once had such high hopes.

It has been said that Stowe suffered more casualties and was awarded more decorations than any other public school irrespective of its size. This may or may not have been true, but hearing that poignant list in chapel it certainly seemed like it.

At the time when James began his first term at Stowe, in September 1941, across the Channel Yvette, now nine – her father in England, her mother and siblings trapped in France – was going back to her local school in Brittany:

My brother and I went off to school wearing the traditional *sarrau* (overall) that all schoolchildren used to wear in France. We also wore our *sabots* (clogs) or *galoches* (wooden-soled boots). At school we were all made to write a letter of loyalty to Maréchal Pétain, and there was a song entitled 'Maréchal, Nous Voilà, devant Toi, le Sauveur de la France'. Needless to say, other words were soon used – i.e. 'Vendeur' instead of 'Sauveur'.*

* The distrusted Pétain became Prime Minister of France on 16 June 1940 as France fell; after an armistice was signed between France and Germany, his government collaborated with the German occupiers. The song title translates as 'Marshal, here we are before you, the saviour of France'. '*Vendeur*' means 'seller'.

A particularly tricky time for the family came at the end of March 1942, when the British mounted a daring raid on the docks at Saint-Nazaire, in the estuary of the river Loire. The main dock was blown up, but the heavily fortified submarine berths remained intact.

We were aware that something important was happening – there were German patrols everywhere, and extra listening devices . . . At school, the children, who were aware of our background and learned that the British had mounted the attack, teased, 'Ton père est là – on l'a vu . . .'* Of course this was very dangerous for us, as the children could have been heard and we would have been reported to the authorities. Fortunately, nothing happened.

You could see that the British attack upset the Germans – they were on edge.

Right across the educational spectrum, children, parents and teachers in the UK did their best to keep their school routines as normal as possible. But this was often a daunting task. Apart from the shortage of teachers – particularly those with special skills such as Latin, science or languages – there was also considerable damage to school premises throughout the country, especially in the cities and suburban districts. It was estimated that about one in five schools suffered bomb damage; thousands of others were used for Civil Defence purposes, principally as rest centres.

Iris, bombed out of her family home several times in the London Blitz, was among the children who had the worst of it educationally:

My school had a direct hit on the room that was designated safe and gas-proof – it happened at night, in October 1940. The next day there was a notice put on the bit of wall still standing to go to another school a few streets away. I was the first one to turn up, as it turned out – I was the first every time. We had old men and women teachers brought out of retirement, and they did their best, but classes were of children of all ages mixed, so no real education came out of it. Just passing time . . .

But when the children started to trickle back from evacuation, some of

* 'Your father is there – we've seen him . . .'

the teachers did too and things got gradually a bit better. Too late for me though, as I started work the day after I was fourteen in October 1941.

Young as she was, Iris was soon doing war work in a factory making scientific instruments for aircraft, and later in the war she filled in the numbers on the dials with radium so that they glowed in the dark.

Mary was also living in London, in a flat close to the severely bombed docklands area, and time and again the family was forced to decamp to the shelter beneath the pub on the corner of their road. As was typical for many children living in badly bombed target areas, Mary's schooling was badly interrupted over several years: 'When the raids started, our school was closed down after lunch because the bombing often came in the late afternoons . . . The main message at school was that we must all work, and continue working, in the safety of our homes.'

Interrupted school routine in city areas seriously interfered with free milk distribution for young children, as well as the provision of vital school dinners – a programme which expanded rapidly throughout the war. For the poor, such medical care as was available to children before the war was delivered mainly in the schools – and even this was not always free. In the mayhem of evacuation, city school closures and bombing raids, the school clinics, which were an important aspect of child welfare, largely disappeared. So, in those early years of war, the health of some children probably did suffer. With many younger doctors called up into the forces, it was not until 1942 that medical and dental care for schoolchildren was reorganized, but after that it operated reasonably well. Moira, living in Inverness, had the personal experience (and the gaps and fillings) to verify this:

Before the war, the dentist used to visit the school once a year . . . and if you needed treatment you were given a blue card to take home for your parents to sign for consent. Extractions were free, but if you wanted a tooth filled you had to pay a shilling. My mother could not afford the shilling, so I had to have my teeth pulled. To this day I have gaps to prove it.

When the war started I was in secondary school . . . I was examined and found to require *thirteen* fillings. The treatment was entirely free of charge.

Years later most of those fillings were still intact, and a dentist compli-
mented me on their quality.

I have often wondered why my teeth acquired an importance in
wartime that they never did during peace.

To the surprise of medical experts braced for the worst, the overall
health of the general population held up well during those six stressful and stringent years. 'The physical condition of Britain's children
improved during the war,' as Angus Calder put it, before adding ominously, 'Their psychological and intellectual development was
another matter.'

Emotionally damaging or not, being huddled together for hours in
badly ventilated shelters, the minimal home heating and the constant
anxiety apparently did no great physical harm. The dreaded epi-
demics did not materialize, and children's health demonstrably
improved through a mixture of better eating habits despite rationing,
fewer sweets, a lot of exercise, and government-sponsored food supplements. Crucially, during the war some 7 million children were vac-
cinated against diphtheria, which had been a terrible scourge in the
pre-war years.

As so many of the then children remembered (perhaps from personal experience), it was head lice (nits) and impetigo (a highly con-
tagious skin condition) that flourished in the war. Unsurprisingly,
both these conditions are associated with overcrowding and poor
hygiene, which were inevitable in that long wartime. So perhaps the
prime cause of these unpleasant ailments was the soap and hot-water
shortages, which made bathing and clean clothes luxuries.

With hindsight, it is the adaptability of schoolchildren that seems
remarkable, far outweighing the episodes of chaotic education, and
not a bad training for later life either. Peter, who was nine when the
war began, lived in the suburbs, close to important train marshalling
yards – a magnet for enemy raiders, who returned again and again.
Peter, his parents and his school were on the receiving end:

One night at about 10 p.m. I heard a stick of bombs come whistling down
near by . . . I shouted to my parents, 'It's the school,' and, wonder of
wonders, next day I found out that I was right. The chemistry lab and the

woodwork room were totally demolished, which is obviously why I failed General Science at School Certificate and have been a total idiot at any kind of handyman job ever since . . .

We had a week off so that arrangements could be made, and then my year was evacuated to another local school, where we had a whale of a time conducting an ongoing war with the inmates.

By the time the doodlebugs arrived the bomb damage to my school had been patched up and things were back to as normal as possible. Then a doodlebug landed right outside the front of the school and everything was shattered once again. We carried on regardless, with broken windows, collapsed ceilings and shattered woodwork. The doors were fixed up with hardboard, and somehow rude nicknames for members of staff were scrawled across them, many of these unofficial adornments surviving for months.

With or without structural damage, where school was concerned nothing seemed unusual any more: not classes of up to sixty children with an age range of as much as five or six years or more; not a teacher struggling to hold the attention of her class as they sat in a gas showroom; not a small group of pupils gathered in a parents' living room, cramming for an exam with a strange teacher. Sally, at a private school in Surrey, routinely spent many hours with her classmates huddled in former wine cellars. 'Our school was previously a large country home, and the cellars served as our shelters. Whenever an air-raid warning sounded we lined up and went down the stone steps to sit on the wine shelves. It seemed quite normal to us.'

Sitting tests and exams in wartime could be either extremely stressful or a lark, depending on a candidate's age and seriousness. As younger children recalled gratefully, you could never be sure of finishing before the siren went – which could prove a blessing. Mary, who attended five different schools in Northumberland, remembered, 'As a six-year-old, I asked God in my prayers to have the siren sound after 2 a.m. so I would be allowed to miss school! Although, if I did, Mother never failed to set me homework at my desk at home.' Her mother's insistence, even in wartime, brought results, as Mary obviously maintained good study habits, later becoming a successful lawyer.

Cramped and makeshift conditions, the frequent tension of sirens, and the problem of broken nights and fatigue must have made all kinds of test an ordeal for most children, at least some of the time. A girl of eleven, at school in the West Country, remembered the summer of 1944: 'We could hear the drone of planes going over on D-Day while we were trying to do our summer-term exams, sitting in the school corridors, which had been reinforced as shelters ... It was hard to keep our minds on what we were doing, not on what was happening above us.'

For older children, anxious about future training and university, sitting exams could be a grim experience. This was certainly true for Mark, who took his Higher Certificate at the height of the attacks by 'buzz bombs' – pilotless enemy planes. Not surprisingly, he recalled that examination in every detail:

We had to write for the whole three hours in an air-raid shelter which was semi-underground, on the school playing field, in west London. My handwriting was neat and easy to read, and I took some pride in it. About halfway through one paper we were interrupted by the fear-inspiring noise of one of those dreadful flying bombs. It became louder and louder, and then suddenly stopped ...

Everybody held his breath. We all knew what to expect – an explosion.

But on this occasion the bomb flew so close to us that we could hear the whistle of the wind around the bomb's structure. Even that became quite loud ...

Then came the expected roar – louder than anything I had ever heard.

The whole shelter was immediately filled with smoke and confusion. Much to our disgust, we were restrained by a teacher, who must have been very strong-minded – he stopped us escaping from the shelter, and even required us to carry on with the exam.

But this was unrealistic, our nerves were shattered. My handwriting was now quite illegible, even to me,

When the time was up, we emerged to see the school buildings still standing, rather to our surprise, but much of the glass broken, and a great deal of interior damage.

Because of the circumstances in which they sat their exam, all the candidates at his school were later interviewed. Mark's handwriting, and what he wrote, must have held up under the extreme pressure better than he imagined, as he was awarded a county scholarship.

The restrictions of wartime, which took so much colour and variety from children's lives, including many outdoor activities, did have a silver lining of sorts: they were heartily welcomed by unsporty children who hated games. The historian Norman Longmate wrote, 'For those with no liking or aptitude for games the war was a great liberator. Even at my games-mad school . . . it was at last possible . . . to work (instead) for a local farmer.'

Whether they enjoyed what limited sports were available or not, thousands of children – girls as well as boys – channelled their energies in other directions and helped with the harvests, fruit and vegetable picking and other farm chores throughout the war. Compensating for fractured schooling and the difficulty of travelling anywhere, Harvest Camps were set up to keep children occupied – and out of the cities – during the long summer holidays. They were extremely popular and productive: by 1943 over 1,000 were up and running, occupying 63,000 children during the summers. Patrick attended a Harvest Camp on the Northamptonshire border with his class of fifth-formers, and thoroughly enjoyed it:

We camped in a meadow, sleeping in bell tents, with a marquee as a mess tent. We were overseen by two masters, and took turns to cook. I distinguished myself one morning by forgetting to put any salt in the porridge.

During the day we harvested flax (linseed), rye and field peas. These were all new to us, as they were not grown in peacetime.

That autumn we were taken daily by coach to harvest potatoes. This is cold, wet, muddy and no fun. There were no fancy mechanical harvesters: the potatoes were simply ploughed up and picked up by hand. Today we would say this was exploiting child labour. But there was no other labour available and, as they said, 'There's a war on.'

Nobody died of it!

Dorothy, a teenager, spent a couple of weeks at a Harvest Camp with her mother in the summer of 1944. She remembered it as a very happy interlude. 'It was a wonderful time. We worked quite hard during the days, but at night there were sing-songs round the camp fire and dances on Saturday nights. It all seems very innocent now, but in those days, when we didn't expect a lot, it was really grand.'

Clubs and hobbies centred on schools either closed down at the beginning of the war or became focused on the war effort – knitting, collecting salvage, plane spotting, stamp collecting. The Scouts and Guides continued where possible, and during raids on cities some older Guides and Scouts put in good practical work, helping out in the messenger services. The Air Training Corps was started in 1941 for boys between sixteen and eighteen. These boys, not far from their call-up, were given uniforms and attended instruction classes, and with patriotism surging the ATC soon attracted a large following. It was swiftly followed by Sea Cadets and Army Cadets, and similar organizations were soon aimed at steering girls' attention towards entering the services as the call-up age for unmarried women was lowered to nineteen.

With no petrol available for private cars, and erratic bus and train services, many children in country and suburban districts routinely faced long walks to and from school. This was considered normal, and neither parents nor children appear to have been troubled by the possible dangers, despite short winter days and the blackout conditions.

Mary was living with her family near Manchester, attending the same school as her brother. It is notable that her conscientious parents had no fear of her walking to school and back even when she was alone:

Our grammar school was a mile away from home, and after the first day I used to walk there on my own. Of course I walked with friends once I got to know the other children. I hated the school dinners, so I would return home at lunchtime – as did my brother usually. Thus I walked over four miles each day. People were not frightened of abductions in those days, and there were very few men around in the day anyway.

However, the US forces came into the area just before the Normandy invasion in 1944, and the traffic increased considerably (perhaps to a tenth of what we endure today). I was only given a bike for my birthday after a good deal of parental heart-searching – because of the traffic – and probably a good deal of scraping of purses too.

When Charlie – aged eleven and living in Greater London – changed schools he also faced a long, tedious walk. He found that imagining himself a star athlete – a popular schoolboy fantasy of the time – gave him encouragement and purpose: 'The distance to my school had now tripled to three-quarters of a mile – and I had to come home for lunch. I soon discovered D. C. Thompson's excellent boys magazines, notably the *Wizard*, the *Rover* and the *Hotspur*, which I devoured voraciously. I fancied myself as the Great Wilson, the superhuman athlete, and sped back and forth to school in a haze of endeavour to better my times.'

For children accustomed to city and suburban life, country walks, even to and from school, often held a special magic. Margaret, who was eight, was living in the country near Newcastle, and she later remembered her long walk to the village school as idyllic. 'I still look back on those country walks with happiness. There was a village pond which we passed each way ... We walked 1½ miles to school and back. School was one huge room divided by screens.' Vera, on her second evacuation, in Devon, said that she enjoyed her long school walk far more than the schooling she received when she got there:

I had to walk 3 miles each way to school, which I loved. I still like walking in the country ... It was a small village school, and there was no room for us Londoners. During the summer our lessons were conducted in the shed in the playground, and in the winter we were put in the passage. We were all about thirteen, adolescents, boys and girls, so we showed off to each other and made our teacher's life hell.

My schooling was ruined by the war, I can honestly say . . . But when my fourteenth birthday came it was time to earn my living and I went straight back to London for the rest of the war. But that's another story!

It is hardly surprising that during the war, for the first time since compulsory education was introduced in 1870, standards dropped. The erratic and unsettled schooling of a large proportion of the school population took its toll. A specialist in education who was studying the progress of children in North Kensington, who were educated during the war amid frequent bombing raids, reckoned that they had 'lost up to five years of formal education'. Educational inspectors for the London County Council came to similar conclusions: they found that many thirteen- and fourteen-year-olds could not read a simple book – twice as many as in similar testing twenty years before. Spelling, arithmetic, history and geography had all suffered.

This falling-off of standards was widespread, though much depended on the individual area: the frequency of enemy raids and the availability of teachers and decent premises. Given the vast range, it is impossible to be more than tentative, but, overall, most children's learning suffered to some degree.

An important factor was absenteeism, which rose throughout the school population. In the cities, bomb damage often made getting to and from school difficult, and older children queued for the family's food, or looked after younger brothers and sisters while their mothers did war work. Some children were kept from school because their one pair of shoes was being mended; understandably, many stayed at home to make the most of their fathers', and other relatives', leaves.

A few favoured and well-disciplined schools – some grammar schools and independent boarding schools like Cheltenham Ladies' College – which stayed as a single unit were able to keep up standards and obtain their usual good exam results. And a mother proudly remembered that her son, educated 'by fits and starts at odd hours, at different secondary schools', nevertheless managed to get excellent grades in his Higher Certificate. For all the adversity of wartime, bright children still found a way through the state system right to the top. Sue, who narrowly escaped a direct hit during a heavy raid on Southampton, was another of them:

I had a really disturbed early childhood – many junior schools, and three changes of secondary. We experienced terrible urban bombing and destruction . . . After one particularly dreadful incident, when many were killed, Mum had had enough, and she, my sister and I took ourselves off to a tiny village near where Mum's sister had been 'in service' . . .

There were very few books in the household ever. (I think there was a copy of *Lorna Doone*, though maybe not.) Yet at seventeen I won an open scholarship to Oxford University – so the war must have done me no harm, at least in the sense of social or personal development.

School-leavers, the majority still only children of fourteen to fifteen, emerged into a dreary, dangerous and uncertain world, with the war affecting all hopes and future plans. As boys and girls took up first jobs, or began whatever training was available, all were aware of a probable stint in the forces looming ahead – particularly after the call-up age was lowered, although the actual call-up of those registered for service proceeded only slowly for some time.

Ironically, the same bleak conditions that so disoriented a middle-class youth with his – or her – eye set firmly on a profession could be a boon to the underprivileged. Joe, who had spent four years struggling from one dead-end job to another in a grim part of post-Depression Manchester, couldn't wait to get his call-up papers. He joined the RAF in 1941, and found his life in the services, and the benefits after the war, a passport to a new and better life. 'I literally never looked back,' he said. 'The war and joining up, and the people I came in contact with, were the best things that ever happened to me.'

Other youngsters, caught up in the drabness and monotony of wartime civilian life, got on with the job and hoped for the best. Ted, sixteen, and living near Hull, was an apprentice plumber and heating engineer at the time when enemy raids on the city were at their height: 'My first job was to reglaze windows. Each of us lads had a handcart of fifty squares of glass or more. We would put the glass in during the day, and the German raiders came over and blew them out at night.'

This was a depressing period for the able pupils who had stayed on in school to take Higher Certificate exams; most career training had to be put on hold, indefinitely. The universities, which had lost over a third of their teachers to the services, were running severely restricted courses; arts faculties had virtually closed down for the duration, and only medicine, teaching and some science and engineering courses were still being offered. Most university students, and sixth formers who had expected to start college courses, resigned themselves to the call-up and to taking their degrees after the war.

Most wartime school-leavers took whatever jobs were available until such time as they were called up or went to work in factories geared up for the war effort. Like many a lad awaiting call-up, Jack was working in a grocery shop, doling out family weekly rations as well as doing deliveries on his bike in between sirens. He and thousands like him faced the same daily grind: getting to work after raids, boring sandwiches for lunch, tiredness, and 'the dratted blackout'.

Jim got his first job, at fifteen, in an office near London Bridge. Like most city workers, he also remembered slogs to work on the mornings after punishing raids. 'The journey was often very tedious – my bus and tram would be rerouted because bombs had fallen or buildings collapsed . . . Sometimes, walking home from work or night school during a raid, the shrapnel from the anti-aircraft-gun shells became more dangerous than the bombs as pieces, still very hot, fell back to the ground. And all this was made more difficult because of the blackout.'

In Manchester, June took a series of temporary jobs before joining the ATS – the (women's) Auxiliary Territorial Service – in 1944. Not long out of school, she never forgot one incident at work:

One of my first jobs, at fourteen, was at Woolworth's. One day I was put on the counter that sold sweets and chocolate that of course were rationed. Along came two soldiers and asked for some chocolate. They didn't have any points, but I thought they deserved them so I sold them some anyway. Two ladies standing near by reported me to the manager, who gave me a real dressing down and said that, what with the sweets I ate and the ones I gave away without points, I was a loss to the firm. A couple of months later he was fired for dealing in the black market in a big way.

Many girls brought up in the country, or with a real feeling for animals, volunteered for the Women's Land Army at the first opportunity. This was a very popular form of war work. Mary, who had started work in a greengrocer's after leaving school, loved country life and had her heart set on it.

Directly I was seventeen I signed up for the Women's Land Army. By the following month I had got my uniform and was sent to a small farm in the south of England. There were just a few cows to milk by hand, and also some poultry and a horse and cart which we used for making hay, all by hand too.

After a year I went to a larger farm close by. There were three of us land girls working together. I was used to horses, so the farmer said I could look after the two big farm horses as well as milking the cows etc. etc.

This was real farming. We grew a lot of corn, potatoes, kale . . . We made huge corn ricks and haystacks, and used to help with threshing . . . We also did hedging and ditching by hand . . .

I got friendly with our neighbouring farmer's family and went out with his son, who taught me a lot about country ways: shooting pigeons and trapping rabbits and skinning them, which was handy as meat was very scarce. I used to admire many of the farmers who were in the Home Guard. They were often on duty at night, and were still up and about at 5.30 a.m. to milk the cows and do all the other chores.

PS. I married the farmer's son – and we are still at the same farm, semi-retired, but we still have our animals around us.

Nearly sixteen at the outbreak of war, Molly lived with her parents in Dulwich. Determined not to be evacuated with her school, she took a shorthand and typing course and, aged seventeen, got her first job in one of the major banks – which turned out to be a first for the bank too:

This was rather fun. I was the first female ever to darken their august doors in the City, and the staff did not know quite how to deal with me. I was, of course, the lowest of the low in terms of office hierarchy, but I was 'female' and as such was treated with great respect.

At that time the daylight raids over London had begun, and often, as the sirens sounded, we would descend to the strongroom below the Bank.

I would travel daily by bus and tube . . . Invariably there were many people lying on the platforms after seeking sanctuary there from the night's air raids. We just stepped over them into the carriages . . .

One day, after a particularly bad raid, there were no buses running so I set out to walk . . . I vividly remember stepping over the great hoses which bisected the main roads, and the acrid smell of the burning that was still going on.

Molly eventually left the bank and started on a three-year training in physiotherapy at one of the big London teaching hospitals. She completed her course with flying colours, despite the dangers of the rocket attacks, and the disrupted journeys.

Girls who had recently left school and started work were much in demand by lonely young servicemen away from home for the first time. 'My cousin and I used to go dancing at Covent Garden Opera House, which was turned into a great dance hall during the war,' one of them remembered. 'It was full of servicemen who looked lost, trying their best to have a bit of fun before going off to war. They all seemed so young – about eighteen years old or so.'

Many young women, and the boys they danced with in makeshift dance halls all over the country, retained happy memories of wartime that balance out some of the remembered drabness and ever present tensions. Nina, who could have stepped straight out of a romantic wartime film, was one of these. Bright and attractive, she had a lot of fun in wartime London, making the most of the feverish gaiety which existed among the danger. While she was still at school she spent night after night with her family in smelly and crowded shelters; later she knew the fear of watching deadly buzz bombs scoot across the skies, liable to cut out at any second. When she first left school she took a job in a department store in Piccadilly, until she was called up for war work at seventeen. She had volunteered for both the WAAF – the Women's Auxiliary Air Force – and the Women's Land Army, but she was turned down because they were full and was instead told to report to a building in Whitehall:

I was assigned as a temporary clerk (the lowest of the low) to the Admiralty, in the second Sea Lord's Department. I worked in a room with ten young sub-lieutenants, but was soon moved to another office because I was very pretty and the boys weren't able to concentrate . . .

About this time the Americans arrived, and through an officers club I met many air-force officers who wined and dined me – then saw me home to my parents. (No hanky-panky in those days!) We were in the thick of all the raids and the buzz bombs and the dread of D-Day, but still – oh what a lovely war!

Just before the end, while she was still working at the Admiralty, Nina met a dashing young British Spitfire pilot. For the girl who had gone through the highs and deep lows of war in London as a teenager, there was a happy ending: 'We married soon after, and are still luckily together after nearly sixty years.'

7

D-DAY AND DOODLEBUGS: JANUARY 1944 TO MARCH 1945

This photograph was taken three minutes after a V1 (doodlebug) hit a row of shops in Clapham, London, 17 June 1944. It gives a chilling picture of the devastation and panic this ferocious weapon caused when it exploded in a built-up area. The boy (bottom right) appears deeply shocked

*There was seldom a day in five years when enemy planes or
flying bombs or rockets were not over some part of the UK. Even
in the remotest areas, bombers of both sides droned in menace as
they sought targets or home bases.*
R. Titmuss, *Problems of Social Policy* (1950)

These were terror weapons, and they frightened us.
A girl of ten, living in 'Bomb Alley', in Kent, during the rocket attacks

Four and a half years into the war, weary civilians were struggling through the dreary winter and early spring of 1944. Sixteen-
year-old Bill, living in the London suburbs, had survived being
bombed out of his home with his parents and sister, followed by basic
emergency services and temporary housing – as well as taking on an
early-morning paper round, before school, to help out the family
finances. That winter he had just been 'conscripted' for Civil Defence
messenger duties. 'This was when the raids on London were less
severe, as they were from 1942 onward. I was there as a back-up in
case the telephone lines went down. All I did was to sit in the shelter
with the wardens, dozing in a chair all night. Not very exciting duty,
just very tiring. In fact, being tired is probably what I remember most
of those drab wartime days in 1943 and '44 – that and the rationing.'

But in the midst of all the gloom, the glutinous dried egg and the
scrapings of butter, there was one bright hope: the opening of the
longed for second front in western Europe. Most people believed it was
bound to happen soon, and persistent rumours and hearsay fed expectations. Everyone was sick and tired of the endless war and its consequences, which no one escaped, and prayed for some decisive move
towards its conclusion. All the signs pointed to an Allied invasion of

255

Europe, which increasingly was felt to be imminent. Catching the nation's desperation, a diarist living in London wrote somewhat wistfully, 'Every time we turn on the wireless we expect to hear that the great invasion of Europe has begun.'

More and more American forces were pouring into the country. Secret military exercises had been taking place for months, and people living in more remote parts of the countryside were well aware that strange things were afoot. In a desolate part of North Wales, mysterious concrete slabs that would play an important part in the Normandy landings were being produced at a site facetiously called 'the jam factory' by curious locals; clumsy, flat-bottomed boats – amphibious landing craft – were being tested by engineers and technicians; and it was common knowledge that a new pipeline was being laid along the seabed, able to supply oil to any beachhead that might be established.

Mary, who was ten, lived in London all through the war, and she has clear personal memories of the long, hard graft that went into making the long-awaited landings in Normandy a success.

My dad worked a six-and-a-half day week making parts for PLUTO (Pipeline Under the Ocean). Then when he came home he went out again during air raids on the 'Light Rescue Squad' – frequently having had to walk to and from work because of bomb damage to the tramlines. And this made problems for Mum too – getting us kids down to the shelter, feeding us all even if there was no gas, reassuring etc.

To my mind, there was a certain coldness from neighbours when their husbands were called up, leaving Dad in a reserved occupation. But did they really have the worst of it? I wonder.

All over the land, along sheltered beaches and stretches of riverbank, as far as possible from prying eyes, men in uniform took part in final preparations for what would be the greatest military invasion ever attempted. Operation Overlord, under the overall command of General Dwight D. Eisenhower, was beginning to take shape. Yet, for all the country's high hopes, the war's ending, like its beginning, would be protracted.

The first intimation of this came from the skies. At the start of 1944,

London and other industrial cities found themselves once more under severe enemy attack. 'The raids that winter were incredibly depressing,' Keith, then nine and living in north London, remembered.

Our small terraced house had been quite badly damaged in the earlier bombing and we had only just got straight, the windows put right etc. Now it was back to the sirens and the Anderson shelter. It had a bad effect on Mum, who was worried about Dad, in the army. He had been on leave, and she knew he was in for some big push . . . D-Day, of course, which he was at, but we didn't know then. She went all quiet, and me and my brother crept about and tried to keep out of her way for a bit.

After three relatively quiet years in the capital, when sirens had become less frequent and raids less destructive, the sudden renewal of prolonged and heavy bombing, known as the 'little Blitz', came as a hard knock to its exhausted citizens. From 21 January until the end of March, London suffered thirteen major air attacks; during February alone, almost 1,000 people were killed.

With renewed strength, and heavier and more destructive bombs, the Luftwaffe went after other vulnerable targets: Hull, Bristol and South Wales were also heavily attacked. The main feature of this series of raids – apart from the considerable loss of life and the destruction – was the ear-splitting noise they created, due to the more lethal German bombs, and more advanced British ack-ack guns.

Morale plummeted. But adults at least had the solace of plentiful cigarettes at last, although matches were still in short supply, and in the great cities – especially London, where ordinary lives were once again disrupted and endangered – gloomy stoicism prevailed. While many families in the areas again under attack made for the nearest shelters, or the underground, many more took the same view as Clive, a lad of thirteen living in west Kensington after several years of evacuation in the Dorset countryside: 'The air raids were happening then several times a week, but not with quite the severity of the Blitz. There were brick shelters in the streets, but we never used them – they were filthy and smelly, and often used as toilets. Mostly I slept through the raids, although when a bomb dropped very close by it made me nervous . . . but a warm bed and sleep always won out.'

After more short, sharp attacks in March, the raids tailed off and then ceased altogether, and by the time that spring took hold spirits had risen again and all hopes were fervently pinned on a second front. Shirley, twelve, whose older brother was in the forces, and who was living with her mother in a rented cottage in the Midlands, captured the buoyant mood: 'The end of this long and bloody war was getting nearer, we knew that, and there are no words to describe the undercurrent of excitement that everyone was feeling then.'

In large areas of the country the American servicemen added a dimension of gaiety, and relative affluence, to the strictly rationed home front: kids eagerly accepted chewing gum and candy, and sparky young girls, long starved of all glamour, were easily won over by offers of highly coveted nylon stockings.

Carrie, evacuated from London to the north Midlands with her family, remembered very clearly the febrile atmosphere of that spring – and particularly the 'Yanks':

The winter before, late in 1943, the rumour went round that the Yanks were coming. They came all right, and our town had never been so alive. My dad came to stay on leave, and believe it or not he brought with him Mum's beloved piano that had been stored for safety in the cellar of a London pub.

The Yanks soon found out about Mum, who was a natural songbird and liked nothing better than a good sing-song. They started to come looking for her . . . She used to invite the boys home for supper if she could get twopennorth of bones to make broth with. They were someone's son, husband, brother or father in a strange country, and Mum was trying to make up for the absence of her firstborn, who was fighting the Japanese in Burma.

I can remember in May, just before they were shipped out for D-Day, their band came to a big park near us. A lot of people had turned up thinking that it would be a military brass band. But soon even the diehards got 'in the mood' when the band really started swinging it.

We watched – and it was brilliant because they were playing Glenn Miller's music and when there was any catchy number that could be jitterbugged to the Yanks who were not in the band grabbed any young girl standing there and proceeded to jitterbug them all round the bandstand.

What a wonderful memory I have of that day . . .

Sadly, a few days after they started moving out. And we all knew why.

Vera, a pretty girl who was living at home near Manchester and longing for a bit of fun, also went out dancing that spring with the lively newcomers from across the Atlantic.

Life had to go on, and by the time I was sixteen, in 1944, I started going dancing in local dance halls and having lots of boyfriends.

An American regiment was stationed near by, and of course we met and danced with these very different people who always had plenty of cigarettes and were extremely generous. One in particular I met – I took him home, he got on very well with my family, he asked me to marry him (I had just turned seventeen) and I said yes, and he had his graduation ring cut down in size to fit me. We carried on going dancing, and the lights used to dim when a waltz was played . . .

I can remember standing there in the dance hall one night and noticing some black American soldiers, and I am so ashamed now to remember how scared I was. This was due to the way we had been brought up. Today I would fight to the death people who are racist, but it was very prevalent in those days and people did not approve of any girl going out with a black guy . . .

My boyfriend went away and I got friendly with a Canadian, so when Carl (the American) returned I gave him back his ring . . . This was just before D-Day. We lost touch after that.

They were all lovely boys, I often think of them. I just hope they got through it.

But territorial disputes could sometimes break out with the American servicemen. Basil, an older boy who was a bit miffed by the large GI presence locally, remembered:

There were two American bases near our town in Lancashire. The Americans would descend on the town at weekends – something eagerly awaited by the local girls. Scuffles broke out near the concert hall and the dance hall between the Yanks and the British servicemen home on leave.

The GIs really tried to make friends with the locals, especially with the children. They organized games of baseball in the park, and did their best to teach us how to play such a strange game.

For all the strict operational secrecy nobody, adult or child, could help noticing the steady build-up of massive military strength. 'Allied forces assembled and covered every field and beach,' a fifteen-year-old lad living on the Dorset coast remembered. Although these troops were concentrated towards the southern coasts, reinforcements fanned out right across the land. Angus, eight, whose father ran a boys' prep school, was living near the Yorkshire coast, where vital military preparations were taking place.

On the run up to D-Day hundreds of troops were billeted in the town. The streets were lined with army vehicles, including tanks. The East Riding being a good tank training area, a lot of fields on the Wolds were cut up with tank tracks as they carried out practice manoeuvres.

The troops were made up from several different countries. A lot of the trucks were given names – my favourites were named after the seven dwarfs. And there was one very sad incident, which really struck me as a child, and which I have never forgotten: two Polish soldiers were working on the engine of a tank when it fell on them, killing both men. They were buried in a nearby cemetery, and a big Polish cross stands over the graves to this day.

All through May, convoys of troops, tanks and lorries clogged roads in the southern counties, and trainloads of supplies jammed the railway lines. A boy who would become one of the major military historians of the period watched, fascinated, as the operation gathered strength along the byways and in the fields of the West Country. It was seeing these pre-invasion forces assemble, he wrote later, that inspired his lifelong military passion. And on a trivial personal level too, plans were being made around the anticipated landings. A girl in the WVS wrote to her mother, only half in jest, 'I feel I must see the dentist before the second front starts.'

At Windsor Castle, the heir to the throne, Princess Elizabeth, celebrated her eighteenth birthday. The friends she had been brought up with – girls who had been equally sheltered within their families –

joined up or took jobs in factories, as was mandatory. But being royal brought its own constraints, even in wartime. Any sort of normal active service that an aristocratic girl would have taken for granted then, and probably thought of as something of an adventure, was out of the question. But the Princess was permitted to enrol in an NCO's cadre course for the ATS, and duly acquired the dreary regulation khaki uniform – with which she was reported to have been delighted.

Younger children were allowed to abandon lessons to watch the convoys of American soldiers moving south for what would be the Normandy invasion. Jill, eleven, who had been evacuated to a village near Southampton, at the very heart of D-Day preparations, remembered it as an extraordinary time – the whole area full of Allied soldiers encamped in any available billet and pasture, and providing lots of excitement for the local kids:

They were a source of all sorts of goodies, chewing gum and innumerable badges which they handed out – the local boys got quite a collection, which they wore very proudly on their belts. They also provided empty drums and excellent caulking material, leading to the appearance of a small armada of home-made rafts jostling for space in the village ponds. When they went off to France, many of them threw change out of the lorries and personnel carriers at us kids – the soldiers didn't think they would need their English coins again.

As the countdown to D-Day approached, the accuracy of the weather forecasting had become crucial. With the invasion scheduled for 5 June 1944, fierce storms blew up, hitting the Channel and coastal areas, and the C-in-C, General Eisenhower, postponed the entire, immensely complex operation for twenty-four hours. It was the right decision – as predicted, there was a lull in the storms, the seas calmed somewhat, and visibility improved. On 6 June, D-Day had come at last. After almost exactly four years, a 'Dunkirk in reverse' (as Angus Calder put it) had been achieved.

British paratroopers had already gone in and the first US troops were landing on the French beaches when Jean, who lived in Ipswich, looked up at the skies from her house: 'Very early on the morning of

6 June I stood in my back garden and saw all the planes and gliders fly from six o'clock in the morning to dusk. Wherever you looked there were planes. It was the start of D-Day, we heard on the wireless.'

Also in East Anglia, ten-year-old Jenny was up early on that memorable day: 'I can remember standing outside the cottage and waving to the pilots. They had just taken off from Ely Aerodrome, up the road from us, so were still flying low – low enough to be flying not far above the cottage roof. People these days can't comprehend just how low those planes flew, or how young the pilots were.'

Later that day, in Cambridge, nine-year-old Carola was walking with her mother through the market place to the shops. 'The threatening sound of planes made me look up. The sky gradually filled with huge Wellington bombers, each towing two gliders. They were in formation, like migrating birds. Later, after the rather sparse news bulletins, my mother told me that they must have been taking the troops to D-Day.'

Philip, seventeen, studying hard for exams, was in class with his schoolmates in Hampshire on D-Day morning. Not far off call-up age himself, he took its implications very seriously. 'The headmaster came into the room to inform us that there had been a landing in France. The second front had started. We listened avidly to every broadcast as a bridgehead was established and the slow advance began. Those annals of war were then imprinted on my mind . . . I was growing up and nearing the age when I would be called up for military service.'

A brother and sister, aged ten and twelve, children of a serving naval officer, who lived on the coast near Portsmouth, had watched some of the troops embarking:

We were allowed access to a very limited part of the beach, and we went down to wave the troops goodbye as they marched into the long, unwieldy-looking landing craft. Even to us, they all looked so young . . . It was just before D-Day, and we knew something big was starting. The Welch Regiment was parading its emblem up and down – a live goat . . . Huge pontoons had been built out into the sea . . . We also saw enormous pieces of concrete being towed by barges. Later we realized that they were the parts of the floating Mulberry harbour.

Another small boy, Michael, aged eight, was living close to the sea in Kent. He also watched, intrigued, as these unlikely concrete flotillas prepared to launch: 'Although we had no idea what it was all for, this fantastic fleet of concrete caissons and floating bridges was on its way to Arromanches . . . to be sunk on the seabed off the French coast to form a harbour for ships bringing supplies to the invasion forces. They were of course the Mulberry harbours.' Michael's prime view of one of the brilliant technical aspects of Operation Overlord had a surprising resonance later on in his life: 'Little did I know in June 1944 that thirty-five years later, as a civil engineer, I would be designing a large harbour on the Libyan coast using much the same techniques. Involvement with this project brought me into contact with some of those very distinguished civil engineers who had created the Mulberry harbours so many years before.'

Across the Channel, where the vital Mulberry harbours were headed, eleven-year-old Yvette, who had been trapped with her English mother and three brothers and sisters at the family holiday home in Brittany for four desperate years, was ecstatic when the news of the landings broke. In her diary of the grim years of occupation she wrote, 'June 6th. DÉBARQUEMENT – Great Excitement! We all imagine that we will be liberated very soon, and follow any news avidly. On the wall of our main room we have a map of Europe, upon which we had been following the progress of the war, especially in Russia, with wool attached to pins.'

Alas, surrounded by badly rattled German troops, doing their best to stay unobserved, the following year was nerve-racking for the family. The Allies were advancing close by, but not yet in control of the region. In August Yvette recorded sadly, 'We are bombed twice by the Americans.' The area was becoming dangerous – and life was hard. Many years later, Yvette remembered those difficult times in painful detail:

The Germans confiscated all bicycles, even our children's bicycle . . . Farmers were made to transport some German ammunition, so that the Resistance would think twice about blowing it up . . . Food was very scarce, and there was no electricity. We would walk along the railway track to see friends or fetch food, as the roads were either mined or flooded to hinder the Allied advance. Bread was a brown sticky mess with maggots, and there was of course a curfew.

The family managed to escape to relatives near Nantes, where they hid for the rest of the war. 'The region of Saint-Nazaire, where we had our house, was finally liberated on 11 May 1945 – three days after the remainder of Europe. We sailed home, to England, to our father, on 25 July.'

The Germans announced the invasion at 8 a.m. on 6 June. At 9.30 came the calm, reassuring voice of John Snagge on the BBC: 'D-Day has come. Early this morning the Allies began the assault on the north-western face of Hitler's European fortress.' After the nine o'clock news that night the first eyewitness account from the French beaches was broadcast. Despite fierce enemy resistance, beachheads had been established; substantial numbers of Allied troops had left the beaches by nightfall and had begun the slow push across France. Casualties, while grave, were far less than the military's worst estimates had suggested.

Many people would remember D-Day, and what they were doing when they heard the news, as a pivotal marker in their lives. That night the King spoke soberly to the country, praising his subjects for all they had endured in the past four years since 'Our nation . . . stood alone . . . with our backs to the wall.'

After the weeks and months of hectic activity, there was a sudden hush. Jenny, who was living in a Hampshire village, remembered that 'The night before D-Day all the roads around my house were full of army vehicles and ambulances. The next day they had vanished – all gone over to France.' Diana, eight, who lived near by, closer to the coast, remembered that the sea was 'black with landing craft on 5 June'; by the next morning they had all mysteriously disappeared.

During the following days there was a stampede outside cinemas to see the first invasion newsreels; many people were emotionally undone by the raw power of their hopes and anxieties, and watched in tears. As subsequent waves of soldiers and tanks poured down the streets to the ports, women came out of their houses and plied them endlessly with food, cigarettes, and tea.

Robert, now eleven, was living in Scotland with his mother and grandparents, barely remembered peacetime, but came to have a gradual awareness of the war and its implications. And he understood the significance of the D-Day landings, which affected him very personally.

At some stage during the war I became aware of the evacuation of children from cities, and counted myself lucky that I could stay with my family. Awareness of these, and other things, crept into my life gradually, as did a deeper understanding of the war and what was going on.

When D-Day arrived I studied the maps in the papers as if my life depended on them. Father was somewhere in France (having gone out to Egypt with Montgomery, been at El Alamein, invaded Sicily, then back briefly to the UK). I had seen him only two or three times since 1940, but I knew he was part of the advancing lines printed daily in the newspapers.

All too swiftly, the sad and tragic consequences of the landings also filtered back, dulling the immediate euphoria. This was war – and it was not yet over. As Allied reinforcements streamed into France, German prisoners of war 'were being herded the other way, through the docks into waiting trains', as a fifteen-year-old boy, who was watching, reported. Tragic news and young, broken bodies came back too.

Dan, ten, who had been evacuated with his sister to Devon at the beginning of the war, was now at home with his family in east London. He witnessed, and never forgot, one of the many casualties of D-Day at close quarters:

I contracted jaundice early in 1944 and was away from school for two to three months. My first day up I walked round the corner from our house to the newsagent to buy a comic and I was astonished to see all the tanks and armoured personnel carriers trundling along the streets. It was 6 June, and the invasion was under way.

Two doors up from us lived a family we were very close to. The daughter was the same age as my sister, her brother Jim a bit older – about eighteen. He went over on the D-Day landings, the first day. He returned about a week later minus one leg and the foot on the other. I feel the tears welling up every time I think of him over these past sixty years. He was a sweet, gentle, quiet boy, but completely broken by this catastrophe – as was his mother, and all the family who helped nurse him.

Tom, who was then nearly eleven, wrote of an agonizing episode that happened within his home. The scene stayed with him – its sadness, as well as its compassion and humanity, marking him for life:

At the time of the Normandy landings my mother and sister and I were living in a large house overlooking the sea in Kent. My father was serving in the army in Egypt. As we had plenty of spare space, several soldiers were billeted in the house during the build-up to the landings. One was a major, with his wife and their small son of about five or six, a few years younger than me.

I have retained a most poignant memory of probably 7 or 8 June. The major was killed on the beaches in Normandy, and the telegram to his wife from the War Office was delivered to our house.

I can still see my mother comforting his wife on the receipt of this dreaded telegram, and have often thought that I learned more that day about comforting those in distress than all the armies of counsellors who nowadays appear on the scene of any disaster.

About a week after the Normandy landings, on the night of 12/13 June, with the country in a mood of restrained relief, a curious sputtering commotion was heard over Greater London and parts of the south-east; earth-shattering explosions followed. This marked the beginning of the V1 and V2 rocket assaults.

Intelligence reports had suggested a year before that a new and far deadlier weapon was on the verge of being unleashed by the enemy, and Churchill had mentioned it in a broadcast in March, warning of 'new forms of attack'. The government had been fearful of mass panic, but the first public reaction was one of astonishment rather than fear. Three days later a heavy bombardment started, with rockets being aimed from bases in the Pas de Calais. And on 16 June the Cabinet ruled that these terrifying weapons should be known not as 'pilotless planes' but as 'flying bombs' – soon to be nicknamed 'doodlebugs' or 'buzz bombs', which helped to lessen the sense of menace and fear that they instilled.

Tim, ten, living in Kent, right on what became known as 'Bomb Alley', the rockets' flight path from the Continent to London, remembered the V1 onslaught beginning – although at the time he had no idea of what he was witnessing:

I suddenly spotted one of the first V1 pilotless planes out of the first-floor window of my home . . . The plane had a coloured light and showed up clearly in the night sky. I think at the time my parents were unaware of what it was. Quite soon the engine stopped and the plane came down in a cornfield nearby. My parents learned very quickly what this new weapon was, and within twenty-four hours or so I was whisked away from home to family in Monmouthshire.

For two weeks, rockets arrived at the rate of about 100 per day, causing terrible destruction and high casualties where they fell. A good proportion were knocked out by fighters and ack-ack emplacements, and more than half did not reach the outskirts of London. Probably the worst-hit area was Croydon, which lay on their route to the City. Areas mainly affected outside London were Kent and East Sussex, although when the Germans took to launching them from conventional planes a few later fell as far afield as Yorkshire and Shropshire.

The doodlebugs' fiery tails were seen very clearly at night. As the rocket passed overhead, the immediate vicinity was safe; it was after the fuel was exhausted and the engine cut out that the tense moments of waiting ensued, with people diving for cover no matter where they were until it crashed. This was followed by a brilliant flash and a high plume of black smoke. It is fair to say that no one, even quite young children, ever forgot being under attack from either the V1s or (later) the V2s.

Margaret and her younger brother lived in the Sussex countryside, right along Bomb Alley. 'When we heard the doodlebugs coming over, we used to run up the back garden path to watch and listen to them going by. We knew that if the engine stopped overhead they would glide down and crash some distance away. The noise they made going over – on towards London – was a low chugging sound.'

Parental anxiety was such that a third evacuation, the smallest of the three main evacuations, was set in motion. By this time many of the earlier evacuees had returned to London, their families believing that, as the major bombing attacks had abated, it was relatively safe. Dora, fourteen, who had been evacuated to Devon and who had settled in very happily with her foster family, remembered that summer of 1944 as being an unhappy time:

When the doodlebugs started, my resentment at being brought home to the smells of cordite and ruined buildings and a very restricted diet on strict rations, not at all like the farm in Devon, really came to the fore and I repeatedly asked my mother why she had brought us home ... It was very depressing, but there was no fear amongst us children as I recall ...

After the country, it was all very strange. I've never forgotten the blue light bulbs in trains and some buses, and the utility seats in some double-decker buses. They were just varnished slats, and if you went round a corner too fast the ones on the outside edge ended on the floor. We all just laughed.

London and its suburbs were being abandoned once more as the V1s continued to get through. Everyone was nervy, on edge, and stories of tragedies and near misses abounded. Soon after D-Day, Mollie, twelve, who had been evacuated to the country with her family, made a quick trip to London with her mother to visit a sick relative.

It was late June, just after the first V1 rockets started coming over ... We were to visit my auntie, who was seriously ill in hospital. I was not very happy about this, because I had an aversion to hospital smells and always used to pass out. So my mother let me go off to the nearest cinema and meet her later.

Meanwhile, there were V1s flying high overhead, all of them going right across London ...

I spotted the roof of the cinema I was heading for at exactly the same moment as a V1 came over – and cut out. I shot into the nearest doorway and covered my head with my coat. The explosion lifted me right off my feet, but apart from the shock I wasn't hurt.

Was that person called God, who my mother had always called upon during the Blitz, looking after me? I had a narrow escape not being in the cinema at that moment. Many people lost their lives.

I was so thankful to see our funny little cottage again when we got home.

One of the great tragedies of that cold, wet and dangerous summer was the direct V1 hit on the Guards' Chapel during Sunday morning service on 18 June, which shocked the nation; many distinguished military personnel and their families were present, and the casualties were high: 119 people were killed, and 200 badly injured. By late August, 1½ million people had left Greater London, some children being evacuated through the official government scheme, many for the second or third time, but most evacuating themselves privately.

Despite the success of the D-Day landings, the Allied advance was arduous and the enemy resistance, in places, fierce and brave. Nevertheless, the British Second Army under Montgomery entered Caen after desperate fighting on 9 July, and on 25 August, to great international rejoicing, Paris was liberated. These hard-won Allied triumphs were celebrated triumphantly on the home front.

Yet still the V1s got through. It was estimated that some 6,725 were launched, of which perhaps 3,000 landed on a target of some kind, although many fell far short of what was intended and crashed in the extreme south-east, frequently in open fields or in suburban areas. A lot were shot down by anti-aircraft guns as they reached the coast. Fatalities were put at six and a half thousand, with huge numbers of casualties and great destruction.

For Sam, living on the outskirts of London, these deadly machines sailing high above him became a common sight, and he would often spot them on his way to and from school. 'We saw many V1s passing noisily over the allotments at the back of our house. I distinctly remember the fire coming out of their tails. We knew that as long as they went on flying we were safe.'

Daphne, fourteen, living in East Anglia, remembered the fear and loathing these alien contraptions spread, as well as the neighbourly desire to help out which so many people recall of those bleak wartime years:

The doodlebugs were a nightmare. When that low, menacing drone was heard in the distance everyone in the village would come outside and look up, listening as the noise got louder, knowing that when the noise stopped the bomb would fall – and there was no way of knowing where.

When it fell to earth and exploded, all the men would get on their bikes and ride towards the area to see what help they could give. It sounds silly now to think that the only form of transport most people had was a bike, but people would go long distances in the pitch black just to see if there was something to be done to help.

Carola, at home in Cambridge with her mother and sister, was all too aware even then of the V1's danger, and later remembered every awesome detail of her family's brush with instant oblivion.

A droning sound, like a queen wasp roused from hibernation in midwinter, woke me. It was early morning, sometime in 1944. The sound of a V1 – a doodlebug – was horribly familiar and never to be forgotten. Soon after came the air-raid warning. The two sounds ran parallel, but, as the siren stopped, the other went on, getting nearer. The ominous silence fell as the engine cut out. Where would it fall? My sister and I had climbed into bed with my mother, and we lay in silent fear. A dull thud told us we had survived.

Bob, a Londoner, was evacuated first to Brighton, then Devon, being brought back home by his parents 'just in time for the Blitz'. His worst doodlebug experience was spine-chilling, even though it occurred in august surroundings:

In the spring of 1944 I was fifteen. I worked Monday to Friday, 8 a.m. to 6 p.m., and Saturdays, 8 a.m. to 12.30 p.m., as an office boy. Then on Sunday mornings, beginning at 4 a.m., I did what was known as W.H. Smith's Rollups, and I had the poshest paper round going – Sunday papers for the famous. I was the Prime Minister's Sunday-morning paper boy, and also did Anthony Eden, Lord Beaverbrook, Lord Alexander and many others. We sent Lord Halifax's to the US. He was then our ambassador in Washington. For this I got the unbelievable amount of 25/6d. (£1.27) – and it only took one and a half hours. Started at Lambeth Bridge, finished near Buckingham Palace. No, I didn't do the Palace!

One Sunday morning that summer I turned off Whitehall into

Downing Street to deliver the last of the papers to the Foreign Office and Mr Churchill. In those days there was a sandbagged barricade, manned by the Brigade of Guards, at the entrance to Downing Street. Whenever I cycled there it was dark, and there was always a cry of 'Halt, who goes there?' I would slow down the bike and shout back, 'Paper boy', then there was a 'Pass, paper boy', the barrier was lifted, and into the street I rode.

One morning a doodlebug cut out over Whitehall just as I was handing the papers to the porter at No. 10. He pulled me inside, and we stood there for those awful, dreaded moments.

Then as soon as the bang went off – horribly close by – he threw me out again.

Living on the outskirts of London, Steven and his friend had a lucky escape – with a humorous musical twist:

We lived in a three-storey house and had a wonderful view all over London – indeed, when the doodlebugs passed over us we would rush to the attic and watch the things explode . . .

One day I was playing – rather appropriately – 'I know that my Redeemer liveth' on my trumpet, my school friend accompanying me on the piano, when there was an almighty explosion very close and the house was instantly uninhabitable. A doodlebug had just missed us . . .

By nightfall – this was the morning – we had been successfully rehoused by a team sent from the rescue organisation . . . And I had even managed to take my trumpet to a place in Kennington to have it repaired!

Paul, nine, who would later become an engineer, showed his technological bent early in life; he remembered that as a child he was both intrigued and appalled by the V1s, for all their menace.

In many ways these were the most fascinating German weapons. They came over by day and by night. In the daylight they were easily recognizable, and at night you could see the afterburn of their jet engine. They were, I think, designed to glide down on to their target once their engine had cut out, so that the resultant explosion spread over as wide an area as possible. However, they did not all work properly and many of them came straight down in a nosedive.

This, to put it mildly, could be disconcerting . . . I particularly remember one evening when all my family were sitting round the dining table and one cut out immediately overhead. We all dived under the table, but fortunately the thing worked properly and glided on to hit the ground some miles away.

Ken, fifteen, who had been happily evacuated to a village in Devon, where he joined the local gang and made friends, did not take kindly to being brought home to his family in London in 1944:

Our small, grimy back garden was a poor contrast with my foster parents' spacious country one . . . I had become so used to village ways that I asked my father where he kept the chickens. 'Life will be different for you now, son,' he said, laughing. And wasn't it just! At weekends I delivered greengroceries to houses, with large wooden boxes balanced precariously on a 'trade bike', dodging the rubble from the doodlebugs. One morning I was knocked off the bike by the explosion of a doodlebug and had to take all the boxes back to the shop for repacking. I also remember another nearby crash from a doodlebug which panicked the milkman's horse into bolting, throwing milk crates left and right. We noticed after that that the horse seemed to get used to buzz bombs, and only showed signs of unease when the engine cut out – which meant that it was about to fall nearby.

Joan, seventeen, whose father was tragically lost at sea earlier in the war, was living with her mother in Portsmouth. All her life she remembered the V1s flying overhead as a fearsome time. 'Seeing the V1 rockets going over and waiting for the engine to cut out – they really did frighten us all. They were truly terror weapons.'

Wendy, ten, had been evacuated from her suburban home to the safety of 'leafy Bucks'; her parents kept her right away from the city over the holidays, but not all her friends were so fortunate. 'The buzz bombs had started in the summer of 1944, and at the beginning of the next term there were two empty desks where classmates had been caught while they were visiting their parents in London during the holidays.'

Peter lived in west London and never forgot the sheer horror of suddenly finding himself and his mother much too close to a doodle-bug for comfort.

My mother and I were walking near the Grand Union Canal when a V1's motor cut out and it started its damaging plunge to earth ... It did not fall towards us but on the Brentford Docks about a mile away. The explosion sent up a cloud of black smoke high in the sky ...

Then a few days later a friend of my parents was shaving before a mirror in his house in south-east London when he heard a V1 come over. He dived under the bed. The V1 fell in the road outside, bringing the house down. He was eventually rescued by Civil Defence workers. He had to be bathed four times to get him clean.

Late in 1944 Tommy started work as an apprentice in an engineering firm in Battersea which had been bombed out earlier in the war and was operating in temporary premises.

Our makeshift office was situated in an old glass-roofed building that had windows on three sides. We had six people working when we heard this buzz bomb more or less over our heads. Someone came running from another office and shouted at us to get out and take cover. With three others I climbed into a brick cupboard with steel-plated doors, used to store historic records. They had just pulled me inside and were closing the doors behind me when the bomb exploded.

After a few moments we heard voices outside calling, 'Are you all right in there?' Then someone tried to pull the doors open. It was difficult, because they had buckled in the blast. Eventually we got out, pretty shaken and covered in cobwebs and rusty flakes.

The doodlebug had fallen about 500 yards away from the office. A row of houses was demolished.

Rockets fell at random, and children were spared neither death nor injury, nor massive damage to homes and schools. They also witnessed the dreadful sights and the grievous casualties which the V1s inflicted when they crashed, as so many did, in crowded urban districts.

Will was sixteen and living in the London suburb of Chingford in the summer of 1944. As he remembered for ever after, he was calmly revising for the School Certificate exams he was to sit the following day when the siren went. Within minutes he had experienced sudden, shocking tragedy; he dealt with it as best he could, bravely and unhesitatingly:

A June evening . . . the siren went at 21.20 . . . I was going to the shelter with my father, an invalid, when we heard the racket of a flying-bomb motor and saw it was low down, heading for us. It cut out and started to dive to the right, and we crouched down as it exploded about 400 metres away. After the tiles, glass and dust had settled, I jumped on my bike and got to the scene of the incident in about six minutes. It had exploded in the back garden of a house where neighbours lived. The son was a friend of mine. The area was absolutely still, no movement . . . My main recollections are of blasted debris and earth and the cloying sweet smell . . .

I found the first victim in the road, a man who was still breathing, and I went on to the next, a woman in a summer dress, obviously dead. I noticed particularly the greeny bronze tinge of their bodies, the effect of the blast . . . People then began to arrive – a girl of my own age, who immediately went into a nearby house and came out with blankets with which we covered the man and the woman . . .

We then went over to a car . . . The driver was slumped behind the wheel, and as the vehicle was shattered we assumed he must be dead from the state he was in. I went to search the ruins of the house for my friend, but could only make my way through the rubble of what had been the front room.

The rescue team arrived. I told them about the family that I believed was buried there, and rode home . . .

The family, the parents and their son, were never found.

For all its terror, with the ever present threat of sudden death or injury, life continued in London and the south-east fairly normally. Young people, eager to get on with their lives, made the best of things. Nina, an eighteen-year-old who was excited, and a bit overawed, to be working in the Admiralty as her first job, looked back on that time, despite its omnipresent danger, with some nostalgia. 'During our lunch hour a group of us would go to the top of the building – in Birdcage Walk, near Whitehall – to see where the V1s were landing.

On other days we would go into St James's Park to listen to the band and watch the birds on the lake. What a lovely war!'

In 1944 Molly was training to be a physiotherapist, and still living with her family in Dulwich. She and her fellow students were working at a unit of Guy's Hospital at Orpington where badly injured service personnel were sent. Her V1 recollection vividly illustrates the sheer horror that could strike, with no warning, at any hour during any ordinary working day.

As I left Dulwich station, near my home, a flying bomb passed in the opposite direction. I heard the engine stop, prior to falling and exploding. I knew it was heading towards the home I had just left.

I phoned directly I arrived at Orpington, and to my relief found that our house had been missed. Sadly, however, the bomb had fallen and demolished the house of good friends. The mother of the family was killed; the rest of the family had not been there at the time. They came and lived with us until they could be housed elsewhere.

At the end of August came the wonderfully heartening news that British troops had overrun the V1 launching sites in the Pas de Calais. With the Allies in control of vital bases, the attacks appeared all but over. But not forgotten – nobody who had lived through them could manage that. A woman who had been close to a major explosion in Croydon, which had caused grave casualties, said recently, 'I was nine, and I clearly remember those seconds, all of us crouching down under the table . . . the engine cut out . . . waiting . . . waiting . . . then the hideous bang . . . I still shiver when I think about it now.' Many people with similar experiences agree. Of all the violent and disturbing memories of air raids that children took from the war, few were more vivid and long-lasting than those of the V1s and V2s.

Part of the area from which the rockets were launched is still maintained as a museum, and visitors to the site nearly fifty years later could still detect an atmosphere of menace and evil emanating from the derelict quarries where slave labourers from eastern Europe had built the launch pads for the attacks on the UK which might have, but did not, devastate the country.

Despite the general relief after the British overran the French launching sites, almost a thousand more doodlebugs were hurled over from launch pads in the Hague. Seventy-nine reached London, but the great danger of mass attack had passed. Yet no sooner had the general jubilation died down than on 8 September yet another – quite different – unearthly, shrieking explosion was heard, the first in Chiswick and a second, immediately after, in Epping.

The number of these explosions increased, and by November some four to six were occurring daily along the same path as the doodle-bugs had taken. At first, the government tried to pass them off as 'gas explosions' to a jittery public, but it was soon clear that this was the arrival of the monstrous V2 rockets: 45 feet long, weighing 14 tons, and travelling so fast that their approach was silent, these were true weapons of mass destruction.

It was doubly unfortunate that these second-generation pilotless rockets started arriving at the same time as depressing news from the Allied front was being absorbed: the daring British airborne landing at Arnhem had failed catastrophically, and further advances on the main Allied fronts were being stalled, or repulsed, by the Germans. With the onset of the even deadlier V2s, there was grave concern that on the home front too the enemy might at last have found a key to the widespread destabilizing of morale. People who were close to a V2 explosion, and fortunate not to have been killed instantly, were badly scarred by this grotesque method of destruction.

A six-year-old girl later recalled how a V2 attack had shattered her family: 'Our house was destroyed on 5 November 1944. My mother and my brother, who was eight, were both killed. But I survived. I was very badly hurt and shocked . . . and I was in hospital for months afterwards. My poor father, who was at work at the time, came home to devastation and thought that we had all been killed.' She was taken by her father to be looked after by relatives in Wales, where she stayed ever since. But her plight on that November day must have been heart-wrenching even to the emergency services, hardened after years of death and devastation: 'I have an interesting letter from the fire service of that time. They collected £15 for me, and I still have the savings certificates. Why they did this for me I do not know, as £15 was a lot of money back then.'

Peter was working in a builder's office in south London at that time, waiting for his call-up papers to arrive. Although he had lived in the London area through the entire war, he found what was to be the last autumn of conflict 'far worse than all the other times I had experienced'.

He spoke for many. The shortages, the drudgery and the constant lurking danger had taken their toll; now, on top of all this, the mightiest and most terrifying weapon of all had to be faced. If the Germans had been able to mount an accurate and sustained V2 bombardment, even at that late stage the war's outcome might have been different.

Peter recalled one V2 incident in particular, probably in November 1944, which unnerved him in a way no previous enemy bombing raids had.

I was going home from work and had got about half a mile from our house. To my horror I turned the corner and saw the damage that had been wreaked by this monstrous rocket . . . It had exploded earlier, in the air, a few roads away from where I lived. At least seven or eight terraced housed had been completely demolished. It all looked like a huge pile of bricks and timber and a tremendous crater where the houses had been. I simply couldn't believe my eyes . . . thinking that I had walked by these houses only this morning on my way to work.

Harry, a schoolboy of eight, and perhaps unaware of the full deadly effect of these monstrous rockets, was less awed by their apparently supernatural powers of death and destruction. He remembered one gruesome occurrence as an adventure he shared with his friends – but he, too, never forgot the awesome sight.

Once, during school playtime, a V2 exploded high above with an almighty bang, leaving a misshapen ball of smoke. We were all told to go home, but less than an hour later we kids were on the spot, by bike. One or two ambulances were already there, by what had been some buildings. The crater was huge, many metres in all directions, stepped, and very deep, and the rocket motor lay at the bottom.

Every piece of glass was shattered in the nearby greenhouses of a market garden. The shrapnel from the explosion radiated out from the crater as far as we could see. Of course we wanted to collect bits, but all the rescue services arrived – there must have been many casualties – and we were told to get right away.

Although they were only thirteen, enterprising twin boys volunteered as Fire Brigade messengers around the time the V1s and V2s started coming over. They had been evacuated more than once, but as true Londoners the boys immediately lobbied to be brought back home – which they were. 'We saw the most terrible sights,' they agreed. 'There were so many appalling incidents near where we lived and did our volunteering.'

For various reasons, the boys did not always work together, so only one of them was involved in this particularly dramatic incident:

One V2 exploded and hit a pub in Shooter's Hill (London). A passing bus was also set ablaze. I was on duty 100 yards from the scene, so I was the first to arrive. Soldiers from the local barracks soon arrived, and we scrambled to try and rescue people. Beside the pub was an ambulance station, also demolished. It was a horrific scene.

The chief fire officer sent me, as the smallest rescuer, down into the pub debris to assist someone crying out for help. I went down with a rope and tied it round a young girl who was so covered in dust that she was hard to recognize. When she was safely brought up the rope was sent down again to lift me out.

It was rather weird . . . I suddenly found myself speaking with an Irish accent. My grandmother was Irish, but I have never spoken with an Irish accent, before or since . . . The fire officer said, 'You've done your bit, Paddy. Get a cup of tea and go home.'

I was then just fourteen.

The following day the chief superintendent of police called at our door to congratulate me for saving his daughter. I asked him how he knew me, and he replied, 'My daughter said you were one of the twins.'

My father then believed me. He had been very sceptical of my story, as indeed was my twin brother. Instead of going on duty with me that day he had taken a young lady to the pictures.

Perhaps because the deadly V2 rockets were still crude and difficult to direct at targets accurately, and it was clear that at last the war's end really was in sight, the total collapse of morale on the home front that Germany hoped for simply did not happen. The public's nerve held.

Attacks were largely confined to Greater London and the south east. In all, 518 of these grotesque rockets – which flew faster than the speed of sound so were invisible before explosion occurred – reached the Greater London area, causing about 3,000 deaths and an astonishing amount of structural damage. But by the end of the year the assaults had dropped to a minimum. Nevertheless, so many homes had been damaged that vital resources had been diverted into urgent rebuilding work.

With characteristic British phlegm, domestic life carried on as normally as possible throughout. And for one woman who was then a child in London the mention of a V2 rocket brings to mind not a casualty, or a shattering explosion, or a demolished house, but *soup*. Geoffrey and his sister were living on the fourth floor of a block of flats in the east of London during the V1 and V2 rocket strikes.

On one occasion my mother had spent hours making vegetable soup, and had just put it out in bowls on the table when the sirens sounded. Usually we ran to friends on the ground floor. But not this time. We should eat first, Mum insisted.

Then, just as we put our spoons in the bowls for our first taste, a V2 fell on Hackney Downs, causing an almighty bang, then a deafening explosion, missing us by a quarter of a mile. The shock waves blasted all the soot down the chimney into our sitting room – and, of course, on to the soup.

We were literally quaking . . . And all Mum could say after such a close shave was 'Look, this soup is ruined.'

8

WAR AND THE FAMILY – AND VICTORY!

At last, at last, Dad's home. A soldier from the Eighth Army is welcomed at the garden gate by his happy family, all dressed up for the occasion, when he arrives home soon after VE Day

The bomb sites were our playgrounds.
An East End child in wartime

My father died on active service on HMS Barham . . . He was thirty-two.
A girl from a service family, brought up in Portsmouth

My elder brother went into the Air Force and we did not see him again for a long time. My little sister was shy and cried when he came home. She did not recognize him.
A boy who lived in East Anglia

In time of war, the family came first. It was the bedrock that under-pinned nearly every child's experience during those six unsettling years – through the evacuations, the wailing sirens, the proximity of death, the shortages, the haphazard teaching. For children crouched in an air-raid shelter dreading what sights the morning would bring, or gorging on half a precious orange, it was mums and dads and brothers and sisters and other relatives who counted. Most people who were then children believe that, whatever their circumstances, the strength and resilience of family life were paramount.

A boy who was seven when the war began spent more than half of those years billeted on reliable foster parents, living above their village shop. But, despite not being at home with his mother and father and older brothers, he said firmly that his parents were never less than central to his life. 'I was evacuated to the countryside in Sussex from south London. I stayed nearly four years. All that time, I never worried about my parents. I knew they would be all right – they were invin-cible. And I knew that deep down they were always there for me.'

Within families, each turned to the other for support, to try to make some sense out of the desperate situation into which they were plunged. As a result, there is hardly a family then in the land which hasn't one or two treasured wartime memories and anecdotes of parents, grandparents, uncles, cousins – telling and retelling them, handing them on to younger relatives, making them a part of family legend. Mary's family, dithering over what to do for the best when war broke out, is one of them: 'There is an apocryphal story that my grandparents told my parents that they could not bring up us children in London during the war. So what did my parents decide? In 1940 they leased a white house on top of a hill in Surrey, right between Germany and London.'

In Wales, Charlie worked out how the vagaries of war set the course of his future life: 'My wife being born in London, her parents Welsh, she was sent to Wales with her mother for safety when the bombing started. After the war, the family stayed on – and we met. So my son always says that if it were not for Adolf Hitler he would never have been born.'

A girl who lived on a large farm in the Midlands came to treasure her father's contrary attitude in exposing her to the full effect of war on the cities: 'My father, who could not join up as he had a heart problem, deliberately took me to London, which he loved anyway, in order to see the barrage balloons and the air-raid shelters in the tube stations and to hear the sirens. Although most children were stopped from going into London for safety reasons, I am very glad to have known it then. At that time the mantra was Business As Usual.'

Rachel too has an amusing fragment of family memoir, redolent of the time: 'I was in Belfast on the night of the Blitz. I spent the whole night, with my family, under my Jewish granny's huge mahogany dining table. We wore silver rose bowls on our heads for protection, and my mother held a mezuzah in one hand and a (fake) rabbit's paw, for luck, in the other. She was certainly hedging her bets!'

As we have seen, the war involved great disruption for families – some relocated themselves, many children were evacuated, menfolk went into the services, relatives moved in with others – and even those children who were not separated from parents and siblings could find the changes disturbing.

In the midst of these comings and goings the inevitable strains and bickering of family life were suddenly less important: the pressing matters of danger and death and survival brought different, basic, priorities and submerged trivial everyday concerns. Most made the best of things and rubbed along. And family foibles and affections could also leaven the bad times with some welcome laughter, as Joyce, who was then about ten, remembered:

My auntie, Mum's sister, wasn't married and stayed with us. One night my mum, auntie, me and my granddad were all in the Anderson at the bottom of the garden. It was noisy overhead – one of the bad raids.

Mum always brought the paraffin stove in because it was so damp and cold. This night we smelled burning, and Mum was sure it was the house hit by incendiaries.

Auntie had her old fur coat on which she wore everywhere. All of a sudden Mum saw smoke then a bit of flame, and it was auntie's coat caught on the stove where she was sat.

We put it out – well, it wasn't the house.

Mum laughed so hard she cried.

Many grandparents found a new, important role as their adult children, long gone, moved in again – with their own young children. Apart from the reassurance of being with relatives, several ration books and heating allowances stretched further, when pooled. Children welcomed their new closeness to grandparents. A little girl whose father was away in the army clearly felt more at ease with her grandparents than with her half-forgotten father, whose rare visits were confusing: 'When our dad was on leave, my brother and I would go to our grandparents' house. We would tell them that we had a strange man at home again who had shaving brushes and soap in the bathroom.'

A lot of these grandparents of the 1940s, grandfathers especially, had no option but to take the place of an absent parent – usually of a father who was away in the forces, or perhaps a mother who had been called up for factory war work. For mothers under forty, unless they had very young children or other pressing responsibilities, war work was mandatory. Although much good work was accomplished, for those who had never worked before this forced work experience was not always a success. Kate's mother found it hard going:

For my poor mum, unused to disciplined work, this must have been quite trying. And for millions of other women too . . . We were living with my grandparents, who could look after me, so she was assigned to the Ministry of Pensions. This was a GREAT mistake! She used to come home saying, 'I made the most awful mistakes today, and they were very cross.'

I can only guess that the Ministry of Pensions never really recovered, and are probably still trying to work out what went wrong!

For families accustomed to fully staffed households – and in 1939, when unemployment was still high, many were – 'Madam's' foray into the workplace could cause dismay – as an eight-year-old daughter recalled:

Nanny's pride made her give in her notice when she discovered that Mummy (smart in her Red Cross uniform) was bringing in the logs for the fire in a wheelbarrow, as all staff and gardeners had left to do active service. Mummy did it all except look after us. Nanny was outraged. She would 'not work in a house that did not have a handyman to do that job'.

She later repented. But Mummy held her to it.

So, after she left, Harry and I had the run of the house, the gardens and the woods when not doing lessons with our governess.

As the years wore on and more and more men volunteered or were called up, it was the women who so often became essential to the family's spirits and survival. As a psychological survey of young children in 1942 put it, 'The magic of the hearth . . . is rooted deep in all human nature, but the mother is the anchor which holds it fast.' Sentimental or no, and always allowing for exceptions, those who were the children of the 1940s indicate time and again that during those wartime years it was the family 'hearth' – and a mother in particular – that got them through.

Domestic resourcefulness took many forms, some trivial and some enduring, and Judy recalled a lighter side. Living in the cottages on her parents' farm were prisoners of war, mainly Germans and

Italians, who helped out with farm labour. 'My mother discovered that one of the men had been King Zog of Albania's former head gardener. He was quickly redirected from farm work to our own neglected garden. Soon after, it had never looked better!'

Anecdotal evidence gathered long after depicts mothers carrying on as normally as possible, cooking and scolding and shopping, getting meals together and children to school, while also coping with bomb damage and generally bearing the main burden of family routine. There is no point in idealizing the mothers' performance, but ordinary family life is what so many of those who were there as children remember and respect.

The anxieties that came with all these maternal responsibilities are obvious. Everything was infinitely more difficult on the home front in wartime, from getting hold of food to heating the bathwater to keeping a family properly clothed. In addition to all the other chores, a lot of women were also doing war work outside the home. Many were also desperately concerned for the safety of husbands and brothers and sons who were away fighting or doing dangerous jobs. A very young child in Coventry could sense his mother's divided emotions as they huddled in their shelter during the devastating night raids: 'I was well aware, even at my age, that my mother worried greatly about my father, who was fire-watching. It was extremely dangerous, as the whole town was in flames and we prayed for the all-clear. We saw little of him except at weekends.'

Faith, who as a teenager lived in London through the worst of the bombing, recalled her mother's unflagging energy and spirit. During the Blitz, joining forces with her aunt and her godmother, they took refuge in the reinforced basement of the family house. But Faith was always aware that during air raids her mother was 'deeply worried' for the safety of her father, who was stationed in the docklands area, in the middle of the most destructive bombing:

He would come home on a three-hour pass whenever he could. I remember he was once reeking of cheese . . . the night before he had been helping put out the blaze in a warehouse full of cheeses that had been bombed.

My mother was constantly worried about him – but she felt herself responsible for the safety and well-being of the household, the rest of us.

She always managed to keep the kitchen range going – with a kettle on, and a stew of some kind simmering. And at the same time she did voluntary work at the canteen in Euston station.

Kate, who was much the same age but living on the other side of London, had similar memories. Her mother and her friend's next door remained cheerful despite the intense strain they were both under with close family in danger, risking their lives, every day:

At one stage my mother had my father working in the Arsenal, me at school in Dartford, and my brother doing office work in the City. My friend next door lived alone with her mother. Her dad was a soldier away with the forces, one brother was in the army in Burma, and the other in submarines. Yet both of the mums kept us well fed, gave us lovely parties, and helped us to make the latest fashion tops out of cheap butter muslin.

For all the civilians on the home front, the drabness and discomfort of war was keenly felt. By the end of 1942 the shortages were beginning to bite, and there was a good deal of grumbling and discontent. A poll conducted in 1943, at a period of relative calm from air raids, found that families were a lot less concerned with the great issues of war and peace than with the frustrations and inconveniences of daily life.

The most irksome of these in most people's minds was the nightly ritual of the detested blackout. Everyone in the country was affected – children quite as much as adults. Maisie, who was six when the war began, remembered that walking home from school or visiting a friend late on autumn and winter afternoons was an ordeal: 'The blackout was quite frightening for young children. No lights could show outside, no torches were allowed unless they were very faint, and it seemed *very* dark.'

In a market town in Wales, the myths of the blackout made Martha nervous. Like all children, she was terrified at the thought of enemy planes, and she made sure she stuck to the rules: 'I was allowed a little torch to find my way with bowl and money to go round the corner from our house to buy chips (no bags or paper supplied then). The torch had to point just ahead of my feet on the ground. (If you

pointed it upward, we thought, the Germans would see it and immediately bomb you.)'

Illustrating how seriously the blackout was taken, Carola's mother,
in Cambridge, was roundly ticked off by the policeman on the beat,
who didn't stand on ceremony either. Carola said that

One evening my sister and I were having our bath together – we always
did, to save what tepid water there was – and my mother was washing our
hair. Suddenly the door of the bathroom on the first floor was pushed
open and a huge policeman in a long black coat stood there.

'There's a chink of light showing through the curtains downstairs,' he
said very sternly. So my mother had no choice but to follow him and pull
the curtains tighter.

Amazingly, we didn't think twice about him walking in on us . . . We
rarely locked our front doors in those days.

In a rural part of Lancashire, where a black face was rarely seen,
Sally recalled the night her mother was confused by a combination of
the blackout and dark skin:

One day an American Army officer came in the street and asked would
anybody cook for about ten soldiers . . . My mum said she would help so
the officer said, 'We'll supply the goods and pay your electric bill.' . . . A
few days later a big butcher's fridge came, plus frying pan, chip pan etc. . . .
Then bags of potatoes, boxes of sausages, bacon boxes, jam, loaves of
bread – anything you could want.

When the soldiers arrived they came for their supper about 6.30. My
mum opened the door and couldn't see anyone at first. She said, 'Is
anybody there?' Blow me, it was a black soldier – you could only see his
teeth, because of the blackout . . .

Every time they came to our house they played games and cards and we
got all their toffees and lollipops and had a lovely time.

After the blackout, the difficulty of travelling caused the most
widespread discontent on the home front. Troop movements and the
transport of vital goods took precedence over civilian travel plans, so
trains ran late and services were frequently cancelled or cut. Because

the railways were so widely used, most trains were overcrowded. To add to the discomforts, there were no reservations, fares were higher, and refreshment cars were removed. Nevertheless, everyone depended on the railways – men and women in the services coming on and off leave, parents visiting evacuated children, and families attempting to keep in touch.

A boy from the Home Counties who visited his grandparents in Yorkshire several times with his mother remembered stations then as being 'spooky, haunted places' – ill lit and teeming with uniforms. There were long queues for a cup of tea and, if you were lucky, a stale bun. But, with no long-distance bus services running, and little or no petrol, parents and children had no option but to brave train journeys for the relief of getting away from the drab and dangerous cities, and to see friends and relatives.

Rose, who lived near London, was frequently taken to stay with her grandparents in their 'long, low white farmhouse' in Wales:

We spent every school holiday there, to get away from the bombing. And those wartime journeys were not pleasant – the trains were crowded and barely lit, with people in the corridors sitting on luggage and kit bags. We children always sat on people's knees. There were long, unexplained stops, sometimes for two or three hours, caused by troop movements or perhaps air raids. The stations were dark and eerie, with no place names. You couldn't tell where you had got to, which was unnerving. And I remember there were women porters . . .

Once, my mother had saved a precious jar of mince and it broke in a suitcase, all over my knickers and clothes. A tragedy!

Jane, too, spent a lot of time on trains with her mother and younger brother, following her army-officer father on his postings:

We travelled all over the country as sort of foot-followers with our mother. I remember travelling to Scotland at midnight from Derby in a train jammed full of soldiers, and having to sit on a padre's knee all night.

My mother was always getting off the train wherever (no signs) and whenever it stopped, to check our at least thirteen items of luggage in the guard's van (no guard) and never being with my very small brother and me when the train started again. I was always completely terrified she had missed it and we would be left on our own.

During the late 1930s car ownership had grown rapidly, but by the time the war started a family car was still a luxury. Petrol rationing began in the autumn of 1939, but, as one man put it:

For us the lack of petrol was not a problem as, in common with most other middle-class families, we did not own a car. Any person who had enjoyed such affluence before the war found it necessary to immobilize their 'pride and joy' by raising it on to blocks in the garage, where it was destined to remain 'for the duration'. Limited supplies of 'Pool' petrol (all brand names disappeared) were available to doctors, other essential users, and some trades people who would not otherwise be able to continue their business activities.

A girl living in Yorkshire remembered the forlorn sight of the prized family car, sitting abandoned on its blocks in the garage for six years, while mice gnawed away at the shiny leather seats.

In country districts, that reliable old standby the horse, which had not then been entirely abandoned, became much more widely used. One family's struggles with their stubborn pony amused and frustrated both adults and children all through the war:

Shortage of petrol led to the reinstatement of the ancient pony and trap. Our pony, Wandy, was so wide that the shafts had to be pulled apart manually to get her between them. She was temperamental – or dogged, depending on how you see it.

Wandy wanted to be on her own, in her paddock, eating grass. Mummy knew all about sailing a boat, and she could drive a car well and fast. Father had been on, behind and around spirited horses all his long life, but never drove. So there was not much common ground.

Living in the depths of the country without a car, and with two children, it was essential that Mummy should learn to drive Wandy in the trap. Hilarious scenes and two red-faced grown-ups ensued. For years. Petrol rationing came to an end without any agreement being reached between Wandy and Mummy.

Father could manage the wilful pony – but only by force and on selected routes. We knew where the critical spots were, and would lead her blind-folded past them. Getting both wheels of a pony trap stuck into a clay ditch is to be avoided – especially if you are short on equine collaboration and the harness is cracked with age.

Friendship, and the need to pull together, blossomed under war-time conditions, even among people who might never have known or spoken to each other in peacetime. In her 1949 novel *The Heat of the Day*, Elizabeth Bowen put her finger on this: 'The wall between the living and the living became less solid as the wall between the living and the dead thinned.' A genuine camaraderie developed during the nightly stints in shelters or the underground as mothers fussed about their older children's behaviour or a baby's crying. Concentrating on the trivia of ordinary life was a distraction from present, acute danger. Neighbours who soldiered through together came to take the place of absent relatives, as Tom, living in a village on the German flight path from the coast to London, saw for himself: 'Before the start of the war my parents, for some reason, never had anything to do with the next-door neighbours. I don't know why, but they hardly spoke. Immediately the war started it all changed and they would look after each other, even down to sharing each other's air-raid shelters.'

As a young resident of one of the worst-bombed areas of London, Iris had mixed feelings about her neighbours. Although her family home was bombed three times, the structural damage was less severe than that of most of the houses near by. 'So we were a little envious of our neighbours who were totally bombed out, as they were rehoused in prefabs – marvellous little bungalows put up on bomb sites, equipped with a bathroom and kitchen and fitted out with taps and sinks. And a lavatory inside. What a luxury!'

Emergency workers noted that when older men and women were dug out of the rubble after an 'incident' (the euphemism for a direct hit) the first thing they asked for was not a cup of tea, or the cat, but their false teeth. Sociability mattered, and if your teeth were 'in' you felt human.

No matter what the circumstances, wartime conditions had done away with much of the old British stand-offishness. Stella, a schoolgirl who lived in the outer city suburbs, said that for the first time her entire street got to know each other: 'When there was a wedding a few doors down the road, all the neighbours donated their food points so that they could buy tinned and dried fruit etc. for the wedding cake. All the men who were not called up in our district acted as ARP wardens. Looking back, it seems that everyone looked out for everyone's good – we got along by all helping each other and pulling together.'

Apart from mild grousing about coupons and keeping fast-growing kids in shoes, Jim, who was a sixth-former in 1943, also recalled an overall attitude of good humour: 'In spite of bombing, food and clothes rationing, shortages of absolutely everything, the impossibility of holidays, women having to do men's work, the black-out etc. there was not a lot of serious complaining.'

However hard daily life became, the feeling was that many people had it worse and that everyone had to get on with it. 'We're all in this together' was the attitude. Undoubtedly, talking helped – as did the certain knowledge that other people had their troubles too. A joke, a moan and a bit of a chat eased the everyday chores. Even young-sters queuing for a paltry piece of fish for the family's supper – or a cinema – might find someone to have a laugh with or exchange a few words of commiseration. Certainly Charlotte, who had just started her first, lowly, job on a public-affairs magazine, took her ritual queuing in good heart: 'Sometimes, on the way to work, I would go to a theatre in St Martin's Lane and rent a fold-up stool which kept a place for me in the queue. I would retrieve this stool in the evening and start proper queuing. The stool cost 6d. The ballet, which I was passionate about, 2/6d. In the process I often made friends with others in the queue.'

In all sorts of ways, it was the glue of family feeling that brought children through those difficult times. Family reunions in wartime had a special poignancy. When the air raids on her home town started, Mary was sent to stay with distant relatives she hardly knew in the country. Her cousin, the same age, was a spiteful child, stealing her precious sweets the moment the grown-ups' backs were turned. Mary cried herself to sleep most nights, and when her parents brought her back home to Newcastle her relief was such that she never forgot it, she said. She willingly put up with the frightening air raids, having to shelter under the dining-room table, because the family was 'together – and happy.'

A serviceman's leave was another kind of wartime reunion – often very brief, and granted only at the last minute. Children frequently stayed home from school to make the most of it. But Tom, who lived in Cornwall, happy though he was to see his father, couldn't help voicing a sly complaint: 'The day before my father was due home on leave from the army, my mother would go around the house getting it spick and span, trying to emulate the national songbird, Vera Lynn . . . It made me feel like leaving home.'

Miserable childhood interludes – and there were many during those years – had to be balanced against the routine of daily family life, which provided a bulwark against the profound disturbances of war. Bob, who lived with his family in the London suburbs, gave a good picture of how he and his family spent their evenings during term time, although even in his comfortable home the tragedy and destruction of war was never far from their minds:

During long winter evenings, after finishing any homework on the kitchen table, we joined Mother and Father round the fire in the living room to listen to the wireless. Variety shows such as Tommy Handley's *ITMA* and Arthur Askey's *Bandwagon* gave a great deal of much-needed amusement.

However, we soon got jolted back to reality by listening to 'the nine o'clock news from London, and this is Alvar Liddell reading it'. We then heard perhaps of the latest air raids on either side of the North Sea or the Channel, with assessments of the damage and casualties, and tallies of aircraft losses on each side . . .

The news boosted or depressed one's spirits depending, of course, on who was doing what to whom.

Another boy, who lived with his grandparents for two years, and who also listened eagerly to the BBC evening news, commented, 'The newsreader's sombre tones reciting planes which failed to return remain with me, as do my grandmother's remarks, hearing of German pilots killed in action as well as ours. She made no distinction: "Some poor woman has lost her son, God pity her."' Other mothers and homemakers, fearful for the safety of loved ones, also despaired at the tragedy and futility of war. Its grief and suffering was falling on families every day.

The wartime mantra of living a day at a time and hoping for the best must have sounded very feeble at times. Tragedy lurked everywhere and few families were immune from the risk of sudden, youthful death. Dick, then a schoolboy, was hit hard, and could never forget his mother's gallant acceptance of her grief. He wrote, 'I lost my only brother in a ghastly gunnery accident while he was on manoeuvres in Scotland. My mother's heart was broken; she never recovered from that terrible blow. Yet she had the grace to write to his commanding officer to say that she didn't blame him. "This is WAR," she wrote, and the thought was that one must expect such horrible things and accept them for the sake of victory against our hated foe.'

Raising children alone in those uncertain times, as so many women did, took courage. Alan, who lived near Hull, and experienced relentless air raids, understood his mother's fear for her husband's safety when she was already shouldering all the hard family work at home. 'My father, being in the merchant navy, was away for about three years before we saw him again. My mum had the task of bringing up two boys, and the fear that her husband would never return. He was the captain of a tanker, used as a fleet refueller, and saw action in the North Atlantic, Russian and Malta convoys. Amazingly, he came through it all unscathed.'

Families in which a relative had been taken prisoner lived in limbo, in constant fear of hearing even worse news. Daphne's father was a POW in the Far East from 1942, after the fall of Singapore, until the end of the war. Somehow, her mother managed to keep up the family's morale through three painful years. 'Looking back, I realize that my mother never for one moment gave us any idea that he might not come back one day. How she managed it I do not know. I certainly remember the excitement when one of the rare postcards arrived from him – only a few, certainly less than ten in the entire period. We were also lucky enough to have a big extended family living locally, so we never felt isolated.'

Families braced for the worst did their best to support one another. Paul, who was about to leave school, was with his sister as she prepared for bleak news: 'In March 1943 I bicycled to the post office with my older sister, who was working for the Ministry of Agriculture. Mum asked me to go with her because my sister had been asked, by telegram, to telephone her fiancé's parents. When she got through she learnt that the RAF officer she was engaged to had been posted as missing after a bombing mission over Germany.'

A girl whose family bore terrible losses said that quite early in the war 'my aunt's fiancé was killed in the North Atlantic. This was our first great blow.' It would not be the last:

My other aunt's very glamorous and gallant husband, who we all idolized, and who was decorated, was killed in France soon after D-Day. Another young uncle – only eighteen – had been killed in 1940. He was a pilot in the Battle of Britain; it was one of his first missions.

The grannies, all the women, spent time alone together behind closed doors when they received the news. But of course we children, watching, knew what had happened.

After, they were very brave and got on with life. There was nothing else to be done. Young men dying was happening in so many families then.

Peter, a schoolboy, who later volunteered for army service in 1944, had reason to be aware of the suffering of families living near by. This was especially bitter at a time supposed to herald peace and goodwill:

During the Christmas holidays at the end of 1941 I worked for a few days as a telegram boy. On 'my' official red Post Office bike, and wearing the heavy leather belt on which was mounted a large yellow pouch containing the then familiar yellow envelopes, I delivered a total of ninety-five telegrams within five days. Although it was Christmas time, by no means all of them were festive greetings . . . I could immediately tell from the face of a recipient that some of them clearly brought the dreaded news of a husband or other loved one. The expressions on their faces said it all.

These personal horrors were being visited on families all over the country. Sheila was brought up by her grandparents, and treated her young uncle more like an older brother. When the war came, she tearfully watched him go off. 'He was in one of the first batches of conscripts to be called up. I was devastated, and cried every night . . . He was shipped overseas to Africa.' Not long after, a telegram was delivered to the family. 'He had been taken prisoner and was in Italy, wounded – not very badly it seemed. This was just before the Battle of El Alamein. So, although we were very distressed, we just hoped and prayed he would be OK and we would see him after the war. The next thing, another telegram saying he had died. I cannot describe the pain and anguish I felt at losing him. He is buried at Bari, in Italy.'

A girl of ten and her mother faced their heartbreaking news together. 'One day, as I dashed into the house straight from school, Mother leaned over the banisters from upstairs and said, "Please come up here darling, I have something to tell you." "Uncle John has been killed," I thought at once . . . And this was indeed what she was going to tell me. He was married, and had three small sons.'

Right across the country another young girl whose beloved uncle had been a special person in her life also looked back and remembered 'the excitement of a ride on the back of an army motor bike ridden by my dare-devil uncle home on leave . . . I must have been about eight. I never forgot. Then the agony in my mother's voice as she took the phone message telling us that this much-loved brother had been killed.'

In East Anglia, sisters of seven and nine approved of their mother's warm common sense in the face of brutal warfare almost literally on their doorstep: 'Early in the war an enemy plane was shot down over fields near our house. When we looked out of the shelter we saw two parachutists coming down – the pilots – with men shooting as they landed near a railway bridge. My mum used to say sadly that if they'd have landed in our garden she would have given them a cup of tea.'

Children who were old enough to follow the events of war, and particularly those who had relatives posted abroad, devoured the papers and kept abreast of the latest war news. Will, an enthusiast for news, said, 'The newspapers were beautiful with their maps with arrows showing the offensive movements of German and Allied armies, and we studied them carefully.' A brother and sister at a grammar school in Manchester also kept up to date with the news: 'We had two newspapers a day at home. One was the *Manchester Guardian*, and my brother and I read parts of both papers every day. I dare say it was fairly selective reading of the easier parts, but we knew something of the progress of the war – and of course we listened to the news on the BBC at one and six o'clock.'

But, with more and more restrictions, nothing on the home front could be taken for granted, even the daily papers. A girl living in the Midlands remembered the creeping effect of wartime shortages and economies:

During the war years, the changes came about so that you hardly noticed them. Take newspapers. They got smaller and smaller. There was no *Sun*, but there was the *Daily Mirror*, even when it got down to two sheets – no sport of course, but room for 'Jane' and other strip cartoons, and my beloved 'Cassandra' . . .

The broadsheet papers were one sheet only, and this was a great hardship at the fish-and-chip shops, but we got used to taking our own paper. Chips were always there even when the fish was scarce.

Whether they were bombed out and living in temporary quarters or still living in the family home, children remember the wartime winters as damp and cold. Clive's description of his home in the cold weather rang true for most children: 'We had limited coal and could heat one room only . . . The bedrooms had lino on the floor, we used to put overcoats over the bedclothes. The bathroom was icy, and the water in the storage tank barely warm. When we had a hard frost in winter the waste pipe froze and the water stayed in the handbasin until the pipe thawed.'

Heavy coats and jumpers and socks – all requiring hefty amounts of coupons – were precious possessions. One wartime winter Rose's stylish and resourceful mother turned her hand to dressmaking – much to her daughter's embarrassment: 'My mother had made herself a suit out of green baize of which I was deeply ashamed . . . One Sunday, my brother and I had gone on to church ahead of her. And I remember praying, "Please, God, don't let her be wearing it today."'

Middle-class children's obligatory afternoon airings continued, although the war intruded even on this harmless nursery pastime. Out walking in the countryside, two children and their nanny got mildly tangled up in a Territorial war-games exercise:

Harry and I were on our 'walk', with Harry in the pushchair, when we came to a crossroads swarming with an army convoy – tanks, lorries full of soldiers, field ambulances, the lot.

From the turret of a tank, Nanny was asked the way to the village hospital. Craning up from her diminutive roundness she demanded, 'Are you the invaders?' As the answer was yes, she said, 'Then I won't tell you.'

The tank said they weren't really, but she held firm. 'Then you'd get shot, madam,' came from deep inside the tank.

'I don't care. I wouldn't tell the Germans, and I won't tell you.'

And off they rumbled – in the wrong direction.

For all the worries of their elders during the war, children were resilient and got on with their play, as children always have, and made their own amusements with whatever was at hand. 'We children were all very happy, playing table games, skipping, or playing ball games outside with our friends,' a girl of about ten said, looking back. In the winters 'We did knitting and embroidery while listening to the wireless; we helped with the household chores with no machines – only a mangle. We made our own entertainment. Very happy with so little really.'

The enemy – Hitler in particular – provided a favourite, scary bogey of childhood play for a generation of boys mucking about with their gangs: 'What will we do when the Germans come? Fancies of fighting a guerrilla war along the lines of the children of Warsaw (depicted in one of my weekly magazines) occupied much of our children's games.'

Mothers had enough on their hands keeping a home together. With no petrol and unreliable buses, there was little opportunity to go anywhere, so children had plenty of unsupervised time to do whatever they wanted with friends in a way undreamed of today. Outdoor play was encouraged, doors were rarely locked, and parents had little or no fear of lurking, malevolent strangers. There is no sign that these 1940s children felt deprived of material goods, as they were; rather, most seem grateful for this miraculous gift of freedom in childhood. As Joanna, evacuated to Scotland with her mother and sister, said:

There were very few toys, though I still had the legacy of pre-war toys that were so beautifully made and attractive that they lasted all through the war. In spite of this we seemed to be always busy. Climbing trees, riding local ponies and walking on stilts, and skipping ropes were a great craze at the time. We used to do what we called 'double throughs', which meant that the rope went round twice before one's feet touched the ground. Once I did 105 – and won the school prize.

We also went for endless walks up in the hills, and gathered blueberries and other fruits in the woods.

There was little to cause our parents any anxiety. Hardly any cars – all very slow-moving – and no child-molesters that I ever heard of.

There were, however, some British children who did not have this untrammelled freedom. Children under German occupation, living in Jersey, where no one was trusted and where walls could have ears, had a very different set of rules. Billy vividly remembered this nerve-racking time:

I was playing war games with toy lead soldiers against my best friend at his house, when the set of our 'battle' suddenly reminded me of a news item. I started to blurt out, 'This is just like . . . Monte Cassino' – but quickly changed it to 'the real thing'.

The irony was that my friend's dad had a hidden radio in his loft, he had told my dad the news, and he had passed it on to me. But my friend didn't know about his father's radio – and I couldn't tell him.

A bit convoluted, but it shows the background of extreme fear and suspicion we were living in.

Listening to the radio was an important part of most children's weeks. *Toytown* (with Larry the lamb, Dennis the dachshund etc.) was adored by younger listeners, who remembered the tunes and nicknames all their lives. All radio programmes were regarded as special. So when Gillian (eight) was taken to the BBC studios by her mother to speak in a live broadcast it was a very memorable and touching occasion for her, and for her family: 'I was to take part in a programme that Vera Lynn was doing at that time for overseas servicemen. It was by special request, and we were able to speak to our fathers just to say "Hello, Daddy, this is Gillian speaking." . . . It was a very moving experience.'

Out-of-school extras such a ballet and piano lessons were unavailable throughout the war, as was most specialist teaching. However, Rose, whose father taught at Eton College, was among the select few children who attended dancing classes and Girl Guides with Princess Elizabeth and Princess Margaret at Windsor Castle. Her enduring memory of those years is a slightly irreverent one:

We had the run of Windsor Castle, although much to our dismay we were eventually banned from roller-skating in the Round Tower. We entered the castle through the Henry VIII gateway. There was massive security, and a new password was given out every twenty-four hours. Our favourite policeman-cum-sentry was called – amazingly – Mr Courtier. He was much admired by the children because he was bald-headed and he could jiggle his helmet up and down.

The grim reality of war could impinge suddenly and chillingly on children playing with friends in peaceful surroundings. A boy who was evacuated to Sussex had built a den with his friends, a hideout made of brushwood, in woods near their village. Meeting there one afternoon, the boys noticed that the apples they had hoarded for outdoor feasts were missing. Then they heard twigs crackling. A young man, wounded and clearly in pain, stumbled into sight. He was a German airman whose plane had been shot down; he had either had a lucky escape or managed to parachute. And he had survived on the boys' apples. He was taken into custody by the local police, and the story ended. But one of those boys, at least, never forgot and many years later he was still chasing old records to try to discover more about the pilot.

Other children also remembered strange wartime encounters with planes. After they were bombed out of their home in Birmingham, Michael spent most of the war years with his mother in Cheltenham, where they lived in three patched-up rooms of a crumbling Georgian mansion. He too came in contact with a downed plane – an incident that was thrilling for a six-year-old unable to comprehend the tragedy of the accident:

When I get home from school, at the far end of our drive there is a small crowd gathered and a fire engine. I march proudly in through the gates and am promptly picked up by a policeman, turned end for end, and marched back out again.

Less than half an hour before, a Wellington bomber and a Tiger Moth trainer have collided overhead. The Wellington has come down somewhere on the other side of the railway bridge, and we have got most of the Tiger Moth about 40 feet from our front door. Its pilot is still in it. The engine is a couple of hundred yards away.

For several years after I shall be able to dig in a flower bed and turn up bits of aluminium, and once a piece of flight instrument dial.

The following eerie episode in the life of a nine-year-old girl is reminiscent of the children's books, extremely popular at the time, by Arthur Ransome:

When the Heinkel bombers had dropped their bombs over Liverpool, they turned for home above us. I was a great tomboy . . . The morning after a particularly vicious raid, our gang went down to the beach to play and we spotted, about a mile offshore and embedded in the sand, the silhouette of a plane.

We found a Heinkel bomber with its nose sunk slightly into the sand. Otherwise, to us, it seemed almost intact, and we were able to take it in turns to climb aboard and sit in the pilot's seat. I can still see the swastika on the wing and remember peering out of the windscreen with great excitement. I was sitting where a German enemy had sat. Where was he now?

Just as the younger children went on skipping, climbed trees, and built dens for their own amusement, and had fun doing it, older children in their teens also found plenty to enjoy in wartime.

Enthusiastic boys who were about to leave school and aching for their call-up papers threw themselves into the war effort, making it a form of recreation: 'To us older schoolboys this war was fun. We became ARP messengers; we could identify warplanes, use stirrup pumps, and discuss poisonous gases. Maps of the world on our bedroom walls, previously used to plot the courses of pioneer aviators, became war maps. Really great news was to learn of a German aeroplane shot down – and riding our bicycles to locate the wreckage before the RAF removed it.'

Cinemas were a sparkling highlight in children's wartime lives. Throughout the war British films flourished, and their quality improved dramatically. *In Which We Serve*, with Noël Coward as both scriptwriter and star, hit exactly the right note of realistic patriotism at a time, 1942, when the country was at its lowest ebb. It was followed by a stream of new films and new stars: James Mason, Rex Harrison, John Mills, Deborah Kerr, Margaret Lockwood, Patricia Roc . . . Entranced by the glamour – and there was little of it in most people's lives – children pored over the anodyne fairy tales in film magazines. A trip to 'the pictures' was worth putting up with inconvenience – a long bike ride, queuing, and even danger. At least Joan and her sister thought so: 'We went to the cinema one afternoon to see *Gone With the Wind*, and when we arrived home all our windows had 'gone with the wind' too – or, rather, been blown out with the force of an exploding bomb quite near. I remember that the glass on every window concerned was blown out in the shape of a leaf.'

In other parts of the country, also under attack from the air, the same bravado was displayed. With very few other organized entertainments around, the magic of the cinema held. 'I was in our Ritz cinema watching a film when a notice came up saying that the siren had gone and if you wanted to leave you could. But nobody left. We all sat there as if nothing had happened, and the film went on.'

In Scotland, Bridie, a bright and enterprising girl who had left school at fourteen, was working for a wholesale grocer's: 'Whenever the Scottish Orchestra was performing, my boss used to give me two tickets which he said he bought by mistake. The first time, I was really embarrassed about it. I was seventeen, no wireless in the house . . . I don't think I had ever heard a piece of classical music. I can remember the programme to this day. I was absolutely enchanted and have loved serious music ever since.'

In London too cultural life kept going, adapting to changed circumstances. Young people who were working, or in the services, learned to make the most of it: 'Concerts were given in the National Gallery at lunchtime, and these became very popular. In the summer you took sandwiches and ate them outdoors after. Theatres continued, but, as air raids generally started about six o'clock, times were altered and some shows were given at about three in the afternoon.'

Stories are still told about actors and actresses who carried on with performances right through an air raid, as a twelve-year-old boy and his father saw for themselves:

We went to His Majesty's Theatre in the Haymarket to see *The Merry Widow* in 1943. There were still some nasty raids going on, and halfway through the first act one started. The theatre shook, the bombs thudded, the anti-aircraft guns roared and dropped their shrapnel. But the really impressive thing was that the wonderfully evocative confidence of the turn-of-the-century operetta continued without the slightest concession to the noise outside the theatre. The performers and orchestra went on as though nothing was happening.

For teenagers of both sexes who were beginning to find their feet in mixed company the war provided innumerable opportunities. In stringent times, any chance for a bit of fun was seized on, and the tensions of war also made for a more tolerant social outlook. As Sylvia, in Scotland, put it, 'There was the lure of the cinema and the Saturday-night dance. These pastimes became more exciting and interesting. I don't think I ever spoke to an Englishman until the war, and suddenly our town became cosmopolitan. The girls enjoyed it, but not always the boys, who thought "their" women were being taken by foreigners – and they probably meant the English.'

For most young people, a bicycle meant freedom. And a present from her mother, who had little cash to spare, meant the world to Rita, who had started war work in a London factory:

A wonderful event for me was that my mother bought me a second-hand bike – cost £3 10s. – from our insurance lady. At work some of us got together and formed a cycling club. One day we went to Clacton-on-Sea. We started at dawn and got back about midnight. We kept right on even through air-raid warnings, although things were relatively quiet at that time (1943). We could not get on to the beach as it was mined and full of barbed wire.

Trevor, who spent much of the war evacuated to Devon, fondly remembered his final billet for, of all things, thumping good parties:

Towards the end of the war we were looked after by my great-aunt who acted as housekeeper to the elderly (very deaf) gentleman who owned the house and had lived there alone.

My aunt would hold 'Taunton cider and Craven A' parties. When I left school at lunchtime (I was sixteen) I went to a local licensed grocer to buy the cider. I had to persuade the owner to let me have a bottle of cider – although I was under age and purchasing it in unauthorized hours. He just said, 'Hide the bottle in your raincoat, sonny.' Great-aunt looked after the Craven A side. And the parties which ensued were hilarious – with her dancing round the table showing her brown satin Directoire knickers.

Impromptu parties were an important part of nervy wartime life under almost any circumstances, and, the get-togethers at Molly's family home in London were happy occasions:

My New Zealand cousins had given their various boyfriends our address, and they made it their base. They were all in the navy, and left their gear at our house when they were off on operations. There was always fun when they were back on a spot of leave. The house would ring with merriment, and we would have dancing and songs round the piano . . . In those times, it was all we could wish for – that these young men were back again, unharmed, at least for a while.

After the heady euphoria of D-Day in the spring of 1944, and the liberation of Paris the following August, hopes for a quick end to the war rose dramatically. But they were to be disappointed: many believe that the last year of the war was the hardest. To weary civilians there seemed no end to it all as the Germans launched powerful and frequently effective counter-attacks as the Allies slogged their way, mile by mile, across Europe.

While the troops fought through and Allied bombers carried out their deadly missions, civilians carried on at home. Early in the spring of 1945, after several false hopes had been raised and dashed, at long last the end of the war was on the horizon. By March the deadly V2s, a last vicious throw of the enemy dice, had ceased. The blackout had been partially lifted the previous autumn, which made the towns and streets slightly more cheery. And, as the din of war quietened, people began to look about them and take stock. The great commercial and shipping centres – London, Manchester, Liverpool, Hull, Birmingham, Southampton, Plymouth and many others – were badly scarred, but they had survived. Despite the loss of life, the injuries and the destruction, the essential services had continued, the work had ground on, and now they were struggling back to normality.

Some found a strange new beauty in these cities: jagged part rooms like sculptures, open to the weather, with bits of tattered wallpaper hanging off, and ragged wild flowers sprouting up through cracks in blackened ruins were common sights. It was a far cry from the pre-war days, but everywhere there was hope. And the children, and everyone else who had removed themselves on and off during these six exhausting years, started to pour back.

Servicemen and -women too were desperate for a return to settled family life, which must come soon. And still strong in the minds of the older generation was the memory of the previous war's end, only twenty-seven years before, and all the thousands of children who grew up without a father, and wives who had to manage without husbands. After the Second World War, although the ordeal was longer and more gruelling at home, many more men did come back.

For most reunited families, the joys of picking up the threads of home life with friends and family were immense, and more than made up for any child's grumbles at missing friends or grandparents. But for the children who were long-term evacuees, used to the independence of being away, reunion could be altogether a more complex matter. 'I never really settled back home,' one of the returning evacuees admitted long after. He added that it was his personal belief, from what he had observed, that long-term evacuees tended to become adults who bottled up emotions and had difficulty with close relationships. Possibly a watchful, self-protective armour had become ingrained. No one can ever know for sure, but it is a tantalizing thought.

Ironically, it was the lengthy and successful evacuations which could be contentious for a family. Most parents did make efforts to visit their evacuated children, and special fare allowances were provided for those who had left the cities with government aid. But such visits were usually brief, and children who stayed with foster parents for three, four and even five years had usually managed well, made friends, and carved out their own lives. The sudden transition back to the parental home came as a considerable shock.

Plunged back into bomb-damaged inner-city streets which they hardly remembered, many children missed the fields and the freedom they had come to take for granted. Leaving friends behind was another wrench. To a fourteen-year-old boy, returning after a long, happy village evacuation to a city worn out by war, early in 1945, the change was depressing:

It never seemed to be as light as in the country, and people seemed sullen and watchful, always miserable, not smiling. A parachute mine – one of the last – came down at the end of our street, blowing out the windows, soot coming down the chimneys. In the morning, coming out of our Anderson shelter, there was a scene of devastation. But there was none of the community spirit of our country village, no consoling. Just a shrug of the shoulder and a feeling of That Could Have Been Us.

Now, as the war which they had come to take for granted was ending, in addition to readjusting to their mother's personality, many children were also faced with a returning father whom they might scarcely recognize. Brothers and sisters who had stayed at home, or who had been born during the war, were also virtual strangers to the returning evacuee.

The reunion could also be hard on parents, who had their own emotional confusions to deal with. Some expected the return of the bewildered little boy or girl whom they had so achingly parted with, labelled and clutching a gas mask, not a developed older child with a mind of his or her own. And any mother – or father for that matter – could so easily resent the affection their child had developed for a foster parent, or for a different way of life.

Polly and her brother and sister, who had spent three 'golden' years on a family farm in Devon, bitterly disliked the abrupt change back to their old life in South London, and both the transition and the way it was handled caused lasting harm to family relationships:

The sad end to all this is that one Friday my mother arrived and took us back on the Saturday. There was no warning – I am sure that Auntie (as we called our foster mother) knew, but she probably had been asked not to tell us.

When I asked my mother why she had brought us home with no discussion or anything, she said, 'That is past, and we don't need to talk about it.' This . . . soured my relationship with her for many years. I never approached the subject again.

While many parents and children were beginning to get to know each other again, all over Europe thousands of displaced people were struggling to get home and to make connections with the families from whom they had been wrenched. Quirky pieces of these pathetic human sagas were emerging from the chaos. And for one British family there was a very happy ending – one that was hard to believe until it happened.

One of my older brothers was a surgeon lieutenant in the Royal Naval Volunteer Reserve; the other joined up as soon as he could and trained as a navigator in the RAF. He was shot down in the Adriatic in November 1944, and as far as the family knew he was missing. We feared the worst. Then, to the family's amazement and great joy, he was mentioned on the German propaganda radio programme, in the following February. He had been moved from Italy to Germany and was one of the last POWs to be released. But he was alive.

Despite the building excitement, by 1945 most people's nerves were raw. The wearing business of keeping a wartime home going had exhausted the women, and it was said later that many demobbed servicemen, used to the harshest living conditions themselves, were nevertheless shocked by the weary, shabbily dressed womenfolk they came back to.

Thousands upon thousands of homes had been damaged and, as repair work in wartime was basic at best, the housing shortage was critical. Returning husbands and older brothers and evacuated children had to learn to fit in to homes – if they were lucky enough to still have them – that were often very different to those they had left behind.

Change of all kind was in the air too. Young women entering the services and the factories at eighteen and younger, free from family constraints, carried out their work and behaved personally as they pleased – a lifestyle that their mothers would never have dreamed of at their age. Wives and mothers had become used to handling family money, and many had experienced the freedom of working outside the home for the first time. With husbands frequently away, lonely wives left at home, and the heady wartime urge to live for the moment, sexual restraint went out of the window. Statistics for Birmingham in 1939–45 show a threefold increase in the percentage of children born to married women but not fathered by their husbands.

During those six long years, the lives of many husbands and wives and parents and children had changed and grown apart. For all the joyful celebrations, there were plenty of hard knocks in store for families. A popular cartoon of the time depicted a small, terrified child cowering behind his mother's skirt and whispering tearfully, 'Mum, who is that man?' as a serviceman rushed to embrace them. But undoubtedly the many pictures of spick-and-span children running down a garden path into the outstretched arms of a soldier, sailor or airman daddy are closer to the truth.

The following memories of a twelve-year-old's demobbed dad's homecoming must ring true for many:

My dad was away fighting most of the time.

A doodlebug crashed at the end of our road. Our house was totally wrecked. My mother and younger brother were on their way to the shelter in the garden and were not hurt; I was inside the house and received many facial injuries from glass and bomb blast. I was dug out by firemen. My mother never received a scratch during the entire war.

Our older brother was evacuated to Wales the whole time, and came home in 1945.

Dad came back from the war safe and sound too. It was a happy day, but a bit strange. He wore a blue striped (demob) suit and a grey trilby hat. We had never seen him in a suit before. But when he took off his jacket and rolled up his sleeves we knew Dad was home and we were all together.

We were far more lucky than some.

Many children tend to remember a father's homecoming as extremely exciting – and sometimes, bittersweet. When, dolled up in a hand-me-down blue linen frock, a nine-year-old girl was sent to the station to meet her father – her mother, felled by the emotion, preferred to stay at home – she did not know who he was. She had only seen him briefly two or three times in six years. And when a tall man in khaki uniform with red braid on his cap stood in front of her on the platform and said 'I'm Daddy', she did as she had been taught and put out her hand.

This strange, unsatisfactory meeting was the beginning of a difficult relationship, she recalled:

Perhaps it would have been in any case, or perhaps my father's absence during those early years made it worse – there is no way of knowing. But I was a spirited child, and deeply resented suddenly having this father around ordering me, and my older brother, about.

As I came to understand in later years, it was also a painful time for my mother, whose loyalties must have been very torn. For six years she had been in sole charge of the home. And now, of course, all of us had to live as a family again – as we did, in time, very successfully. But after one of my many battles with my father, soon after the war, I vividly remember overhearing my mother saying to him wearily, 'Oh, do please stop treating us like the Fourteenth Army.'

The disharmonies of daily living, and getting used to a man about the house demanding a mother's attention, took some time for most. And with so much readjustment on all levels there must also have been considerable marital tension in the post-war years. One twelve-year-old boy got through an uncomfortable period with fortitude, although he was miserable at watching his parents' unhappiness:

When my father returned from the war my parents never really got on again. I saw that for about five years they lived separate lives and it was too late for the relationship to mend. My mother left home and took my sister, and I stayed with my father. I think when it happened we both sat down and drowned our sorrows in a pot of tea.

Since this sad event – a direct result of war, I believe – I've learned to accept life as it comes and never lay the blame on another.

Also, although there are no hard facts, the sad truth is that a good number of servicemen took their demobilization as an opportunity to desert their families. They disappeared in the immediate post-war muddle – and never returned. This left wives and children in near poverty and the lasting hurt and emotional damage for most of them can be imagined. A boy who was eleven when the war ended said that his father 'never came back. He deserted us – my mum, my younger sister and me. We became thoroughly peripatetic, moving to various family members, sleeping where we could. We remained without any settled home for about five years.' Although many similar situations undoubtedly did not, this boy's story ended surprisingly well: after he had been dragged in and out of numerous schools, and had lived all over the place, his natural aptitude was spotted and he won an early scholarship to university.

Putting all the pieces together as a family in an uncertain, if peaceful, world would never be simple. And the expectations of a glowing peacetime future must have been high – perhaps even fanciful. Although it is fair to say that many more families happily readjusted after the war than did not, the considerable domestic stress is reflected in the divorce rate, which rose sharply during and immediately after the war. In 1938 there were just under 10,000 divorces; by 1945 the number had risen to 25,000.

But during the early spring of 1945 most of these reunions and family accommodations still lay in the immediate future. For the present, everyone was intent on the approaching victory, and had no wish or need to look further ahead.

For the momentum had quickened. Early in March 1945 the Americans crossed the Rhine, closely followed by Montgomery's troops. This heartening news was still being celebrated when on 12 April President Roosevelt's death was announced. It was received with shock and sadness, and this remarkable leader was mourned on both sides of the Atlantic.

But the war news continued to be good; the end must come soon . . .

Yet even at this late hour there was more suffering – true horror this time – to be absorbed, however disbelievingly. In April, the Nazi concentration camps at Buchenwald and, a few days later, at Belsen were overrun by the Allies. The complexity of Nazi evil was unravelling in front of a horrified world. The true understanding of what this war was all about was, in a sense, only just beginning.

Many years later, adults who were then children retained crystal-clear mental pictures of photographs of those camps. Some said these were the clearest and most lasting of any images or memories of war that they still had. More than one spoke of having experienced immediate physical revulsion on first seeing the bestial pictures. One girl had to be taken out of church while listening to a sermon graphically describing them, and was violently sick.

Even very young children looked and listened and never forgot. Photographs splashed over every newspaper shrieked the horror across the world: the piles of naked emaciated corpses, the men in ragged striped prison uniforms caged behind barbed wire. 'Sick with disgust and fury' was how one popular tabloid described British troops who were at the scene of the atrocities.

Andrew was nearly eleven in 1945, and expresses what so many of his contemporaries thought and felt then and still feel today:

The first time I remember being really painfully conscious of 'death' as a concept was towards the end of the war in Europe, seeing the German concentration camps on the newsreels at the cinema, and a little later the results of Hiroshima and Nagasaki – both on a scale and degree of horror that stunned even a war-hardened eleven-year-old London kid who had lived through the Blitz . . . It took the sheer unmitigated horror of the concentration-camp obscenity to even begin to comprehend man's inhuman capability towards his fellow man.

And yet the pace of victory in Europe was now unstoppable. When the long-delayed announcement finally came, on the evening of 7 May, its reception by each citizen, of whatever age, was unique – as personal as that individual's experience of the war:

I was on the late shift that day. We knew it was going to happen at any moment. Cycling home, at the crossroads I saw Mary walking down the hill. I wobbled over to the side.

'It's over,' she called, hurrying, not stopping.

I went on. I felt flat. Nothing else.

Tim's room was the way he left it. We didn't have the heart to move anything. His cricket bats, the books, the school pictures. The crystal wireless set he had made out of an old cigar box.

He was nearly nineteen when he died in 1940. He had volunteered for the RAF immediately, and he took to flying. He was very good they all said. He would have been twenty-four.

I had been dreading the end all along. Other people's sons, husbands, brothers coming back.

I think Mary knew this.

The official announcement also specified that the following day, 8 May, would be a national holiday, and mark the official celebration of Victory in Europe – VE Day. The Board of Trade did its sedate best to contribute to the festivities by announcing in its fussy way, 'Until the end of May you may buy cotton bunting without coupons, as long as it is red, white or blue, and does not cost more than one and three a square yard.' Within hours, VE Day was being ushered in on the stroke of midnight by a glorious cacophony of hooters and blaze of lights which burst forth from ships assembled in Southampton Docks. The great celebration party was on.

All over the country, in towns and villages and market squares, with simple picnics or fireworks and bonfires and parades and parties, there was heartfelt rejoicing. Even those grieving for the loss of loved ones must have been grateful for this hard-won peace. This was the day the nation had longed for, despaired of, and struggled towards for six hard years. Bunting, flags, music, dancing, singing, hoarded drink of any kind – and many tears of sadness as well as joy – were on show for all the world to see on that sunny May day.

A small girl in East Anglia remembered 'us all going to a victory party. It was a lovely summer's day, a farmer had lent a field, and there was a hay wagon. We took our own lemonade, because of the rationing . . . I can still recall the happiness felt by all that day.' In Wales, Martha was amazed at the show of public lighting, which she could not remember: 'The big four-sided clock on the town hall was lit up – it seemed like a great moon high up in the sky.' Kate and her friends had the time of their lives at a party in the church hall, 'falling in love with our brothers' pals, they looked so gorgeous in uniform.'

Along wide stretches of the coast, still guarded by pillboxes and rusting barbed wire, fires were lit – 'bonfires with flames leaping right up, making it as light as day in some places, and rockets also, donated by the navy defence' – as had been the custom to mark a great victory for centuries. The King and Queen and the princesses, Mr Churchill at their side, made appearance after appearance on the balcony at Buckingham Palace, responding to the huge celebrating crowds packing the Mall and clambering over statues and fountains.

Though many young children could not have had much idea of what it was all about, it was still a day, and a night, never to be forgotten:

My parents were very rigid about bedtimes, and when VE Day came, with a victory parade through our village, a bonfire and fireworks in the evening, they still thought we should be in bed at our usual time. Some old friends spent the entire day persuading them that this was, please God, a once-in-a-lifetime occasion and we must be allowed to stay up.

We were.

And I can still picture the parade and the bonfire, and the drunken man being helped down the road singing, 'It's a long way to tickle Mary . . .'

A family of six children in the middle of Oxford when the celebra-tions were in full swing watched it all happen, 'VE Day was wonder-ful – street parties and everyone singing. We all went to the town centre to join in the fun, and it was still warm even at ten o'clock at night – we only had thin summer dresses on. People were running up and down the High Street and throwing people into the river. Groups of men even lifted the few cars that there were shoulder high and carried them about!'

For those who had lost loved ones, there were painfully mixed feel-ings: profound relief that it was all over, as well as bitter regret that many of the men and women who had died in the supreme effort to make that day a reality were not there.

Joan's father was killed early in the war. Brought up by her mother and surrounded by other relatives, she was young and resilient and adapted. At some inner core, she would mourn the father she barely knew all her days, but on VE Day, caught up in the excitement of the moment, she laughed and danced and was deliriously happy with all the rest. For her mother, however, the present, and the future, were much darker. 'I was eleven when the war ended,' Joan said:

They opened the pleasure pier, and an army band played for dancing with all the lights on. But my mother was crying, and I got cross with her . . .

I now realize she had spent four years, since my father died, alone bringing me up, half starved and frightened, all the while knowing she had lost her one love. She had to face the peace without him. Her hopes of house ownership and a decent life completely destroyed. And the widow's pension, small as it was, was actually taxed as 'earned income'.

Few community festivities, at least in the towns, were complete without a victory street party – trestle tables loaded with sandwiches and cakes and jellies which resourceful mothers had laid hands on, rationing or no. But young children can be contrary, and one little boy evidently did not enjoy his much: 'Being a very shy, solitary child I did not want to go to our inevitable street party. However, my parents insisted, and I have still got the photo of this occasion, showing a poor forlorn little lad, looking over his shoulder to see where his parents were standing across the street.'

Street parties – and more elaborate feasts – were in progress, or being planned, everywhere. Families celebrated in whatever way suited them. One girl's rather formal parents took the opportunity to revert to a sketchy post-war version of their normal pre-war dining:

To celebrate, my younger brother and I were going to have dinner for the first time with the grown-ups. Our friend the butler had recently been liberated from his call-up in the air force, so the plan was to reinstate normality. Following this norm, the female members of the family were required to wear long dresses.

Clothes rationing would not allow for luxury, so the yards of white muslin that had dressed my brother's cot was recycled to concoct a long dress for a twelve-year-old me. At twelve one is not very well proportioned; the growing gets going in odd places. Thin (yellowing) muslin does not make a sylphide of just any skinny growing girl. The trouble was my feet. No dainty satin slippers to peep timidly from under the hem. They were colossal and square-toed in solid gym shoes. The stifled guffaws of the red-faced butler from behind his screen put me on the track to the enjoyment one can cause by not being elegant.

As the heady jubilation of victory in Europe began to fade, the sober realization that the war was not, after all, finally over began to set in. Allied troops were still fighting bitterly against the Japanese, and were winning there too – but had not won yet. Those whose husbands and fathers were still on active duty in the Far East were quick to resent the implication that the long hard struggle was now at an end. Children felt this too. An older girl whose father was in the Far East, reported as missing, was deeply aware of this injustice: 'At VE Day, when most people felt that the war was over, I remember feeling annoyed and angry that the other war was being ignored.'

Demobilization had already started in the European theatre when President Truman, who had succeeded President Roosevelt, gave the awesome permission to use the ultimate weapon of mass destruction, the atom bomb. The first A-bomb was dropped at Hiroshima on 6 August, and three days later a second bomb was dropped on Nagasaki. Whatever the moral implications of Truman's decision, the hard truth is that the immediate objective was achieved. On 14 August 1945 the Japanese surrendered, and the Second World War was over.

In a country already growing used to peace, this final ending set off yet more frenzied celebrations – more singing and dancing, more parties, more flags and bunting, more delirious waving crowds. One girl, out to enjoy the thrill of this historic moment, was determined to make it a night to remember:

My older sister took me up to the centre of London for the impromptu celebrations. It was magical! Peoples of all nations in their various uniforms were surging through the streets, singing and dancing around the coloured fountains in Trafalgar Square and the lights were on everywhere. We tried to get down the Mall to Buckingham Palace, but the mass of celebrating happy people was just too dense for us to get through.

What a party!

What a memory!

Now, yet more exhausted servicemen began to embark on the long journey home. Fighting in the alien heat and undergrowth of the jungle, struck by malaria and monsoon rains as well as the enemy, many had thought they would never see their homes again – as their fallen comrades did not. And it is fitting that a girl whose father was one of these servicemen, and among the last to return, has the final words on homecoming of a child of war:

As the eldest, I remembered my father very well, though inevitably the boys – my two little brothers – did not. The first phone call after he landed in Southampton after nearly four years, was very special. We bought flags to celebrate his return home, and all the neighbours decorated their houses too.

Looking back at the photos of that time his face was very gaunt and he was very thin. But I don't think I noticed that.

He was Daddy – and he was home.

8th June, 1946

To-day, as we celebrate victory, I send this personal message to you and all other boys and girls at school. For you have shared in the hardships and dangers of a total war and you have shared no less in the triumph of the Allied Nations.

I know you will always feel proud to belong to a country which was capable of such supreme effort; proud, too, of parents and elder brothers and sisters who by their courage, endurance and enterprise brought victory. May these qualities be yours as you grow up and join in the common effort to establish among the nations of the world unity and peace.

George R.I.

This scroll from King George VI was intended for all schoolchildren in recognition of their six years of childhood on the home front during a 'total war'

Epilogue

A short while ago one of my oldest friends said, 'You know, we grew up in a world war – and we never had any counselling . . .'
'No,' I said, 'but did we get laughs?'
We did indeed!
A woman who started school in 1939, aged five

How many nice Jewish boys spent the war in a quiet Scottish mining town and acquired a thick Scots accent to bring back to north London?
A child whose father was a tailor, evacuated to Scotland with his family

Those of us who survived the war are a special breed. We don't like throwing things away. We buy things we don't actually need at the moment when we see them again. We tend to store, because we don't always believe we will find them again. We keep things far too long. And we never waste. I think most of us survivors are resilient and adaptable.
A woman who started on a successful career in wartime

Like many other children of war, I agree with the writer of that last comment. Her assessment seems to fit most of us who were children during those critical years. And she does not romanticize: she goes on to paint a rather sombre picture of her seventeen-year-old self in 1941 when she landed her first job, looking after the classified ads of a weekly journal:

I can't say I was happy. I was working hard and trying to get myself into journalism . . . I had given up my university evening course because it was too exhausting with the day's job and evenings at the air-raid shelter. I also worked as a part-time air-raid warden. Life seemed serious and difficult. And the war and the shortages – particularly food – seemed endless. I longed for it all to be over so I could get on with my life.

The war was no picnic for any of us. Five years of casualties, of official telegrams informing of death or capture or wounding of close relatives – husbands, sons, fathers, brothers, uncles, cousins – brought grief to so many families and sapped so much emotional energy. And men, women and children going about their daily business in familiar streets were also enemy targets in this war. Few were entirely spared risk, injury or death.

For the survivors, nothing could ever be the same again. This included the children: their attitudes also had been deeply affected, perhaps skewed for life, by the atmosphere of death that they were intimately aware of, even if they could not describe it. Andrew, who was five when the war started and who lived in north London throughout, reflected that

There began the stirring of a fatalistic attitude to life. As children, we were surrounded by death, immersed in death – in the sky, on the films, in the papers, on the radio, and in the street. Very often in our own street, or in a street down which we walked or cycled on the way to school or a playground. Death coming to members of our family, or the family of our school friends, or people we had known or seen, friends of our parents. In the accepting way of children, we accepted. We didn't know any different. But we were affected.

A boy in Sussex, who had lived on Bomb Alley, the path the rockets took as they hurtled towards Greater London, and who had witnessed more than one bomber crash and its consequences, said thoughtfully:

When I was a child, danger was an everyday thing – just part of life. Consequently we kids became unaware of it; it wasn't anything strange . . . We did some pretty terrifying things ourselves too. It was part of the time . . . We would sometimes find live bullets from ack-ack guns lying about in the fields, take them back to our garden shed, clamp them gently in a vice, and with a hammer and nail strike the cartridge end and fire them out of the door. There was so much sheer brutality, we didn't think twice about it.

An only daughter from a privileged background collided brutally with the horror of bombing, the casualties and the fact of early death. She came, she said, to take all this for granted:

Before the war I had been so sheltered. If there was an accident when we were in the car and passing, it was 'Avert the child's eyes', I must be protected . . . Then suddenly, it was war, and I was watching people being pulled out of bomb craters, badly injured and covered with dust and debris . . .

And the death of the young was very real; it was all around us. I seemed to know a lot of boys in the air force . . . boys I would have tea with at home, laughing and chatting, so proud of their uniforms. And the next thing – they had been killed. I remember one especially: it was his first flight, over Crete.

This was all part of everyday life.

Of all the trials of war on the home front, separation from beloved relatives was undoubtedly the hardest to bear – both at the time and, for some, far into adult life. Profound emotion is unpredictable, and can surface in unexpected ways. The reaction of a successful career woman to tragic family news some sixty years later gives one small clue to the depths a child's unhappiness can reach. 'The day my husband's fatal illness was diagnosed I cried bitterly,' she said. 'Then it suddenly came to me that the last time I had felt so utterly without hope was when I was evacuated from Newcastle to Carlisle on my own and cried myself to sleep every night.'

A twelve-year-old boy who was evacuated to Wales from London escaped the bombing, but, like many other children, he was not spared the tragedy of war, and its long-lasting effects have burdened him ever since: 'In my case, the war meant the break-up of my family as a whole unit, because my father was killed on active service in 1943 and I was brought up by my mother in a one-parent family. This was a schism in my life that has never really healed.'

Of all the many aspects of family separation in wartime, little is heard of younger children who stayed at home while older brothers and sisters were sent to the country. In one woman's case, the insecurities and confusion stemming from being left behind are still with her:

I, along with numerous other young children who were left behind at home, surely felt the anxiety of separation from their siblings who had been evacuated just as acutely as being separated from fathers and older brothers and sisters going away to fight for their country. Looking back now, I know that the war years left an indelible mark on my psyche, and to this day I am unable to cope with key people in my life leaving the safety of my 'world'.

Few men and women who were children during the war can have escaped having their subsequent lives influenced by family separation in wartime. As Richard Titmuss wrote in 1950, 'Perhaps more lasting harm was wrought to the minds of men, women and children than to their bodies. The disturbance of family life, the separation of mothers and fathers from their children, of husbands from their wives, of pupils from their schools ... perhaps all these indignities of war have left wounds from which it will take time to heal and infinite patience to understand.'

Private domestic bitterness which was nurtured in wartime privations has continued to shadow some unfortunate children. A girl who was twelve when the war began was one of them. She lived in a city in the midst of bombing throughout; she was never given the option of evacuation; she put up with inadequate schooling, and she was too old for the perks of the green ration book. 'There was the black market in goods, and people would talk about where this or that could be had. But we couldn't afford these things ... It was the injustice of everything that I felt, and still feel,' she said vehemently. Such injustice, she believed, was hard to bear in wartime, as she knew other children in her street who appeared better fed, or who were sent to relatives in a peaceful area in the country. There must have been many men and women who felt similarly ill-treated by a society which they believed should have protected them better, and who carried these hurts and grudges through their later years.

Schooling was a problem throughout the war. Many wartime schoolchildren expressed long-lasting regret at their disrupted education, some believing that they never caught up and that their chances for advancement in life were blighted from the start. A girl whose schoolmaster father attempted to coach her during his rare leaves from the army said that the effect of the war on her education was 'shattering – and this must be true of nearly every child to some extent.'

For children who were well into their teens in September 1939, the war meant that all future plans were affected. 'We had our youth totally altered by those six years – not only for that period, but for ever more,' one woman wrote, her hopes for a Civil Service career dashed by her call-up papers. After the war, her family situation made it impossible for her to take up the opening. Youthful hopes for professional training or higher education were nearly all put on indefinite hold for those who left school at seventeen or eighteen during the war, unless they involved medicine or one of the sciences.

Whatever their circumstances, few children in Britain were entirely spared the tribulations of war. Yet many believe that hardships of separation, of frightening air raids and of strict rationing often had a positive side too, and may even have strengthened the child's inner reserves. Most of us came through these adversities, however hard, and learnt early in our lives the valuable lesson that discomfort and unhappiness can be borne.

Of course the tragedy of the death of a parent or sibling in war must be treated in a different light, though it should be said that, however deep the hurt, bereaved children would not have felt alone. As we grew up, nearly all of us had friends whose fathers, or older brothers, did not come home. It was a fact of life, and we children knew it.

So what *were* the positive things that we took from our wartime childhoods?

A boy who was four when the war began was evacuated to East Anglia to stay with his grandparents, but brought back to the city to begin his schooling. One of his significant, and rather charming, early memories is of being looked after by an elderly relative who would take him out into a London garden square and read to him – mainly from Charles Dickens. 'Pretty heavy stuff for a four-year-old!'

When the siren went, they trooped down into the shelter in the middle of the square and she continued with the story during the air raid. 'I owe her much, as she engendered in me a lifelong love of books and reading,' he said. (Lots of wartime children devoured books. All the classics – Trollope and Jane Austen especially – became extremely popular. And with 400 libraries bombed, book buying increased – particularly among the young.)

In addition to his quirky introduction to great literature, he pondered other lasting effects of his wartime childhood:

I think those years instilled in me a sense of frugality, an appreciation of things hard earned and striven for. A strong sense of community spirit. A gradual realization of the horrors of war – not at the time, as my feelings were more of excitement at everything that was happening, but later in life. The deprivation, the drabness and the danger were all somehow character-building.

I was lucky enough as a child not to lose any family or friends or to be bombed out, and the qualities I took from growing up in wartime have stood me in good stead through the years.

Oh, but I do have a lifelong fear of balloons! I am sure that it's because when they pop it reminds me of the bombs exploding.

Evacuation and war work and the chaos in bomb-damaged cities produced a unique social scrambling of class and age and place of origin on the home front. But, despite the disruption, all this was stimulating, and sensibilities were heightened even in the young. Many who were involved agree that the very mention of dried egg, or a few bars of 'The White Cliffs of Dover', is enough to transport them right back into that uniquely charged atmosphere. A lot of wartime catchphrases do the trick, and a couple of boys who were both about five in 1939 pooled some of their mental triggers and came up with a list of their own:

'I don't mind if I do' (Colonel Chinstrap); 'Can I do yer now, Sir?' (Mrs Mop); 'It's being so cheerful as keeps me going' (Mona Lot); 'Careless Talk Cost Lives'; 'Be Like Dad – Keep Mum'; 'Dig for Victory'; Ovaltine and Horlicks tablets; Kardomah cafés; land girls; German prisoners of war; the

Home Guard; working on local farms; the ARP; Fougasse cartoons; searchlights; headlamp visors; wardens; air-raid shelters; ack-ack; sandbags; sirens; Spam; condensed milk; dried egg; whale meat; blackout; gas masks; 'Utility' goods; ration books; coupons; points; identity cards; listening to Churchill's speeches . . .

One of them added, 'And the good humour of my whole family – particularly my uncle Bob, who frequently had us in fits of laughter with his Cockney stories of the Blitz.' We could all probably add to the list.

Another of the wartime boys admitted sheepishly, 'I'm almost ashamed to say I actually enjoyed my war years. I had never consciously known anything else.' Many feel the same. As one girl wrote, half humorously, 'I, and lots of my contemporaries carry some burden of guilt for having found it the most magical and exciting of times.'

It seems wrong now to have enjoyed wartime in the midst of so much hardship and loss of life. But in many ways it was a thrilling and adventurous time for the young, and most of us were touched by the sense of national emergency and the uncomplicated patriotism.

The lack of material goods, toys and entertainments was more than compensated, many of us now feel, by the blessed freedom we had to come and go, climb trees, pedal off on our bikes, and play outside with friends for hours on end with minimal grown-up supervision. Despite the war, people felt at ease in their surroundings – and safe. Remembering how she mucked about with her sisters, making up their own games, a woman said, 'We were completely unspoilt, and we learnt to be resourceful.'

In wartime, as always, it was largely the luck of the draw that determined who saw bad times and who came through relatively unscathed. There are children who insist that they suffered so badly from deplorable treatment by foster parents, or even relatives, during evacuation that it left deep scars which lasted for years. Others speak of foster parents with genuine affection. One long-ago evacuee said that many years later she returned to the village she had been sent to and, after strenuous efforts, managed to get in touch again with her foster parents' daughter and arrange a very happy reunion.

For the clever and the fortunate, the war's interruption of their plans for the future could have a positive outcome. The government gave priority – and grants – to returning young servicemen and servicewomen if they were qualified and wished to take up full-time post-war education. This could, and did, transform the lives of thousands of able young men and women from poorer families who could never have afforded a college education before the war.

A boy who spent the first day of war as a carefree fifteen-year-old, picnicking on the beach with his family, and ended the conflict as an army officer in the Middle East, took an optimistic view overall. 'When I got home at the end of the war,' he said, 'everything felt different. Despite the tremendous problems with housing – so many young people and families literally had nowhere to live – there was a great feeling that it was a new beginning and, for a brief time, that anything was possible.'

Politically aware older children and young adults were caught up in the sudden optimism. The push for sweeping social reform which had fermented in the bitterness and poverty of the thirties was at last being addressed, and in 1948 the National Health Service and the National Insurance schemes were launched. Attitudes within society that had held for a thousand years had been transformed by wartime conditions, and would never fully change back. The children of war who played tag on bomb sites and put up with long hours in Anderson shelters would emerge as adults into a vastly changed social order.

But, although balanced by the blessing of peace, there was still a hard slog to come on the domestic front. In addition to other shortages, bread and potatoes were both rationed briefly. During the bitter winter of 1947 the country's fuel supplies almost ran out, and a lot of children remember water frozen in washbasins during those icy months. For younger children like this boy, life in those early post-war years was very puzzling after the heady buzz of victory: 'I am nine years old. We have just won the war. We rule half the world. Everything is going to be marvellous from now on. Seven years later I have come home on leave at the end of my first term at Dartmouth (Naval Training College). I have brought my ration book with me.'

As we all had drummed into us, making the best use of everything was essential. None of us who remember rationing – which continued in some form until 1953 – can countenance waste of any kind.

'The war taught us to be economical. I now regard waste as ignorant and common,' one woman said firmly. Young children, who had never known anything else, grew up believing wartime shortages and restrictions were normal. We learned to look on the bright side too – grateful for not being bombed out like the family across the road, and ecstatic to find there was a whole orange for tea.

One boy said that certain habits had never left him:

Wartime conditioning still affects my life. Some of it is idealistic – like wishing we could all 'pull together' again – but some of it is ingrained habit. I notice how I still utilise everything: I automatically scrape out a butter tub or a cream carton, as we all did then. And I mentally divide up the food on my plate throughout the meal so as to match the bits I 'like' with bits I 'don't like' – a throwback to having to eat what was available and making it as palatable as possible.

Ironically, despite all the austerity, a boy who was evacuated aged nine from the east of London to the West Country said that it was in the depths of wartime deprivation that he got his first glimpse of worldly goods and gracious living. Young though he was, its impact did much to determine the later course of his life: 'The house of the solicitor for whom my foster father worked was an utter revelation to me – large rooms, beautiful furniture and pictures, polished silver, and a housemaid to look after it all. It was my introduction to a world far outside my working-class, dockside experience, and it was a world I was determined to enter when I grew up.' Which is what, in time, he did, turning on its head the idea that all beautiful objects, and a healthy bit of personal ambition, were banished for the duration.

So what, overall, did we take from our wartime childhoods? Perhaps the drab and disciplined routine of a normal wartime family life, with none of the frills, proved a sound preparation for the ups and downs ahead. Perhaps the old-fashioned values of the time – of patriotism, pulling together, and hard work – stood us in good stead through whatever it was that life threw at us, as well as the monumental changes of future decades. A former child of war, who had watched injured neighbours being pulled out of bomb-blasted houses, spoke from the heart:

Looking back, war made children brutally aware of the fundamentals, the fragility of life, the vulnerability. He or she may not have expressed it, but it was real to a child then, and deeply felt. Whatever their background, children were told, 'It's wartime – you've got to get on with it'. And that is what we have continued to expect of ourselves. We learnt self control; we didn't express feelings. Life was too serious for all that. We had to be stoic, to take it all in our stride, and we did.

As one of the women whose words opened this epilogue suggested, a lot of people who were then children describe themselves now as 'resilient'. We had to 'get on with it' – there was no choice – and we have done. An informal survey of other long-held attitudes inculcated by the war came up with dislike of waste, adaptability, gratitude for what we have, independence, and ingrained qualities of thrift; as well as a mania for hanging on to any old piece of used wrapping paper . . .

Though the insecurities, the unhappiness and the nightmare fears which the war engendered may have undermined some children's later lives, for many of us these seem a lot less important than the qualities that we gained. And we had fun too. There was the excitement of hearing the ack-ack guns firing and foraging for pieces of warm shrapnel, and the simple joy, unheard of today, of watching night fall on a blacked-out and starry world.

Many of us now are grateful for the values and the grit that we took from those long-ago wartime childhoods.

We are, after all, the survivors.

SELECT BIBLIOGRAPHY

The number of published works concerning the Second World War is enormous and, though many have been consulted in the preparation of this book, the following have been of particular use and may be of interest to readers:

Bowen, Elizabeth, *The Heat of the Day* (London: Jonathan Cape, 1949)

Brendon, Piers, *The Dark Valley* (London: Jonathan Cape, 2000)

Calder, Angus, *The People's War* (London: Jonathan Cape, 1969)

Card, Tim, *Eton Renewed* (London: John Murray, 1994)

De Courcy, Anne, *1939: The Last Season* (London: Thames and Hudson, 1989)

Delafield, E. M., *Diary of a Provincial Lady* (London: Folio Society, 1979)

Lambert, Angela, *1939: The Last Season of Peace* (London: Weidenfeld & Nicolson, 1989)

Longmate, Norman, *How We Lived Then* (London: Hutchinson, 1971)

Maxtone Graham, Ysenda, *The Real Mrs Miniver* (London: John Murray, 2001)

Mowat, Charles, *Britain Between the Wars* (London: Methuen, 1955)

O'Neilla, Gilda, *My East End* (London: Viking, 1999)

Panter-Downes, Mollie, *London War Notes* (London: Longman, 1972)

Patten, Marguerite, *Victory Cookbook* (London: Chancellor Press, 2002)

Priestley, J. B., *English Journey* (London: William Heinemann, 1934)

Roffey, James, *The Evacuation of British Children during the Second World War* (Retford, Notts: Evacuees Reunion Association, 2004)

Titmuss, Richard M., *Problems of Social Policy* (London: HMSO, 1950)

Ziegler, Philip, *London at War* (London: Sinclair-Stevenson, 1995)

As a young person male, female. Some things are good some are bad!.

Life is not perfect. You gain experience as it evolves.

It is education — learn from the good and the bad

Patience is the name of the game. <u>EMBRACE YOUR LIFE</u>.

<u>PHYSICALITY PLUS</u>
<u>MENTALITY</u>.

TAKE THE FLACK!
   EDUCATION.

ALICE, LEO IN THE
   RIGHT PLACE.

P.S. After serving an apprenticeship working for my Dad. _I wanted freedom!_

Len Gosside and family moved in to Whalley Avenue Chorlton. He worked for Manchester City Council

I got the office address of the council. Got a job. They put me on the North side of Manchester.

I DID IT! TWO BUSES 94 from Chorlton to town, the another bus to North Manchester!

This was growing up!

Later got a transfer to Hulme Moss Side. All the terraced houses had been knocked down. 4 Storey Flats. Ridiculous!